DOSTOEVSKY'S

Occasional Writings

DOSTOEVSKY'S

Occasional Writings

SELECTED, TRANSLATED & INTRODUCED BY

DAVID MAGARSHACK

NORTHWESTERN UNIVERSITY PRESS
EVANSTON, IL

Northwestern University Press
Evanston, Illinois 60208-4210

First published in 1963 by Random House, Inc., New York, and by
Random House of Canada, Ltd., Toronto. Copyright © 1963 by David
Magarshack. Northwestern University Press edition published 1997 by
arrangement with Mrs. E. D. Magarshack, care of Curtis Brown Group
Ltd., London. All rights reserved.

Printed in the United States of America

ISBN 0-8101-1473-9

Library of Congress Cataloging-in-Publication Data

Dostoyevsky, Fyodor, 1821–1881.
    [Selections. English. 1997]
    Dostoevsky's occasional writings / selected, translated, and introduced
by David Magarshack.
        p. cm.
    Originally published: New York : Random House, c1963.
    Includes index.
    ISBN 0-8101-1473-9 (paper : alk. paper)
    1. Dostoyevsky, Fyodor, 1821–1881—Translations into English.
I. Magarshack, David. II. Title.
PG3326.A16M3 1997
891.78'308—dc21   97-15418
                                                                              CIP

The paper used in this publication meets the minimum requirements of
the American National Standard for Information Sciences—Permanence
of Paper for Printed Library Materials, ANSI Z39.48-1984.

CONTENTS

INTRODUCTION

NO GREAT WRITER EVER SUFFERED SUCH A CRUSHING FALL
as Dostoevsky did in 1847 after the acclaim of his first
novel, *Poor People,* by Visarion Belinsky, the most influential critic of the time. It is true that the twenty-six-year-
old Dostoevsky was himself responsible for the fact that
the Petersburg literary world had turned away from him.
He had been too arrogant, he had treated his fellow writers, who were only too anxious to recognize his genius,
with a contempt that his own literary achievements, astonishing as they were, warranted but little. From the
very beginning of his literary career he had cut rather an
absurd figure among the aristocratic crowd of writers
such as the young Turgenev, the frenchified dandy Dmitry Grigorovich, with whom he had shared lodgings for a
short time, the great patrician Count Vladimir Sollogub,
and the rest of the brilliant literary lions of the day. With
Belinsky alone could he compare in social status, for, like
the critic, he too was the son of a poor doctor. But his
friendship with Belinsky did not last. The stories he had
written after *Poor People,* which, with that characteristic
inability to judge his own work while engaged in writing
it, he had thought would consolidate his reputation, had a
very lukewarm reception. Indeed, so disappointed was
Belinsky with *The Landlady,* published in 1847, that he
expressed his belief that he had made a great mistake in
acclaiming Dostoevsky as a writer of genius. Dostoevsky
had just then resigned his commission in the army; he
was in debt to moneylenders and had to live on the mea-
ger advances Andrey Kraevsky, the editor of the monthly
Home Annals, allowed him for his short stories. What his
position was like at the beginning of 1847, when he wrote
his first essay for the *Petersburg News,* can be gathered
from one sentence in a letter he wrote to his elder brother
Mikhail: "They have created a doubtful reputation for
me," he declared, "and I don't know when there will be an
end to this hell, this poverty, this work that has to be delivered by a certain date— oh, for a little rest!"

Introduction

It was in this desperate situation that Dostoevsky eagerly accepted an offer from the *Petersburg News,* a paper that allowed itself to depart from its usually austere preoccupations with scientific and social problems (it was closely connected with the Academy of Sciences) only with the publication of a bi-monthly *feuilleton,* to take over this task of amusing its readers by some lighthearted comments on the latest Petersburg social events. It was Count Vladimir Sollogub, whom Dostoevsky described during his short-lived period of fame as "some silly little aristocrat," who took pity on his plight and recommended him to the editor of the *Petersburg News* as a regular contributor to the paper. But it was the regularity with which the copy had to be delivered that made Dostoevsky give up his job of *feuilleton* writer, for the task of delivering his writings by a certain date drove him frantic with despair. He therefore contributed only four essays to the paper between April 13 and June 15, 1847. He signed the first essay with the letters "N.N." and the others with his initials, "F.D."

These essays express not only Dostoevsky's state of mind at that difficult period, but also the ideas that were to occupy him during most of the rest of his life, for instance: his hostile attitude to Europe and to those Russians who regarded European civilization as the only way of solving the Russian political and economic problems; or the great cleavage between the vast majority of the illiterate peasants, the so-called common people, and the small educated section of the population, to whom the opera, the ballet and the concerts by celebrated European virtuosos meant so much; or, finally, his contempt for the Russian landowning aristocracy. All this already becomes evident from his first essay, which contains only sparse comments on the latest literary events, such as the publication of Goncharov's first novel, *An Ordinary Story.*

With the ruthless censorship prevailing at the time, best characterized, perhaps, in the phrase one of the censors used to Turgenev: "I promise you not to touch a single letter, I shall merely kill the spirit," it is no wonder that

Introduction

Dostoevsky, who was just then an active member of two revolutionary "circles," could not as much as hint at the things that were uppermost in his mind in the year that preceded the disclosure of his political activities and his arrest. Many years later, Turgenev described the general situation in Petersburg in those days in the following words: "You look round, bribery is flourishing, serfdom seems as firm as a rock, the barracks are always there in the foreground, justice is unknown, rumors of the closing down of the universities are rife and are partially confirmed when the news leaks out that the complement of students at each university is to be reduced to three hundred, no decent book can be ordered from abroad, a sort of a black cloud hangs over everything that can be called learning or literature, and spies are everywhere." *When the news leaks out* . . . In his second essay, Dostoevsky remarks dryly that after commenting on the filthy weather, the most offensive question one can ask in Petersburg is "What's the news?"—a question, he explains, that is accompanied by "a feeling of desolation" in those who ask it. It is, indeed, only "an empty phrase" requiring no answer, since the answer might reach the ears of the ubiquitous spies.

It is all the more surprising, therefore, that Dostoevsky should have expatiated at some length in the same essay on a subject that was to become political dynamite sixteen months later—the subject of the Petersburg "circles." Dostoevsky himself was a member of the Petrashevsky "circle," which was composed of young men holding all sorts of political opinions and led by Petrashevsky, a minor official of the Russian foreign office and a disciple of the French utopian socialist Charles Fourier. One cannot help admiring the skillful way in which the young Dostoevsky skates over thin ice in this particular passage of his essay, an ability which he was to display to perfection a year and a half later during his interrogation by the tribunal that tried him for treason. Thus, he remarks with feigned innocence that in a "circle" one can always receive a prompt answer to the question of what is the news. And after de-

ix

scribing rather flippantly the sort of innocuous circles that abound in Petersburg, he goes on to give a devastating picture of Petrashevsky's "circle," in which "heated debates about matters of importance are conducted, a few harsh truths are uttered," and in the end "it all peters out." . . .

His dissatisfaction with Petrashevsky, which was soon to lead him to organize a much more revolutionary group of people bent on action, becomes clear from his veiled portrait of the Fourier disciple as the man "with a good heart and nothing else besides." It is followed by another veiled autobiographical passage in which Dostoevsky's former "well-wisher and benefactor" (a hint at his brother-in-law, a middle-aged high Moscow official who had married his seventeen-year-old sister and who, as the executor of his father's estate, refused to let him have a lump sum for his share in it), also appears under the same name of Julian Mastakovich in two of his early stories. He ends his second essay with a story published in *Home Annals* in March 1847, a story he might well have written himself, so typically Dostoevskian is it.

The most sensational literary event of that time—the publication of Gogol's *Selected Passages from a Correspondence with Friends*—Dostoevsky mentions only in passing at the end of his second essay, merely remarking that the particularly significant thing about it was "the consensus of opinion among almost all the newspapers and periodicals." The "consensus of opinion" with which he entirely agreed was hostile to Gogol's reactionary views as expressed in that book. What Dostoevsky did not know was that barely two years later he would be arrested and sentenced to four years' hard labor in a Siberian prison for reading at a meeting of the Petrashevsky circle Belinsky's violent condemnation of the *Selected Passages* in the critic's famous open letter to Gogol.

The last two essays, apart from their autobiographical asides, such as the descriptions of the mood of dreadful despondency in which Dostoevsky was constantly sunk at that time, are notable for his insight into character, his veiled challenge to the authorities to give a lead to the people who were anxious to contribute to the general welfare by any kind of useful activity, and, lastly, for the long passage in the fourth essay on the tragedy of the general feeling of frustration among the younger generation which forces many of them to spend their lives as idle dreamers. Dostoevsky himself had been through a similar period of ecstatic daydreaming, the brief but intense romantic period of his obsession with Schiller and the ideas of abstract justice, from which he emerged to take an active part in the attempt to bring an end to the reactionary regime of Nicholas I by demanding the liberation of the serfs, the abolition of censorship and the reform of the judiciary.

This attempt ended in catastrophe. He was arrested on April 23, 1849, incarcerated in the Peter and Paul Fortress with twenty-two other members of the Petrashevsky circle, sentenced to death, reprieved, subjected to a mock execution ceremony on the Semyonovsky Parade Ground in the early morning of December 22, and, three days later, was put into chains and sent to Siberia to serve a four-year sentence of hard labor in the Omsk prison. After his release from prison, he had to serve another four years as a private in one of the Siberian line regiments in Semipalatinsk. There he fell in love with the wife of a minor official and subsequently married her a short time after her husband's death. He returned to Russia in August 1859 and was allowed to reside in Petersburg once more at the end of that year.

It is characteristic of Dostoevsky that immediately on his arrival in Petersburg he began taking an active part in the political life of the country. The changes he found on his return were of cardinal importance: Nicholas I as well as his reactionary policies were dead, and his successor, Alexander II, was about to carry through several liberal reforms, including the liberation of the serfs. A wave of hope swept through the Russian radical circles, resulting in exaggerated optimistic predictions that, as Dostoevsky declared in his first announcement—or "manifesto," as he preferred to call it—of the forthcoming publication of his own political and literary periodical, *Time,* all these reforms would usher in a period of "peaceful" collaboration between all classes of the population and particularly between the forty-odd million liberated serfs and the handful of their former aristocratic masters.

As an ex-convict, Dostoevsky was not allowed to become the editor of his monthly, but even though his elder brother Mikhail was the "official" editor, it was Fyodor, of course, who was in actual control of *Time.* He was the author of the three manifestoes to its readers in September 1860, October 1861 and October 1862, as well as of the one of his second periodical *Epoch* in September 1864. These manifestoes are of the utmost importance for an understanding of Dostoevsky's political and social ideas. The remarkable thing is that these ideas remained essentially the same in spite of the fact that during the next sixteen years he changed from a mild liberal into a diehard conservative. Thus already in his first manifesto of September 1860 Dostoevsky emphasized, as he was to do a few months before his death in his Pushkin speech, the "universal" character of the Russian "idea" which he was convinced would provide "the synthesis" of the ideas that are "developing in Europe with such stubbornness." A curious statement (if he only knew how familiar it was to become a hundred years later, though in a sense quite contrary to what he had in mind), followed by a still more curious statement to which he adhered all his life, namely that for some mysterious reason the Russians "spoke all languages, understood all civilizations, sympathized with the interests of every European nation and realized the reason and wisdom of phenomena quite alien to them." Still another statement, formulated in the very first public announcement he wrote for *Time,* was to become one of his most firmly held convictions at the end of his life, namely that the Russian common people possessed "the ability to assume a reconciliatory attitude toward the things that divide the foreigners." This, in turn, led him afterward to the belief that the "European contra-

Introduction

dictions" would eventually be "reconciled" by the genius
of the Russian people.

The political ideas outlined by Dostoevsky in his articles and manifestoes in *Time* revolved around his rather
hazy demand for "a return to the soil," by which he meant
a gradual recognition by the educated section of the Russian population, which, according to him, had been slavishly imitating the West, of the innate spiritual values of
the Russian common people. He strongly objected to the
patronizing air, as is apparent from his article *Pedantry
and Literacy*, with which the "enlightened" Russians regarded the illiterate peasant. His experience in the Omsk
prison, where for the first time in his life he was thrown
together with the "common people" and could study them
at close quarters, taught him that the hatred of the peasants for their masters was so deep and irreconcilable that
any attempt on the part of the well-meaning liberal section of educated Russians to bridge the gulf that separated them from the now emancipated peasants was
doomed to failure unless they renounced their often quite
unconsciously superior attitude toward the illiterate mass
of the people. His call for "a return to the soil" was, therefore, an appeal to the Europeanized Russian for understanding and humility. This appeal was bound to fail and
its failure eventually drove Dostoevsky to abandon his role
of arbiter between the mainly atheistic Westerners, who
looked to Europe for a political solution of their difficulties, and the Slavophiles, the fanatical Moscow party led
by the mystical poets Khomyakov and the brothers Kire-
yevsky and the even more fanatical Konstantin Aksakov,
whom Dostoevsky attacks in his article *The Latest Literary Controversies*. At the time of his editorship of *Time*
and after the suppression of *Time* for an article on the
Polish insurrection, *Epoch*, Dostoevsky showed no signs of
the religious obsessions, such as his violent Anti-Catholi-
cism, that marked his last period, during which he finally
broke away from his radical and revolutionary past and
joined the camp of the Slavophiles.

But, while sitting on the fence so far as the Western-

xiii

ers and the Slavophiles were concerned, Dostoevsky never hesitated to challenge the extreme party of the radicals, the so-called utilitarians or "nihilists," and particularly the literary critics grouped around the *Contemporary,* owned and edited by his old friend the poet Nikolai Nekrasov. The chief representative of the utilitarians on that monthly was the brilliant young critic Nikolai Dobrolyubov, to whose views Dostoevsky devoted the whole of his article published in *Time* in February 1861. Dobrolyubov's chief claim to fame was his study of Ostrovsky's plays dealing with the life of the Moscow merchants. This study was published under the general title "The Realm of Darkness." In it Dobrolyubov put the blame for the greed, the moneygrubbing, the lies and the superstitions of the Moscow merchants on the social and economic conditions under which everyone in Russia was forced to live, and in his last essay, "A Ray of Light in the Realm of Darkness," he hailed the young heroine of Ostrovsky's tragedy *The Storm* as a rebel against those conditions in spite of her deep religious faith, on which the real action of the play hinges. It was Dobrolyubov's "utilitarian" view of literature (which has become the "official" view of literature in Russia today) that Dostoevsky demolishes in his article *Mr. ——bov and the Question of Art.* In fact, this essay perhaps more than anything else may explain why Dostoevsky is still held in disrepute in Soviet Russia while the much more reactionary writers of his day, such as Leskov, for instance, have been forgiven.

The failure of *Epoch* after the death of Dostoevsky's elder brother, his desperate financial situation following upon this failure, his second marriage to his stenographer Anna Snitkin, the four years from April 1867 to July 1871 he and his wife spent abroad, his going over to the conservative camp with the increasing revolutionary outbreaks in Russia, and his editorship of the reactionary weekly *The Citizen* on his return to Petersburg were the main events in Dostoevsky's life in the interval between his last manifesto in *Epoch* and the publication of the *Small Sketches* in 1874 in a symposium of articles and stories in aid of the famine-stricken peasants in the province of Samara. By that time he had published three of his great novels, *Crime and Punishment*, *The Idiot* and *The Devils*, and became acknowledged as one of the major Russian novelists. He and his family (by that time he had a daughter and a son) spent the summer in the watering place of Staraya Russa. To get there from Petersburg he had to travel by steamer across Lake Ilmen. *Small Sketches* is mainly an account of such a trip. It is one of the rare pieces of descriptive writings which Dostoevsky published during the last six years of his life. It is authentically Dostoevsky both in the characters he is describing and in the attitude he adopts toward them.

Among the twelve extant articles on the political events in Europe Dostoevsky contributed to *The Citizen* during his editorship of the weekly in 1873-74, one deserves particular attention inasmuch as it is completely free of his pervading chauvinistic bias. It is the article dealing with Maréchal Achille Bazaine's trial for treason; Bazaine had surrendered the fortress of Metz to the Germans without a fight. The article is certainly remarkable for Dostoevsky's insight into the weaknesses of the French party system. Written a hundred years ago, its conclusions seem to be as valid today as they were at the time. It also shows, incidentally, how clear-sighted Dostoevsky could be when not blinded by his own political opinions. The article was published before the end of the trial. Like Dostoevsky, the marshal was sentenced to death and then reprieved, but he did not serve his prison sentence, having escaped to Spain, where he died in 1888, seven years after Dostoevsky's own death.

In February 1865 Dostoevsky published in *Epoch* the first installment of a satirical attack on the "utilitarians" —the "theoreticians," as he referred to them in his article *The Latest Literary Controversies*—under the somewhat cumbrous title *The Crocodile, an Extraordinary Event, or an Amusing Incident in the Amusement Arcade*. The article provoked an angry rejoinder from the liberal press, which accused him of lampooning the high priest of the utilitarians, Nikolai Chernyshevsky, the virtual editor of the left-wing monthly, who had only recently been exiled to Siberia. Dostoevsky indignantly denied that Chernyshevsky had been the prototype of "the gentleman swallowed whole by a crocodile" whom he represented as preaching the utilitarian doctrines out of the crocodile's belly. Still, there probably was more than a grain of truth in this accusation, for Dostoevsky took it so much to heart that he never finished his story. In 1878, however, he turned the tables on his chief political enemy, the famous satirist Mikhail Saltykov, who wrote under the pseudonym of Shchedrin, by publishing in *The Citizen* his brilliant and, on the whole, good-humored satire *The Triton*. After the closure of the *Contemporary* by the authorities, Saltykov-Shchedrin became joint editor with Nekrasov of *Home Annals*, and Dostoevsky's jibe in *The Triton* at the satirist for suspecting a police spy in every man he met was probably quite justified. *The Triton* is preceded by the following short introduction: "After an interval of three months, we received last July the following article, the meaning of which is not quite clear to us. Besides, we find it very hard to give any credence to the incident described in it, especially as according to experts there is no pond on Yelagin Island. However, though we do not entirely understand the meaning of the story, we have decided to publish it."

Unlike the other hitherto untranslated articles in this volume, *The Triton* does not suffer from the diffuseness of style which Dostoevsky himself admitted to be the chief blemish of his writings. This blemish is particularly noticeable in his articles, which were written in an even greater hurry than his novels. But the ideas he expresses in them certainly provide the reader with an excellent opportunity of obtaining an insight into the mind of one of the greatest creative writers of our time. This alone is enough to justify their publication.

D.M.

FOUR ESSAYS

FROM

The Petersburg News

FOUR ESSAYS

I

APRIL 13, 1847

THEY SAY IT IS SPRING IN PETERSBURG. Is it? Still, perhaps it is. Indeed, all the signs of spring are there. Half
the town is down with 'flu and the other half has at least a
cold in the head. These gifts of mother nature fully convince us of her renascence. So it is spring! The classical
season of love. But, the poet says, the season of love and
the season of poetry do not arrive at the same time, and
thank God for that. Farewell poetry; farewell prose; farewell literary monthlies, with or without political trends;
farewell newspapers, opinions, something or other, farewell and forgive us literature! Forgive us our transgres-
sions as we forgive yours. But why on earth do we talk of
literature before anything else? I cannot give you an answer, gentlemen. Let us get rid of our heavy burdens first
of all. We have brought the literary season to an end—
somehow or other, and a good thing, too, though it is said
to be a *natural* burden. Soon, perhaps in a month's time,
we shall tie all our books and journals into a bundle and
not open it again till September. We shall then have something to read in spite of the saying "A little of the good
things of life is enough." Soon the *salons* will be closed,
the evening parties, no more evening parties, the days will
grow longer and we shall no more yawn so charmingly beside elegant fireplaces in stuffy rooms, listening to a story
whose author, taking advantage of our innocence, is so

3

eager to read on the spot or talk about; we shall no longer have to go to the lectures on modern French literature by Comte de Suzor, who has gone to Moscow to assuage the savage breasts of the Slavophiles; the Olympic Circus of Alexander Gwer will no doubt follow him with the same aim in view. Yes, indeed, with the departure of winter, we shall miss a great deal, we shall not have many things, we shall not do many things; we have made up our minds to do nothing during the summer. We are tired; it is time we had a rest. It is not for nothing that Petersburg is said to be such a European, such a businesslike town. It has done so many things; give it a chance to calm down, to have a rest in its country residences, in its woods; it cannot do without woods, at least during the summer. It is only in Moscow that they "rest before work." Petersburg rests *after* work. Every summer it gathers its thoughts while on holiday; even now it is probably considering what it is going to do next winter. In this respect it is very like a certain literary person who, it is true, has written nothing himself, but whose brother has been trying to write a novel all his life. However, while we are preparing for a journey, it behooves us to look back on our past, on the road we have traversed, and at least to say good-by to something, at least to look back once again on what we have done, or who has pleased us particularly. Let us see what has pleased you particularly, gentle reader. I say "gentle" because in your place I should have given up reading essays long ago and this one in particular. I should have done so because so far, I think, as I and you, too, are concerned, there is nothing in our past that pleases us. We all seem to be laborers carrying some heavy burden, willingly hoisted upon our shoulders, who are only too glad to be able to carry it at least till the summer season with due decorum and in a civilized European way. What don't we do out of sheer imitation! For instance, I know a gentleman who could not make up his mind to put on galoshes however muddy the streets, or a fur coat however hard the frost: this gentleman had an

4

overcoat that fitted him perfectly around the waist and gave him a truly Parisian look, and he simply could not bring himself to put on a fur coat, or disfigure his trousers by wearing galoshes. It is true that in this gentleman's opinion European civilization was epitomized in a well-cut coat—that's why he adored Europe so much for its enlightenment; but he fell a victim to his Europeanism, having left a request in his will to be buried in his best pair of trousers. He was buried on March 9, to commemorate the day of the Forty Martyrs, when buns in the shape of larks are sold in the streets. Now, we had, for instance, an excellent Italian opera, and I suppose next year we shall have, if not a better one, a much more sumptuous one. All the same, I don't know why, but I can't help feeling that we keep the Italian opera just for the sake of prestige, as though it were some kind of duty. If we did not yawn (it seems to me, though, that we did yawn a little), we at least behaved with such propriety and decorum, we kept our opinions to ourselves so cleverly, we foisted our enthusiasm upon others so restrainedly that we really could not help looking bored and worried by something. Far be it from me to decry our ability to live in the civilized world. In this respect the opera was of great benefit to the public, having quite naturally sorted out the melomanes into enthusiasts and ordinary lovers of music. The former went off to the gods where the air became as incandescent as in Italy, while the latter sat in the boxes, fully conscious of their importance, the importance of an educated audience, the importance of a thousand-headed hydra which enjoys great influence, has a character of its own and is capable of delivering its own judgment, and were not surprised at anything, for they knew beforehand that this was the chief virtue of a well-educated and well-bred man of the world. So far as we are concerned, we entirely share the views of this second category of the audience. We ought to love art quietly, without being carried away and without forgetting our duties. We are men of business; sometimes we are "too busy" to go to the theater. We

have still so many things to do. That is why I cannot help
being vexed with people who believe that they simply have
to go crazy, that it is their bound duty to counterbalance
the general opinion of the public *on principle* by their enthusiasm. Be that as it may, and however sweetly the
primadonna Borsi and the tenors Guasco and Salvi may
sing their rondos, cavatinas, etc., we dragged ourselves
to the opera just as though we were dragging a cartload of
firewood; we were tired out, we were utterly exhausted,
and if we did fling bouquets on the stage at the end of the
scene, we did so simply because the opera was drawing
to an end. Then there was the famous violinst Heinrich
Wilhelm Ernst . . . It was with an effort that the whole
of Petersburg came to his third concert. Today we are saying good-by to him. We do not know whether there will be
any bouquets! But opera was not our sole entertainment.
We had lots more. Excellent balls and fancy-dress balls.
But having heard our marvelous artist describe on his
violin the other night what a southern fancy-dress ball is
really like, I was completely satisfied with his description
and did not go to our highly respectable northern fancy-
dress balls. The circuses were a great success, though.
Next year, too, I understand, they will be no less successful. Have you noticed, gentlemen, how our common people
enjoy themselves on their holidays? In the Summer Gardens, for instance. A huge, dense crowd moves along
slowly and sedately—all in their Sunday best. Occasionally the shopkeepers' wives and young girls venture to
crack a few nuts. Somewhere in the distance a band is
playing loudly, but the main character of the festivities is
a kind of universal expectancy. On all faces a very naïve
question is written: what next? Is that all? Except that
somewhere in the crowd some drunken German cobbler
starts kicking up a row, but even that does not last long.
And it seems as though this immense multitude feels an-
noyed at these new customs, at these metropolitan amusements of theirs. They cannot help imagining a *trepak*, a

6

balalaika, an unbuttoned, tight-fitting pleated peasant coat with stand-up collar, vodka galore, in short, everything that would let them display themselves, let themselves go as they had been used to, in accordance with their national spirit. But what prevents them is the feeling of decorum, the feeling that it is not the right time for this sort of thing, and the crowd disperses sedately to their homes, not, of course, without dropping into a bar on the way.

I can't help feeling, gentlemen, that there is something here that is not unlike ourselves, except, of course, that we should not reveal our disappointment in so naïve a fashion. We would not ask, is that all? We would not demand anything more. We know very well that for our fifteen rubles we have received a European entertainment. This is enough for us. Besides, such patent celebrities come and visit our country that we cannot possibly express any dissatisfaction. We had learned not to be surprised at anything. If an opera singer is not Rubini, then he's not worth wasting our money on; if a writer is not a Shakespeare, why waste time reading him? Let Italy train artists and let Paris give them a start. We have no time for cherishing, training, encouraging and giving a start to new talents, such as a singer, for instance. Why should we waste time on it when they are sending them from there ready-made and covered with glory? How often does it happen in our country that a writer is not understood and turned down by one generation to be recognized decades afterward by a third subsequent generation, so that the most conscientious of old men just shake their heads in astonishment. We know perfectly well our national character. We are frequently dissastisfied with ourselves, we are often angry with ourselves and at the obligations Europe has thrust upon us. We are skeptics; we would very much like to be skeptics. We try to avoid any show of enthusiasm peevishly and indecorously, doing our best to protect our skeptical Slav soul from it. It is true that occasionally we do feel like enjoying ourselves, but what if it isn't the right thing to enjoy? What will people say about us in that case? It's not for nothing that we have become so fond of the rules of propriety.

However, let us leave all that; let us rather wish ourselves a good summer during which we could have such great fun, such a wonderful rest. Where are we off to, gentlemen? To Reval, to Helsingfors, to the South, abroad, or simply to some country residence? What shall we do there? Go fishing or dancing (summer balls are so excellent!), be bored a little, carry on with our office work in town and, generally, combine the useful with the pleasant. If you should wish to read, take two volumes of the *Contemporary* for March and April; there, as you know, you will find a novel, *An Ordinary Story;* read it if you have not had time to read it in town. It is a good novel. The young author has observation and great intelligence; the idea seems somewhat old-fashioned and bookish to us, but it is cleverly put over. Still, the author's special desire to preserve his idea, to explain it at great length gives the novel a sort of peculiar air of dogmatism and aridity, makes it even a little long-winded. This fault is not made good even by Mr. Goncharov's light and almost volatile style. The author believes in reality and depicts people as they are. His Petersburg women are particularly good.

Mr. Goncharov's novel is very interesting, but the annual report of the Society for Visiting the Poor is even more interesting. We were particularly pleased about the appeal to the general public; we are glad of any joint efforts, particularly a joint effort for some good cause. This report contains many interesting facts. The most interesting fact to us, however, was the extraordinary dearth of the society's funds. But we must not give up hope: there are many honorable people about. Let us mention the orderly soldier who sent in twenty rubles in silver. To a man of his income that must have been an enormous sum. What if we all contributed proportionately? The society's methods of distributing the contributions are excellent and prove it to be a free philanthropic organization which

Four Essays

has a profound understanding of its purpose. But what
about philanthropy out of a sense of duty? The other day
we happened to pass a bookshop and saw in the window
the last issue of the humor magazine *Yeralash* (*Medley*).
In it there is an excellent cartoon of a philanthropist out
of a sense of duty, the man who at home

> Hits poor old Gavrilo
> For a crumpled *jabot*
> Across his mustache and face,

but is suddenly filled with sincere compassion toward his
neighbors when out of doors. We shan't say anything
about the others, though there is a great deal we could say
about them that is both to the point and characteristic of
our modern manners. We could tell the editor of *Yeralash*
the following poignant story on the subject of philanthropy. A certain landowner is talking very warmly to his
friend about his love for humanity and tells him how
anxious he is to do everything in his power so as to conform with the spirit of the age. "You see, sir," he says, "my
house serfs are divided into three categories: the old
servants, venerable fellows, who served my father and
grandfather faithfully and well, belong to the first category; they live in well-lit clean rooms, enjoy every con-
venience and eat what is left over from their master's
table. The second category includes servants who are neither deserving nor venerable, but who are simply good
fellows; I keep them in one well-lit room and on festival
days they have pies for their dinner. The third category
consists of scoundrels, swindlers and all sorts of thieves; I
do not give them pies but lessons in morals every Saturday.
For dogs a dog's life. The scoundrels!"

"How many are there in the first two categories?" his
friend asked.

"Well, to tell you the truth," he replied, looking somewhat embarrassed, "I haven't had anyone so far who . . .
er . . . You see, the peasants are such brigands and
thieves that they do not deserve any philanthropy. . . ."

9

II

APRIL 22, 1847

ONLY A SHORT WHILE AGO I could not imagine a Petersburg citizen except in a dressing gown and a nightcap sitting in a shut-up room with his doctor's strict orders to take something in a tablespoon every two hours. I don't expect that all of them were ill. Some were forbidden to be ill by their duties. Others were saved by their strong constitutions. But at last the sun is shining and this is undoubtedly the greatest piece of news everyone has been waiting for. The convalescent is at a loss what to do: he takes off his nightcap hesitatingly, gets dressed thoughtfully and at last makes up his mind to go out for a walk, armed to the teeth, of course, that is to say, in a sweater, a fur coat and galoshes. He is pleasantly surprised by the warmth of the air, the kind of festive look of the crowds and the deafening roar of the carriages on a roadway no longer covered with snow and slush. On Nevsky Avenue, at last, the convalescent swallows a mouthful of new dust. His heart begins to throb and something in the nature of a smile twists his lips, till then skeptically and questioningly closed. The first Petersburg dust after the deluge of slush and something very moist in the air is, of course, in no way inferior to the delight of the ancient smoke of native hearths, and the convalescent, whose look of skepticism has vanished from his face, makes up his mind to enjoy the spring at long last. Generally speaking, there is something good-natured and ingenuous about the Petersburg citizen who makes up his mind to enjoy the spring at long last. On meeting a friend, he even forgets the usual question, "What's the news?" and changes it to a more interesting one: "How do you like this splendid weather?" And, as is well known, after the weather, especially if it is filthy, the most offensive question to ask anyone in Petersburg is, "What's the news?" I have often observed that when two Petersburg friends meet in the street and, after greeting each other, ask with one accord, "What's the news?" there is a piercing feeling of desolation in the sound of their voices, whatever the intonation they started their conversation with. Indeed, this Petersburg question conceals a feeling of utter hopelessness. What is so unforgivable, however, is that very often the man asking this question, a Petersburger born and bred, is completely indifferent to the answer, for he knows that it is merely an empty phrase to which he will get no reply, that there is no news, that he has put this question at least a thousand times completely without success and is therefore not in the least perturbed at not getting an answer. But he asks it all the same and even seems to show some interest in it, as though some sense of decency forces him to take part in some public enterprise and show that he, too, has some public interests. But so far as public interests are concerned . . . Not that we don't have any. Of course we have. We all love our country ardently. We love our native city of Petersburg, we love to have some fun, if any should come our way. In short, we have a great many public interests. What we are really interested in, though, are *circles*.

It is indeed a well-known fact that the whole of Petersburg is nothing but a collection of an enormous number of small "circles," each one of which has its own constitution, its own rules, its own laws, its own logic and its own oracle. This is, in a way, the creation of our national character, which is still a little shy of social life and prefers to stay at home. Besides, for social life one must possess a certain art, one must provide so many conditions for it—in short, it is much better at home. One feels more natural there, much more at rest, one needs to possess no art for it.

In a "circle" you will always receive a prompt answer to your question, "What's the news?" The question immediately assumes a private meaning and is answered either by some piece of gossip or a yawn or by something that makes you yawn cynically and patriarchally. In a "circle" you can live to the end of your useful life happily and without worry between gossip and a yawn, up to the very moment when influenza or malaria pays a visit to your domestic hearth and you bid a stoic and indifferent farewell to it in happy ignorance of what has been happening to you and why it has all been happening. You will die at dusk, in the dark, on a tearful day, a day without a gleam of light, in complete bewilderment of how it has all come to pass that you have lived (you have lived, haven't you?), achieved something, and now for some obscure reason have to leave this pleasant and tranquil world and take up your abode in a better one.

In some "circles," though, the members conduct heated debates about matters of importance. A number of well-educated and well-meaning persons gather with enthusiasm, fiercely banish all innocent amusements, such as gossip or preference (this is not true of literary circles, of course), and with quite incomprehensible animation discuss all sorts of important subjects. Finally, having discussed, talked about and solved a number of problems of general importance and having reached a unanimous decision, the entire "circle" lapses into a state of irritation, into a kind of unpleasant state of limpness. At last they all suddenly get cross with one another, a few harsh truths are uttered, and a few harsh and bold personalities come to the fore, and in the end it all peters out, calms down, acquires a full measure of common sense and gradually gathers once more into the innocuous "circles" of the first category described above.

It is, no doubt, pleasant to spend your life in this way, but in the end one cannot help feeling hurt and vexed by it all. I, for example, feel vexed with our patriarchal circle because it always produces a man of a most insufferable character. You know this man very well, gentlemen. His name is legion. He has a good heart but nothing else besides. Just as though it really is something extraordinary to possess a good heart in this day and age! As though one simply has to possess it, this eternal good heart! The man who possesses this excellent quality makes his appearance in the world fully convinced that his good heart will be quite sufficient to make him happy and contented for the rest of his days. He is so convinced of his success that, on entering upon the journey of life, he scorns any other means. He has no notion of any impediment or restraint. He is always frank and outspoken. He is the sort of person who wears his heart on his sleeve.

This sort of man is extremely inclined to become fond of a person suddenly and make friends with him. He is absolutely convinced that everyone would immediately become fond of him in turn for the only reason that he had grown fond of them. The good-natured fellow never imagines that it is not enough to grow very fond of people, but that one must possess the art of making people fond of you, without which nothing is of any avail, without which life is no life both for his own loving heart and for the unfortunate fellow whom his heart has chosen for the object of its uncontrollable affection. If such a man gets a friend, this friend at once becomes a piece of furniture, something like a spittoon. Everything, every bit of rubbish inside him, as Gogol expressed it, is flung from his lips into his friend's heart. His friend is obliged to listen to everything and sympathize with everything. Whether he has been deceived in life, whether he has been deceived by his mistress or lost all his money at cards, he at once forces his way unasked, like a bear, into his friend's heart and pours into it without restraint his trivial worries, quite often without noticing that his friend himself is worried to death, that his friend's children had died, that his wife had run away, that, finally, his friend had got sick and tired of his loving heart and that his attention is most tactfully being drawn to the fact that a solitary walk in such excellent weather would have a most beneficial effect on him. Were he to fall in love with a

13

woman, he would insult her a thousand times before becoming aware of it in his loving heart, before becoming aware (if, indeed, he is capable of becoming aware of anything) that the woman is weary of his love, that she hates being with him, that he has become loathsome to her, that he has poisoned her whole existence because of the unimaginative propensities of his loving heart. Yes, it is only in solitude, in some dark corner and most of all in a "circle" that this wonderful work of nature is produced, this specimen of our "raw materials," as the Americans say, on which not a particle of art has been spent, in which everything appears in its natural colors, pure and undefiled, without restraint or hindrance. In his complete innocence such a man forgets, and indeed does not even suspect, that life is an art in itself, that to live means to make a work of art of oneself; that it is only when his interests are those of society's, when one shows sympathy for society as a whole, for its direct and spontaneous demands, that it is not by drowsiness and indifference, which lead to the disintegration of society, that it is not in solitude that his hidden treasure, his capital, his good heart can be ground and polished into a precious, sparkling and genuine diamond!

Good Lord, where are the old villains of the old melodrama and novels, gentlemen? How nice it was when they were about in the world! And therefore how nice it is now to find that right here next to you there lived a most virtuous man, who defended innocence and punished wickedness. This villain, this *tirano ingrato,* was born a villain, ready-made in accordance with some secret and utterly incomprehensible predestination of fate. Everything about him was the personification of evil. In his mother's womb he was already a miscreant; moreover, it is quite likely that his forebears, foreseeing his appearance in the world, deliberately chose a *surname* that fully corresponded to the social position of their future offspring. By his surname alone you realize that this man walks about armed with a knife and stabs people to death for the sheer pleasure of it, for nothing at all, goodness only knows why. Just as though he were a machine made to put the whole world to the fire and sword. That was excellent; at least understandable! But today our novelists talk about goodness only knows what. Today you are somehow suddenly faced with the fact that the most virtuous man, a man, besides, who is quite incapable of committing a crime, suddenly appears to be a perfect villain without even being aware of it himself. And the really annoying thing about it is that no one notices it, there is no one to tell it to, and the man lives long and honorably and finally dies so greatly honored and exalted that you can't help envying him, and quite often he is sincerely and tenderly mourned, and, what is so funny, mourned by his own victims. In spite of it all, there is sometimes so much common sense in the world that it is quite impossible to comprehend how it could all take place among us. Think how much there is of it to spare in an idle hour and all to make people happy! Take, for example, the case of my good friend Julian Mastakovich, a former well-wisher and even to some extent benefactor of mine, who seems to have the intention of getting married. To tell the truth, it would be difficult to get married at a wiser age. He has not got married yet; his wedding is not due for another three weeks. But every evening he puts on his white waistcoat, his wig and all his decorations, buys a bouquet and a box of sweets and goes to visit Glafira Petrovna, his fiancée, a seventeen-year-old girl, full of innocence and complete ignorance of the world. The very thought of the last circumstance brings a most lascivious smile to Julian Mastakovich's sugary lips. Yes, indeed, it is most agreeable to get married at such a sensible age! In my opinion, if I have to be quite frank about it, it is indecent to be married while still a young man, that is, till the age of thirty-five. Immature old age! But when a man is almost fifty—a good position, steady income, propriety, good form, physical and moral rotundity—what could be better? And what a marvelous idea! A man has been living, living for a long time, and at last he grabs happiness. . . . For this reason I was completely at a loss to understand why the other day Julian Mastakovich kept pacing his study, his hands behind his back, with such a dull and dingily sour look on his face that if there had been anything sweet in the character of the civil servant sitting in a corner of the same study and dealing with a highly important and urgent matter, it would have turned sour on the spot and inevitably from one look of his superior. It is only now that I realize what was the matter. I don't really feel like talking about it: the whole thing is so unimportant and nonsensical that it would never occur to any right-thinking person to take it into account. In Gorokhovaya Street there is an apartment on the fourth floor of a house. I had intended to rent it some time ago. Now it is occupied by a widow of an assessor, a rather good-looking young woman. She has a very pleasant appearance indeed. What, therefore, Julian Mastakovich was so worried about was how he could still go on visiting Sofia Ivanovna after his wedding to discuss her court case with her. Sofia Ivanovna had lodged a petition in the courts about two years ago and Julian Mastakovich, who had a very good heart, acted as her solicitor. This is why his grave face was creased in such deep wrinkles. But he put on his white waistcoat at last, picked up the bouquet and box of sweets and drove off to see Glafira Petrovna with a joyful countenance. Some people are lucky, I could not help thinking as I thought of Julian Mastakovich. In the prime of his declining years a man finds a female friend, a girl of seventeen, who understands him perfectly, an innocent and well-educated miss, who had left her boarding school only a month before. And such a man will live a happy and contented life! I could not help feeling envious. As it happened, it turned out to be a filthy and overcast day. I was walking along the Haymarket. But, gentlemen, I am a publicist and I have to talk to you about the latest and most burning news—I'm afraid I had to use this ancient, well-worn cliché, which no doubt came into being in the hope that the Petersburg reader would tremble with joy on hearing some burning piece of news, such as, for example, that Jenny Lind had left for London. But then what's a Jenny Lind to a Petersburg reader! He has lots of other interesting things. . . . But, unhappily, gentlemen, he has nothing of his own. Nothing at all. So there I was, walking along the Haymarket feeling terribly depressed. It was a damp, misty morning. Petersburg got up feeling angry and malicious, like an angry society woman who is green with malice because of what happened to her at the ball the night before. Petersburg was bad-tempered from head to foot. Whether he had had a bad night or a particularly bad attack of jaundice, or caught a cold in the head, or lost his shirt like a stupid youngster at cards that lasted from the evening before so that he had to get up the next morning with empty pockets, feeling vexed with his bad, pampered wives, his rude, lazy children, the grim, unshaven mob of servants, his Jewish creditors, the scoundrels of councilors, calumniators and all sorts of other scandalmongers—it is difficult to say; but he was so angry that it made one sad to look at his huge, damp walls, his marbles, bas-reliefs, statues, columns, which also seemed to be angry with the filthy weather, shivered and chattered with the damp cold, with the bare, wet granite of his sidewalks, which seemed to have cracked under the feet of passers-by out of sheer malice, now, finally, with the passers-by themselves, looking pale-green and stern, terribly angry with something, mostly beautifully cleanshaven and hurrying hither and thither to carry out their duties. The whole Petersburg horizon wore such a horribly sour look. . . . Petersburg was sulking. . . . It was clear that, as happens in cases like that with some irate gentlemen, he wanted very badly to vent his accumulated vexation on some stranger who is unfortunate enough to cross his path, to pick a quarrel, to finally have it out with someone, to haul someone over the coals in a most thorough manner and then run off somewhere and never again be forced to remain in this Indo-Germanic swamp. The sun itself, having gone off during the night for some obscure but compelling reasons to the Antipodes and hastening back with such an amiable smile, with so magnificent a love, to kiss his sick, pampered child, stopped in his tracks halfway; he cast a bewildered and pitying glance at the dissatisfied grumbler, the peevish, unhealthy-looking child, and rushed off behind the leaden clouds. Only one bright and joyful beam, as though begging to be allowed to have a look at the people, fled playfully and for a brief moment out of the deep violet haze, danced playfully over the roofs of houses, flashed across the somber, damp walls, broke into thousands of sparks in every raindrop and vanished as though resenting its own solitude—vanished like a sudden feeling of rapture that inadvertently finds it way into a skeptical Slav soul, of which it is at once ashamed and which it refuses to acknowledge. At once dull dusk spread all over Petersburg. It was one o'clock in the afternoon and the city clocks seemed to be at a loss to explain why they were forced to strike such an hour in such darkness.

At that moment a funeral cortege came along the street, and, in my role as a journalist, I at once recalled the fact that influenza and fever were almost the most hotly discussed questions at the moment in Petersburg. The hero of the cortege, in a sumptuous coffin, was solemnly and decorously, feet foremost, on the way to the most comfortable apartment in the world. A long row of Capuchins, breaking the fir branches in the road with their heavy boots, spread incense all over the street. The plumed hat on the coffin proclaimed ceremoniously the rank of the dignitary. His decorations followed after him on cushions. A son-in-law or perhaps a cousin of the deceased, a colonel, already gray-headed, wept aloud disconsolately beside the coffin. As is the custom on such an occasion, strained, mournful faces could be glimpsed in a long row of carriages, the hiss of never-dying gossip could be heard, and the gay laughter of children in their white *pleureuses*. I felt rather depressed and vexed and,

having no one to haul over the coals, greeted with a very
sour expression and even a highly exasperated look the
courteous attention of a rather phlegmatic and palsied
four-legged beast who was standing quietly in a taxi stand
chewing the last remnants of hay it had stolen from a cart
beside it. Having nothing special to do, it decided to play
a joke on some human passer-by, that is to say, to choose
preferably one who looked very stern and preoccupied,
and having apparently taken me for one of them, it
grasped me lightly by the sleeve, drew me toward it and
then, as though nothing had happened, showed me, who
had been startled out of my depressing morning reverie,
its virtuous bearded muzzle. Poor old hack! I came home
and was about to sit down to write my chronicle, but instead, not knowing how myself, I opened a magazine and
began to read a short story.

The story described a Moscow lower-middle-class family. Love, too, was discussed in that story, but I do not like
to read about love, gentlemen. I don't know about you.
And so I seemed to have been transported to Moscow, my
far-away native city. If you haven't read this story, gentlemen, you ought to read it. Is there any better news I can
tell you? That, for instance, new omnibuses are flourishing on Nevsky Avenue, that the Neva had been the topic
of discussion for a whole week, that they still go on yawning in the *salons* on the appointed days in expectation of
summer? Is this what you want? But I daresay you have
got tired of such news long ago. You have just read the
description of a Northern morning. Depressing, isn't it?
So why not read in this bleak hour of a bleak morning
this story of a poor Moscow family and the breaking of a
family mirror? I seem to have seen in my childhood this
poor Anna Ivanovna, the mother of the family, and I know
Ivan Kirilovich, too, quite well. Ivan Kirilovich is a good
man, except that, when tipsy, he likes to play all sorts of
little jokes. His wife, for instance, is ailing and is afraid of
death. He knows that, of course, and starts laughing in
the company of his friends and talking jestingly, if a little

vaguely, of his intention of getting married again when he is a widower. His wife tries her best to control herself and even tries hard to laugh it all off, for that's the sort of man her husband is. The teapot gets broken, no doubt it costs money, but she can't help feeling ashamed when her husband calls her a fool and starts reproaching her in the presence of strangers. At Shrovetide, Ivan Kirilovich was not at home. A number of young friends of Olinka, their eldest daughter, came, as though by stealth, to have some fun in the evening. There were many young men and boisterous children, among them a certain Pavel Lukich, a character out of a Walter Scott novel. Pavel Lukich got them all excited and proposed that they should play blind-man's buff. Poor ailing Anna Ivanovna had a feeling that there was going to be trouble, but was prevailed upon by the rest and gave her permission for the game. Dear me, gentlemen, only fifteen years ago I myself played blind-man's buff! What a glorious game! And that Pavel Lukich! It is not without good reason that Sashanka, Olinka's black-eyed friend, whispers, as she clings to the wall, trembling with expectation, that she is lost, so terrible is Pavel Lukich even if he is blindfolded.

It so happened that the young children hid in a corner under a chair and made a noise near the mirror. Pavel Lukich rushed at the noise toward the corner, the mirror swayed, broke away from its rusty hinges, flew over his head and fell on the floor, smashed into smithereens. When I read it, I felt as though I had smashed that mirror myself, as though it was all my fault. Anna Ivanovna went pale; they all ran away, seized by panic. What's going to happen now? I was impatiently and fearfully waiting for the arrival of Ivan Kirilovich. I was thinking of Anna Ivanovna. He returned home drunk at midnight. He was met on the front steps by grandmother, an old Moscow character, a terrible mischief-maker, who whispered something to him, no doubt about the *misfortune* that had befallen them. My heart began to throb, and suddenly the storm broke, at first with thunder and lightning, then

gradually dying down. I heard Anna Ivanovna's voice—
what's going to happen now? For three days she was bed-
ridden and a month later she died of consumption. But
how's that? Surely not because of a broken mirror. Is it
possible? Well, she did die, though. A kind of Dickensian
charm fills the description of the last moments of the gentle, obscure life of that woman. Ivan Kirilovich, too, is
good. He nearly went out of his mind. He ran to the drug-
store himself, quarreled with the doctor and kept lament-
ing about whom his wife was leaving him for. Yes, it
brought back many things to my mind! In Petersburg, too,
there are many such families. I personally knew a man
like Ivan Kirilovich. There are lots of them everywhere. I
have brought up the subject of this short story, gentlemen,
because I intended to tell you a story too. . . . But another time . . . By the way, about literature. You have
heard, I suppose, that many people are very pleased with
the winter literary season. There were no loud cries, no
particularly heated arguments, though a few new magazines and newspapers did make an appearance. Everything seems to be much more serious, more austere; there
is more harmony in everything, more maturity, more
thoughtfulness and agreement. It is true, Gogol's book
created a great deal of noise at the beginning of the winter. What is particularly significant is the consensus of
opinion about it among almost all the newspapers and
periodicals whose opinions usually clash with each other.

Sorry, I forgot the most important thing. I remembered it all the time while talking to you, and then it
slipped my memory. Ernst is giving another concert. The
takings will be in aid of The Society for Visiting the Poor,
and the German Philanthropic Society. We need not even
mention the fact that the house will be full, we are quite
sure it will.

III

MAY 11, 1847

Do YOU KNOW, GENTLEMEN, the value of a man in our vast capital city who always has in reserve some piece of news no one as yet knows and, in addition, possesses the gift of telling it in a pleasant manner? In my opinion, he is almost a great man, and there can be no doubt at all that to have such a piece of news in reserve is better than possessing a fortune. When a Petersburg citizen learns some rare piece of news and rushes off to tell it, he already feels in the grip of a kind of spiritual voluptuousness; his voice grows weak and trembles with pleasure; and his heart seems to bathe in an attar of roses. At that moment, while he has not yet conveyed the news and while he is still running along Nevsky Avenue to see his friends, he all at once divests himself of all his troubles; he even (my observation proves) is cured of all his incurable diseases, he even forgives his enemies with pleasure. He is infinitely gentle and great. Why is that? Because at that moment a Petersburg citizen realizes his own dignity and his importance and does justice to himself. Moreover, you, gentlemen, and I, too, probably know many people whom, but for the present peculiar circumstances, we would not have admitted at any other time to our foyer to pay a visit to our valet. It's bad! The man realizes himself that it is his fault and that he is like a little dog who hangs his tail and ears and waits for a more favorable opportunity. Then the right moment comes and the man rings your doorbell boldly and self-confidently, walks past the surprised footman, shakes hands with you without the slightest embarrassment and with a radiant face. You realize at once that he is fully entitled to act like that, for he has come to tell you some piece of news or some society scandal or some-

22

thing else exceedingly pleasant, since a man like that would not have dared to come to see you otherwise. And you listen to him not without pleasure, though you may not at all be like Gogol's society woman who had a dislike of any kind of news but listened with pleasure to the story of how the married woman she employed to teach her children English had thrashed her husband.

Scandal is sweet, gentlemen. I often think that if a man appeared in Petersburg who discovered how to make social life more pleasurable—something that never happened anywhere before—he would have made a fortune. But I'm afraid we all have to be satisfied with more homely entertainers, hangers-on and funny men. There are real masters among them. Human nature is certainly wonderful! Without any desire of playing the hypocrite, a man will suddenly turn himself into the most insignificant insect. His face suffers a sudden change and, instead of moisture, is covered with a kind of radiant unguent. He suddenly grows much smaller than you in height. His independence is completely gone. He gazes into your eyes exactly like a pug waiting for some tidbit. And as if this were not enough, in spite of his excellent cutaway coat, he lies down, in a fit of communal bonhomie, on the floor, wagging his tail joyfully, yelping, licking your hand, not eating his tidbit till he is ordered to do so, and, what is most agreeable and really funny, does all this without losing his sense of dignity. He preserves it, unsullied and piously, even in your own opinion, and it all takes place in the most natural way. You are, of course, a Regulus of honesty, an Aristides, at any rate; in short, you are ready to die for truth and justice. You can see through your man, while, for his part, the man knows perfectly well that he is transparent—and everything goes on swimmingly. You feel good and the little man keeps his dignity. The point is, gentlemen, that he sings your praises. It is, no doubt, not very nice to be flattered, it is annoying, it is disgusting, but you soon discover that the man isn't flattering you at all, that he is merely pointing out the things you yourself admire in your person. Which means that the man is intelligent, tactful, that he is a man of feeling and a connoisseur of the human heart; for he discovers in you faculties that the world perhaps refuses to recognize in you, no doubt, out of envy and quite unjustly. You can never tell, you say to yourself at last, perhaps he is not a flatterer at all, but just a little too naïve and sincere; why, anyway, turn down a man the very first time you see him? And such a man gets everything he wants to get, like the Jewish peddler who implores the gentleman not to buy his merchandise. Why buy it? Let the gentleman just have a look at it, perhaps just to see how bad it is and then go on his way. The peddler unwraps his goods and the gentleman buys everything the Jew wanted to sell him. And our Petersburg little man does not act out of baseness. Why such fine words? He is not a low scoundrel, he is clever, charming, sociable, eager to receive, questing, a man of the world who, it is true, is not abreast of the times, but who possesses a soul like many another man, if not exactly like all men. And another reason why this is so good is that without such a man we should all have died of boredom or torn each other to pieces. Double-facedness, chicanery, duplicity, I admit, are bad things, but if at this very moment everyone appeared as he really is, it would be a damn sight worse.

All these useful reflections occurred to me at the very moment Petersburg went out to show off its new spring fashions in the Summer Gardens and on Nevsky Avenue.

Good Lord, one could write a whole volume on the people one meets on Nevsky Avenue alone. But you know all that from your own agreeable experience, so I do not think it is necessary to write books about it. Something else occurs to me, namely that people spend a terrific amount of money in Petersburg. It would be interesting to know whether there are many people in Petersburg who have enough for everything, that is to say, people who are really well-to-do. I don't know if I am right, but I always imagined Petersburg (if such a comparison is permissible) as a spoiled younger son of a highly respectable father, a man belonging to a past age, rich, generous, sensible and extremely good-natured. Papa at last retires, goes to live in the country and is happy—happy to be able to wear his nankeen coat without violating the rules of decorum. But his son has been left to face the world alone, his son has to study every conceivable subject, his son has to be a young European, and he, Papa, who has only a vague idea of education, has set his heart on his son's becoming the most educated young man in town. His son at once gets a smattering of high life, acquires European airs and grows a mustache and an imperial. Papa, completely failing to notice that his son has grown up and acquired experience and independence, that in one way or another he wants to live his own life and at twenty has learned more from experience than his father, living according to the customs of his forebears, had acquired during the whole of his life; horrified, aware only of the imperial and of his son's helping himself freely to the money in his father's spacious pocket and observing, too, that his son is a bit of a freethinker and egoist, Papa grumbles, is angry, accuses both education and the West, and is most of all vexed at his son for "teaching his grandmother to suck eggs." But his son wants to live and he is in such a hurry that one cannot help wondering where he gets all his energy from. To be sure, he is throwing money about right and left.

The winter season is at an end and Petersburg, at least so far as the calendar is concerned, now belongs to spring. Long columns in the newspapers are beginning to be filled with the names of those who are going abroad. To your astonishment, you notice at once that Petersburg is more upset about his health than about his pocket. I must confess that when I compared these two upsets I was thrown into a panic, to such an extent that I began to imagine that I was not so much in a capital city as in a hospital. But I immediately realized that there was no need for me to worry and that the purses of the provincial papas are still sufficiently spacious and bulging.

You will soon be able to see the sheer magnificence of life in the country residences, the simply inconceivable splendor of the costumes in the birch-tree copses, and how happy and contented everyone will be. I am even quite convinced that even the poor will at once become happy and contented at the sight of this universal joy. At least they will be able to see free of charge what you will not see in any city of our vast empire.

By the way, about the poor. It seems to me that of all the possible kinds of poverty the most disgusting, the most horrible, dishonorable, base and abominable kind of poverty is that which afflicts people of the upper classes, infrequent though it is, the kind that follows the squandering of the last penny but forces people to drive about in carriages, bespattering with mud the pedestrian who earns his living by honest labor and in the sweat of his brow, the people who in spite of everything have servants in white ties and gloves waiting upon them. It is a kind of poverty which is ashamed to beg and yet is not ashamed to accept money in a most arrogant and dishonest way. But enough of this filth! We sincerely wish the Petersburg citizens to have a good time on their vacations and to abstain from yawning. It is a well-known fact that in Petersburg yawning is as much an illness as influenza, hemorrhoids, fever, an illness for which no cures, not even Petersburg fashionable cures, are of any avail. Petersburg gets up yawning, performs its duties yawning and goes to bed yawning. But he yawns most of all at his fancy-dress balls and at the opera. The voices of the wonderful singers are so pure and sonorous that they begin to echo pleasantly throughout our vast empire, in all our cities, towns, villages and hamlets. Everyone already knows that Petersburg has an opera and everyone is full of envy. And yet Petersburg is a little bored in spite of it all, and toward the end of winter, opera is beginning to be as boring to him as—for example—the last winter concert. The last remark does not refer to Ernst's concert, given in aid of some excellent charity. What happened was rather strange. There was such a crowd of people at the theater that many people, anxious to save their lives, decided to have a walk in the Spring Gardens, which, as though on purpose, had just been opened to the public, and for this reason the hall was far from full. But that was due to some misunderstanding. The collection plate for the poor was full. We understand that many people sent their contributions but did not go to the concert themselves because they were terribly afraid of a mob. Quite a natural fear.

You cannot imagine, gentlemen, what a pleasant duty it is to talk to you about Petersburg news and to write a Petersburg chronicle for you. Why, it isn't really a duty at all, but one of the greatest of pleasures. I don't know if you will appreciate my joy. But it really is pleasant to meet, sit down and have a talk about public affairs. I am sometimes even ready to burst into song from sheer joy when entering some social gathering and seeing such exceedingly well-bred and respectable people gathered together, sitting and discussing something decorously without at the same time losing their sense of dignity. What they are discussing is another matter. Sometimes I even forget to follow the trend of the general conversation, entirely satisfied by the general air of social decorum. My heart is filled with most respectful enthusiasm.

But I have so far been unable to grasp the meaning of what our well-bred, upper-class people talk about, the people who are not members of a "circle." Goodness only knows what it is they talk about! Something, no doubt, quite inexplicably charming, for they are all such charming and respectable men of the world, but it is difficult to grasp all the same. It is all as though the conversation were only just starting, as though the instruments were only just being tuned; you sit there for two hours and they are only just starting. Occasionally you get the impression that they are talking about some highly serious subjects, something calling for thought; but afterward when you ask yourself what they were talking about, you simply cannot find an answer: was it about gloves, the state of agriculture, or about whether "a woman's love is lasting"? So that I am afraid I must admit that sometimes I can't help feeling bored. It is as if you were walking home on a dark night, looking dejectedly this way and that, and suddenly heard the sound of music. A ball. Yes, a ball! Shadows flit about behind the brightly lit windows, you can hear the rustle of dresses and the scraping of shoes, you even imagine you can catch the seductive whispering of the guests, there are gendarmes at the main entrance, you pass by feeling a kind of elation, excitement; some vague desire has awakened in you, a dark craving for something. You seem to have caught a glimpse of life, and yet all you carry away with you is a pale, colorless motif, an idea, a shadow, almost nothing. And you pass by as though distrusting something; you seem to hear something quite different. Through the colorless motif of an everyday life you seem to hear quite a different one, something piercingly alive and sad, as in Berlioz's* ball at the Capulets'. Doubts and a feeling of utter desolation wring your heart, the same feeling of desolation which is characteristic of the long refrain of the doleful Russian song that touches such a familiar chord in our hearts:

> Listen. . . . Other sounds are heard. . . .
> Sounds of despondent, desperate revelry.
> Is it a highwayman singing there,
> Or a maiden weeping in the sad hour of parting?
> No, it is haymakers homeward from work.
> Who has made their song? How? Look,
> All around dense forests, Saratov steppes. . . .

* Berlioz gave a number of concerts in Petersburg in February and March 1847, including a piece from his Romeo and Juliet symphony.

The other day was a holiday. A national Russian holiday to welcome the arrival of spring, when Russian garlands are woven all over. But in Petersburg the weather was cold and dead. It was snowing. The buds on the birch trees had not yet opened and, anyway, the hail had torn down the buds the day before. The day was like a day in November when one waits for the first fall of snow, when the Neva roars and is whipped into waves by the wind, which howls and whistles through the streets, making the lamps creak. I can't help feeling that on a day like this the Petersburg citizens are terribly ill-tempered and melancholy, and my heart contracts even as I write this article. I cannot help feeling that they are all sitting lazily at home, depressed and bad-tempered, some whiling away the time by slandering their neighbors, others spending the day quarreling with their wives or poring meekly over some official documents or playing preference through the night, dozing off and waking with a start to begin another game, or making coffee in some solitary, depressing room and lulled to sleep by the fantastic bubbling of the boiling water in the coffee pot. It seems to me that the people in the streets are not in the mood for festive days and public interests, that on such a wet day they are oppressed with care, except perhaps for that peasant with the big beard who seems to feel happier when it rains than when it shines, and that gentleman with the beaver hat who has gone out on such a cold, wet day to put some money in the bank. . . . In short, it is bad, gentlemen, bad! . . .

I V

JUNE 15, 1847

IT IS MID-SUMMER, hot, the city is deserted; everyone is in the country, living on his impressions, enjoying nature.

There is something inexplicably naïve, something moving, even, about our Petersburg countryside when suddenly and quite unexpectedly it reveals its hidden powers, clothes itself in verdure, dresses up in all its finery, bedecks itself with flowers . . . I don't know why it reminds me of an unhealthy-looking ailing girl whom you sometimes regard with pity, with a kind of compassionate love, and sometimes even do not notice at all, but who suddenly, in a twinkling, and, somehow, quite unexpectedly becomes wondrously, inexplicably beautiful, so that, astonished and struck dumb, you cannot help asking yourself what power has made those always sad and wistful eyes gleam with such fire, what has brought out the blood in those pale cheeks, what has filled the tender features of that face with such passionate desire, why that bosom is heaving so, what has so suddenly evoked the strength, vitality and beauty on the face of that woman, made it radiant with such a smile, made it become animated with such joyous, sparkling laughter? You look about you, you are searching for something, you are trying to guess . . . But the brief moment passes and tomorrow perhaps you will again meet the same sad and wistful look, the same pale face, the same characteristic meekness and timidity of movements, lassitude, weakness, dull anxiety and even traces of a sort of debilitating vexation at that momentary animation. But why comparisons? Who wants them now? We have gone to the country to live a contemplative, spontaneous life without comparisons and opinions, to enjoy nature, to rest, to laze about to one's heart's content and leave behind the unnecessary and troublesome worries of life, the nonsensical rubbish heap of existence in sumptuous apartments, till a more convenient time. I have a friend, though, who assured me the other day that we could not even laze about properly, that we did so painfully and uneasily, without any real enjoyment, that our rest was a sort of feverish one, anxious, gloomy and dissatisfied, that we could not rid ourselves of analysis, comparisons, skeptical views and mental reservations, while perpetually worried by some everlasting, never completed, important business; that, finally, we were getting ready to leave for some restful vacation as if it were some grim and difficult business and that if, for instance, we wished to enjoy nature, we would put down in our diaries a week before that on such and such a day we would be going to enjoy nature. This reminds me very much of that careful German who, on leaving Berlin, very calmly jotted down in his diary: "On passing through Nürnberg must not forget to get married." A German, of course, always has some system in his head and he does not appreciate how disgraceful such a decision is out of gratitude for it. But one cannot really help admitting that sometimes there is no system whatever in our actions, that things happen as though in accordance with some oriental predestination. My friend is to a certain extent right: we do seem to be dragging our cart of life along as though we had not the strength to do so, as though we did so out of a sense of duty, as though it were too much for us, and we are ashamed to admit that we are not up to it and that we are tired. As though we had really gone to the country for a rest and to enjoy nature. Have a good look at the useless things we have taken with us beyond the toll gate. Not only have we not left behind our old things that had served us so well during the winter; we have brought with us all sorts of new things: we live on our memories, and any old scandalous story, any old affair is furbished up to do duty for something new. Otherwise we are bored, otherwise we will have to try what a game of preference is like in the open air to the accompaniment of the nightingale's song, which, as a matter of fact, we do try. Besides, we are hardly constituted to enjoy country life and our countryside too, as though knowing the stuff we are made of, we had forgot to organize things to our advantage. Why, for instance, is a most unpleasant characteristic so strongly developed in us (a characteristic that is perhaps quite often useful in our kind of society) *to test and weigh* without any need, just by force of habit, a little too accurately *our impressions;* sometimes to weigh only impending, future pleasures, to appraise and find satisfaction in them beforehand in our daydreams, to be satisfied with fancies and, quite naturally, to be quite incapable of dealing with the real thing afterward? We always crush and pull to pieces a flower in order to get a stronger impression of its fragrance and we are indignant when instead we only get an acrid smell. And yet it is hard to say what would happen to us if we did not have those few days in a year and if we did not satisfy our everlasting and insatiable passion for spontaneous and natural life by the diversity of natural phenomena. And how are we to avoid getting tired or suffering a total collapse when we never cease chasing after impressions like a rhyme to a bad verse, tormented by a desire for external, spontaneous activity and in the end terrified to a point of physical sickness by our own illusions, our own chimeras, our own reveries and all those extra remedies with which people nowadays try somehow or other to fill the insipid emptiness of their everyday, colorless lives.

Our passion for some sort of activity reaches a point of feverish and uncontrollable impatience; we all long for some serious occupation, many of us are full of an ardent desire to do good, to be of some use, and we gradually begin to realize that happiness is not the same thing as being able to afford to sit about twiddling one's thumbs or just to do something for the sake of a change when the occasion arises, but consists of continual and tireless activity and the development of all faculties and capabilities in practice. Are there many among us who do their work, as they say, *con amore?* It is said that we Russians are lazy by nature and love to shun work and that if it is thrust upon us, we make a mess of it. But is that so really? What experiment has this unenviable national characteristic of ours proved? Altogether too great a clamor has recently been raised about our general laziness and inactivity, and people have been urging each other a little too much to engage in better and more useful

work, though, to be quite frank, merely urging each other
on. As a consequence, we are ready to accuse our fellow
citizens for no reason whatever of not biting hard enough,
as Gogol had once observed. But take the first step toward
a better and more useful activity yourselves, gentlemen,
and show it to us in any form you like; show us what to do
and, above all, make us take an interest in it, let us do it
ourselves, give our own individual creative abilities free
play. Are you capable of doing that, you who are so keen
on urging us on? You are not, so why accuse us and
waste words? The trouble is that if anything has to be
done, we only become aware of it, as it were, from the
outside. It never arouses any particular sympathy in us
and it is in this that the peculiarly Russian characteristic
reveals itself: to do something badly and unconscientiously
because we do not really care how it is done and then, as
they say, go to seed completely. This national characteristic of ours can be seen in everything, even in the most
unimportant facts of social life. If, for instance, someone
has not sufficient means to live in some sumptuous apartment in grand style or to dress decently, to dress as *everyone* does (that is, as very few can afford to do), then our
room is very often turned into a pigsty and our clothes
reduced to a point of indecent cynicism. When a man is
dissatisfied, when he has not the means to show what is
best in him, to express himself fully (not out of vanity,
but because of the most material necessity to realize, ful-
fill and justify his *I* in real life), he at once gets involved
in some quite incredible situation; he either takes to the
bottle in a big way, or becomes a gambler and card-sharp,
or a rabid duelist, or goes crazy from sheer arrogance
while at the same time despising arrogance in his heart
and even resenting the fact that he had to get into trouble
because of such a silly thing as arrogance. And before
you know, you come to a conclusion, an almost unfair,
offensive but seemingly very probable conclusion, that we
have little sense of personal dignity; that we have little of
necessary egoism and that, finally, we are not accustomed

to do a good deed without a reward. Entrust, for instance, some accurate, systematic German with some business, a business that is against all his aspirations and inclinations, and merely explain to him that it will provide him with a livelihood and give him a decent job, help him to reach his desired goal, etc. The German will at once set to work, bring it to a satisfactory conclusion, and even introduce some special, new system in his work. But is that good? To a certain extent it is not, because in such a case a man goes to another terrifying extreme, lapses in a sort of phlegmatic immobility, which sometimes does away with the man completely, putting in his place a system, a duty, a formula and blind obedience to his forefathers' customs, although these are completely out of tune with the spirit of the present day and age. Peter the Great's reform, which introduced free activity in Russia, would have been impossible with such an element in our national character, an element that often assumes a naïvely beautiful but sometimes extremely comic form. A German is quite capable of being engaged till he is fifty, meanwhile teaching the children of a Russian landowner, saving up his pennies and at last marrying his heroically faithful Minchen, dried up from remaining a virgin too long. A Russian, on the other hand, would not be able to keep it up; he would rather fall out of love or go to seed, or do something else equally drastic—and here one is fully justified in reversing the well-known proverb "What's good for the German is death for the Russian." And are there many Russians who possess the means of doing their work properly and with love? For all work requires a will to do it well, requires love in the man who does it, requires this man to devote himself to it entirely. And are there many Russians who have discovered what their real activity is? For some activity requires the possession of means, security, and, besides, a man may not be inclined to some kind of work: he gives it up and then the whole thing goes to rack and ruin in no time. It is then that what is known as dreaminess arises in the characters who are

34

eager for activity, eager for life, eager for results but are weak, feminine, tender. And in the end the man is no longer a man but a kind of strange being of a neutral gender—a *dreamer*. And do you know what a dreamer is, gentlemen? It is a Petersburg nightmare, it is a personified sin, it is a mute, mysterious, gloomy and wild tragedy, with all its frantic horrors, catastrophes, peripeteias and unhappy endings—and we are not saying this in jest, either. You sometimes come across a man who looks absent-minded, with a vague, dull look in his eyes, often with a pale, crumpled face, always busy with something terribly burdensome, some kind of difficult, abstruse problem, looking exhausted by some apparently hard work but actually producing absolutely nothing—such is the dreamer from the outside. A dreamer is always a difficult sort of person because he is unpredictable to a degree: sometimes too cheerful, sometimes too gloomy, at times rude, at others very considerate and tender, one moment an egoist and another capable of the most honorable feelings. These gentlemen are no good at all in the service, and though they sometimes get jobs, they are quite incapable of doing them and merely waste their time, which is really worse than doing nothing. They have a profound aversion to anything of a formal nature, and in spite of or perhaps because of being such mild and peaceful individuals and afraid of being attacked, they are themselves formalists *par excellence*. But at home they are quite different. They usually live in complete solitude, in some inaccessible quarters, as though they were hiding from people and the world, and, generally, there is something melodramatic about them at first sight. They are gloomy and taciturn with their own people, they are absorbed in themselves and are very fond of anything that does not require any effort, anything light and contemplative, everything that has a tender effect on their feelings or excites their sensations. They are fond of reading and they read all sorts of books, even serious scientific books, but usually lay the book down

35

after reading two or three pages, for they feel completely satisfied. Their imagination, mobile, volatile, light, is already excited, their senses are attuned, and a whole dreamlike world, with its joys and sorrows, with its heaven and hell, its ravishing women, heroic deeds, honorable activity always with some superhuman struggle, with crime and all sorts of horrors, suddenly possesses the entire being of the dreamer. His room vanishes, and so does space; time stops or flies so quickly that an hour counts for a minute. Sometimes entire nights pass imperceptibly in indescribable pleasures; often in a few hours he experiences the heavenly joys of love or of a whole life, huge, gigantic, unheard of, wonderful like a dream, grandiosely beautiful. By some mysterious power his pulse quickens, tears gush, the pale, moist cheeks blaze with feverish fire, and when the dawn breaks in at the window with its rosy light, he is pale, sick, worn-out and happy. He flings himself on the bed almost unconscious, and, as he falls asleep, for a long time he can feel a sort of morbidly delightful physical sensation in his heart. The moments of sobering-up are dreadful; the unhappy wretch cannot bear them and immediately takes his poison in new and larger doses. Again a book, a musical motif, some old memory from real life, in a word, one of the thousands of the insignificant reasons, and the poison is ready, and once more his imagination begins to roam over the emblazoned, fanciful canvas of his quiet, mysterious dream world. In the street he walks with a drooping head, paying little attention to his surroundings, sometimes completely oblivious of reality even there, but if he does notice something, then the most ordinary trifle, the most insignificant fact assumes a fantastic coloring in his mind. Indeed, his mind seems to be attuned to perceive fantastic elements in everything. Closed shutters in broad daylight, a misshapen old woman, a man approaching him waving his arms and talking aloud to himself, as one, incidentally, often comes across in the street, a family scene in the window of a dilapidated wooden house—all these are almost adventures.

His imagination is attuned; at once a whole novel or a short story is born. But quite often reality produces a painful, hostile impression in the dreamer's breast, and he hastens to hide himself in his precious golden corner, which, as a matter of fact, is often dusty, untidy, unswept and dirty. Little by little our reprobate begins to shun crowds, to take no interest in general affairs, and gradually and imperceptibly the talent of real life becomes blunted in him. He quite naturally begins to believe that the pleasures that his uncontrolled imagination gives him are fuller, more splendid and more enchanting than real life. At last, in his delusion, he completely loses the moral judgment that enables men to appraise the full beauty of the present; he is at a loss, he gets flustered, he lets the moments of real happiness slip by, and, in his apathy, he folds his arms indolently and does not want to know that a man's life is continual self-contemplation of nature and actual reality. There are dreamers who actually celebrate the anniversary of their fantastic sensations. They often note the dates when they were particularly happy and when their imagination presented them with the most agreeable fancies, and if they happen to walk along a certain street at the time, or read some book, or catch sight of some woman, they do their utmost to repeat the same experience on the anniversary of their impressions, copying and trying to recall the minutest circumstances of their rotten, impotent happiness. Is not such a life a tragedy? Is it not a sin, a horror? Is it not a caricature? And are we not all more or less dreamers? . . .

Life in the country, full of external impressions, nature, movement, sun, greenery, women, who are so kind and pretty in summer—all this is very beneficial for the sick, strange and gloomy Petersburg, in which youth passes away so quickly, health deteriorates so quickly, hopes fade so quickly and man, too, undergoes a radical change so quickly. The sun is such a rare visitor, greenery such a precious thing, and we are so used to our wintry quarters that the novelty of customs, the change of place and mode of life cannot but have a most beneficent effect upon us. The city is so magnificent and so empty. Some eccentrics, though, like it in summer more than at any other season of the year. Besides, our poor summer is so brief; you don't even notice how the leaves turn yellow, the flowers fade and wither, the days become damp and misty; unhealthy autumn is here again and the flurry and scurry of life is resumed as before. . . . An unpleasant perspective—now, at any rate.

FIVE ARTICLES

FROM

Time

Time, JANUARY, 1861

Introduction

IF THERE IS A COUNTRY IN THE WORLD which to other
countries, distant or contiguous, is more unknown or un-
explored, more than any other country enigmatic and
mysterious, this country is undoubtedly Russia to its
Western neighbors. Neither China nor Japan can have
been hidden with such a veil of mystery from the inquisitiveness of the European countries as Russia has
been in the past or is at present or will be for a long time
in the future. We are not exaggerating. China and Japan
are, to begin with, too distant from Europe, and, secondly,
the access to those countries is often very difficult; Russia,
on the other hand, is wide open to the rest of Europe, the
Russians conduct themselves without the slightest reserve in their dealings with Europeans, and yet the character of the Russian is perhaps less distinctly comprehended by the European than the character of a Japanese
or Chinese. To Europe, Russia is one of the riddles of the
Sphinx. The *perpetuum mobile* or the elixir of life will be
discovered sooner than Western Europe will comprehend
the Russian truth, the Russian spirit, character or turn of
mind. In this respect even the moon has been explored
more thoroughly than Russia. At least it is absolutely
certain that no one lives on the moon; on the other hand,
it is known that people do live in Russia and even that
they are Russians, but what kind of people? This is still a

41

mystery, though the Europeans are quite convinced that they have long since understood us.

At different times our inquisitive neighbors have made great efforts to understand us and our mode of life; materials, figures and facts were collected; investigations were set on foot, for which we are exceedingly grateful to the investigators, because their work has been very useful to ourselves, too. But all sorts of efforts to deduce from these materials, figures and facts anything fundamental, intelligent and sensible about a Russian, anything synthetically true—all these efforts always founder against some sort of fateful obstruction which seems to be there expressly for that purpose. When Russia is under discussion a kind of stupor descends on the very people who invented gunpowder and numbered so many stars that they became convinced that they could snatch them out of the sky. Everything proves it, beginning with trifles and ending with the most profound investigations of the fate, meaning and future of our country. They do know something about us, though. They know, for instance, that Russia lies between certain longitudes and latitudes, that she abounds in certain raw materials, etc., that there are places in it where dogs are used for driving. They know, too, that besides dogs there are people in Russia, very strange people who are like other people and yet seemingly unlike anyone; they seem to be Europeans and yet at the same time also barbarians. They know that our common people are quite intelligent and yet possess no genius; that they are very handsome, live in wooden cottages, but are incapable of higher development because of the hard frosts. They know that Russia has an army, and a big one, too, but think that the Russian soldier is an automaton made out of wood, that he walks on springs, that he is incapable of rational thought and has no feelings, and that this is why he is so steadfast in battle, but has no idea of independence and is inferior to the Frenchman in every respect. They know that Russia had an Emperor Peter, who is called Great, a monarch not without abilities but only half educated and carried away by his passions; that he was educated by Lefort, a native of Geneva, who transformed him from a barbarian into an intelligent human being and suggested to him the idea of building a navy and cutting the Russian beards and *caftans,* that Peter did, in fact, cut the beards and that as a consequence the Russians became Europeans. But they also know that if Lefort had not been born in Geneva, the Russians would still be walking around with beards and there would therefore be no reorganization of Russia. But these examples will suffice; the other information is almost of the same kind. We are saying this quite seriously. Just open up the books written about us by viscounts, barons and mostly by marquesses who have paid a visit to Russia, books that have been sold in tens of thousands of copies all over Europe, read them attentively and you will see whether we are speaking the truth, whether we are joking or not. And what is so interesting is that some of these books were written by quite remarkably intelligent people. The same kind of feebleness which is manifested in these attempts of foreign travelers to cast an intelligent eye over Russia and grasp her chief idea, we see in the absolute incapacity of almost every foreigner who is forced by circumstance to live in Russia, sometimes even for fifteen or twenty years, to look about and see what is actually happening round him, get acclimatized in Russia, grasp something thoroughly, and get some idea that in any way approaches the truth. Let us, to begin with, take our nearest neighbor, the German. All sorts of Germans come to our country: foolish ones and intelligent ones, scholars who arrive with the serious intention of finding out and describing and in this way doing something useful for science, and ignorant people who come to our country with the more modest but honest intention of baking rolls and smoking sausages—all sorts of Webers and Lüdekens. Some of them even make a point of accepting "as a rule and even as a sacred duty" that they should acquaint the Russian public with all sorts of European rarities and consequently arrive with all sorts of male and female giants, with learned marmots or monkeys, specially trained by Germans for Russian delectation. But whatever the difference between a learned and an ordinary German so far as their ideas, social position, their education and their purpose for visiting Russia, in Russia all these Germans at once agree about their impressions. A kind of morbid feeling of mistrust, a kind of fear of reconciling himself with what he sees that is quite unlike himself, an absolute inability to realize that a Russian cannot turn himself into a perfect German and that it is therefore impossible to judge him by one's own standards, and, finally, open or secret but at all events boundless arrogance in the presence of Russians—these are the characteristics of almost every German in his attitude toward Russia. Some of them come to Russia to act as agents of Russian landowners; others come as naturalists to catch Russian beetles and acquire immortal glory thereby and preside over all sorts of learned conferences; others still, after attending conferences for fifteen years, make up their minds at last to do something useful for their contemporaries and describe in great detail the nature of the rocks that are going to be used for the plinth of the future memorial to the thousandth anniversary of Russia. Some of them are exceedingly kindhearted, and these nearly always begin to study Russian, grow very fond of the Russian language and literature, become at last fluent Russian speakers, not without herculean efforts, of course, and in an excess of enthusiasm, wishing to be of great benefit to themselves, the Russians and humanity at large, they decide to "translate Kheraskov's *Rossiade* in Sanskrit." However, not all of them translate the *Rossiade*. Some arrive with the intention of writing their own *Rossiade* and publish it in Germany. There are famous works of this kind. You read this *Rossiade*— serious, matter-of-fact, clever, even witty. The facts are true and new; a profound view is taken of some facts, a view that is both original and accurate just because it is

44

more convenient to observe Russian facts if you don't
happen to be a Russian, to observe them in a detached
way; then, suddenly, when it comes to expressing an
opinion about something very important, something fundamental, without which no theories about Russia, no
facts acquired by most conscientious studies, can give
any idea of it, or give at most a confused, not to say
muddleheaded, one—suddenly our scholar is puzzled,
comes to a stop, loses the trend of his argument and concludes with such a piece of absurdity that the book seems
to be torn out of your hand by itself and sometimes even
finds its way under the table.

The French visitors are quite unlike the German; they
are diametrically opposite. A Frenchman will not start
translating anything into Sanskrit, not because he does
not know Sanskrit—a Frenchman knows everything, even
if he has learned nothing—but because, in the first place,
he comes to our country in order to cast the most pene-
trating look at us, to pierce with his eagle eye all our
secrets and then pronounce his final, categorical opinion
of us; second, because he already knew in Paris what he
was going to write about Russia; he may even write an
account of his travels before he has even been to Russia
and sell it to a publisher, and only then come to visit us
—to show off, to captivate and to fly off. A Frenchman is
always sure that he has no one to thank for anything, even
if one really does something for him, and not because he
has an evil heart, but, on the contrary, because he is
absolutely convinced that it isn't he who, for example,
has been entertained, but that he has himself by his
appearance made everybody happy, comforted and re-
warded everybody, and satisfied everybody he happened
to meet on his travels. The most stupid and dissolute of
them, having spent some time in Russia, leave us absolutely convinced that they have made the Russians happy
and to some extent changed Russia. Some of them arrive
with serious, important intentions, staying for as long as
twenty-eight days, an immense period, the number of

days showing the great conscientiousness of the explorer, for in such a time he could carry out and even describe a voyage round the world. After snatching his first impressions of Petersburg, in the description of which he is not entirely unsuccessful, and, incidentally, casting a critical eye over the English institutions as well, teaching, in passing, the Russian boyars (*les boyards*) table-rapping or blowing soap bubbles, which is very charming and a great improvement on the majestic and swaggering boredom of our assemblies, he finally makes up his mind to make a thorough and detailed study of Russia, and leaves for Moscow. In Moscow he has a look at the Kremlin, gives a thought to Napoleon, praises the tea, praises the beauty and the health of the people, sheds a tear over their premature depravity, over the lamentable results of the attempts to inoculate them with European civilization, over the disappearance of national customs, for which he will immediately find proof in the change of ten guitar-shaped hackney cabs for one that is wagonette-shaped, resembling a European cabriolet; then he launches a violent attack on Peter the Great, followed quite naturally by the story of his own life, full of the most remarkable adventures. Everything can happen to a Frenchman without, however, harming him in any way, so much so that after telling his readers the story of his life, he will at once proceed to tell them a Russian story, a true story, of course, taken from Russian national life, with the title "Petroucha," having two advantages: first, that it gives a true picture of Russian life, and, second, that, at the same time, it gives a true picture of the life of the Sandwich Islanders. He will, of course, take notice of Russian literature, too; he will say a few words about Pushkin, who, he will remark condescendingly, was a poet not without gifts, a wholly national poet, who successfully imitated André Chénier and Madame Deshoulières; he will have a word of praise for Lomonosov, will speak with some respect of Derzhavin, observing that he was not an untalented fabulist who imitated La Fontaine, and will express his special sympathy for Krylov, a young writer, prematurely snatched away by death (followed by his biography), who successfully imitated Alexandre Dumas in his novels. Next our traveler bids farewell to Moscow, continues his travels, expresses admiration for the Russian *troikas* and at last makes an appearance somewhere in the Caucasus where he joins Russian Cossacks in shooting Circassians, strikes up an acquaintance with Shamil and reads *The Three Musketeers* to him. . . .

We repeat: in saying all this, we are not at all joking or exaggerating. And yet you cannot help feeling that there is a grain of parody or caricature in our words. It is of course true that there is not a single thing in the world that cannot be regarded from a comic point of view. Everything can be derided, we shall be told; you can say something that is not exactly as it is, quote the same words but not express them in the same way. Agreed. But take the most serious view expressed by foreigners about us and you will be convinced that nothing of what we have said is exaggerated.

2.

But we must make a reservation. The last absurd cries concerning us by foreigners were mostly made while in a state of excitement, during the recent conflicts, which have now, thank God, come to an end for a long time, if not forever, during a war, amid tumultuous shouts of battle. However, if a summary of former opinions were made, the conclusion would be almost the same. The books are available: one can look them up.

Well? Are we to accuse foreigners for holding such an opinion? Accuse them of hatred of us, of obtuseness? Laugh at their short-sightedness, their narrow-mindedness? But their opinion has not been expressed once or by any one person: it has been expressed by the whole of the West, in every shape and form, both coolly and with emotion, by shouters and by perspicacious men, by scoundrels and by men of great honesty, in prose and in verse, in novels and in histories, in *premier Paris* and from orators' rostrums. This is therefore almost a general opinion and it is rather difficult to accuse everybody. Besides, what are they all to be accused of? Of what crime? Let us declare quite frankly: not only is there no question of any crime here, but we regard such an opinion as quite a normal one, that is, as the direct result of the course of events, in spite of the fact that it is, of course, completely false. The point is that foreigners cannot possibly understand us differently even if we try to dissuade them. But why try to dissuade them? To begin with, it is highly improbable that Frenchmen would subscribe to *Time* even if Cicero himself were to be one of our contributors, though perhaps we would not have had him as one of our contributors. They will therefore not read our reply. Neither would the Germans. Second, it must be admitted that they really do possess a certain inability to understand us. They don't even understand one another very well.

Even today the Englishman is not convinced of the reasonableness of the existence of the Frenchman. The Frenchman pays him back in the same coin, and with interest, in spite of any alliances, *ententes cordiales*, etc. And yet the one and the other are Europeans, representatives of Europeans. How, then, can they be expected to fathom us Russians when we are a puzzle to ourselves (at least we are constantly posing puzzles about ourselves to ourselves). Have not the Slavophiles set riddles to the Westerners and the Westerners to the Slavophiles? We are addicted to rebuses even to this day. Read the announcements concerning the publication of periodicals and you will be absolutely convinced of that. And how can they possibly fathom us when one of our chief idiosyncrasies is that we are *not* Europeans, and they cannot judge people except by themselves. What is so confusing about it all is that to this very day we ourselves keep presenting ourselves to them as Europeans. What could they understand in this confusion, especially looking at us? Can they be blamed for still not having enough facts about us to form an impartial opinion of us? Have we attracted their attention by anything special, anything original? On the contrary, we seem even to have been afraid to admit our originalities, we hid them not only from them but also from ourselves; we were ashamed of carrying about some distinguishing mark on us and could not become wholly Europeans however much we tried; we reproached ourselves for that and, as a result, hastened to agree with them and did not attempt to disabuse them. And, anyway, what Russian did they see? By whom did they judge? It is true they had been meeting many Russians continually for a century and a half. Together with the rest, Mr. Grech traveled to Western Europe and wrote his Paris Letters from there. About Mr. Grech we know that he made an attempt to make the French change their minds about us, conversed with Sainte-Beuve and Victor Hugo, as becomes clear from his own letters. "I told Sainte-Beuve *straight*," is how he expresses himself. "I told Victor Hugo *straight*." You see, Mr. Grech had told Sainte-Beuve or Victor Hugo (I do not remember whom—I have to look it up) *straight* that literature which preached immorality, etc., etc., made a great mistake and was not worthy of the name of literature (the words may not be the same, but the meaning is— I vouch for it). I suppose Sainte-Beuve had to wait fifty years to hear this sort of copybook truth. I expect Sainte-Beuve must have opened his eyes wide on hearing this! Still, let us set our minds at rest: the French are a very courteous people and we know that Mr. Grech returned safe and sound from Paris. Besides, perhaps we are not mistaken in saying that one cannot judge all Russians by Mr. Grech. But enough of Mr. Grech. We referred to him only in passing. To business! Others besides Mr. Grech had been to Paris. From time immemorial our retired cavalry officers made an appearance there, gay and good-natured fellows, who when on parade astonished our public by the beauty of their figures, encased in buckskin, and afterward spent the rest of their days not in the

49

performance of the burdensome duties of the service but in pursuit of pleasure. Thousands of young ne'er-do-wells who went abroad, too, have seen no service, but were greatly worried about their estates. Many of our native landowners went there, too, with all their families and mountains of luggage; they climbed good-naturedly up the towers of Notre Dame, viewed Paris from there and, unknown to their wives, chased after grisettes. Deaf and toothless Russian ladies, who had completely lost the use of their native tongue, which they never really knew, spent the rest of their lives there. Our mothers' darlings (which, translated into French, are: *enfants de bonne maison, fils de famille*), on their return to us, knew all the secrets about Palmerston and all the dirty gossip in France to the last society scandal, and, at dinner, they asked their hosts to tell their servant to pour them a glass of water so as not to have to utter two words in Russian even to a butler. Mr. Grigorovich personally bears witness to one of these facts in one of his recent stories. But there were some of them who knew Russian, who even studied Russian literature for some unknown reason and produced comedies on the Russian stage, such as Alfred de Musset's *Comédies et Proverbes*, under the title of—well, for instance, *The Racans* (an invented title, of course). Since the subject of *The Racans* characterizes a whole class of society appearing in such comedies and at the same time represents a special genre of works of the same kind, let me tell you all about it in a few words. A long time ago, in the last century, there flourished in France a most vulgar versifier with the name Racan, who was not fit to polish even Mr. Sluchevsky's boots. A certain marquise, a fool of a woman, gets carried away by his poems and expresses the wish to meet him. Three mischievous fellows arrange to go to see her, one after another, under the name of Racan. No sooner does she see one Racan off to the door than another one calls at her house. The whole wit, the whole point, the whole pathos of the comedy consists in the look of stupefaction on the face of the marquise at the sight of Racan in three persons. The gentlemen who concocted (sometimes at the age of forty) such comedies after *The Government Inspector* were absolutely convinced that they were conferring most precious gifts on Russian literature. And there were not only one or two of such gentlemen; their name is legion. To be sure, none of them writes anything. The author of *The Racans* is almost an exception; but, on the other hand, every one of them looks as though he were going to write *The Racans* on the spot. By the way (forgive the digression), any one of our columnists could have written a most diverting article if he had only taken the trouble to tell us about the subject matter of all these comedies, stories, "proverbs," etc., etc., which still appear sporadically in Russian literature. District police officers who refuse on principle to marry daughters of army generals—are they not the same kind of Racans, in a different way, of course, and only a little more malignant? I know, for example, of one short story that has as its subject a swallowed watch that continues to tick in a man's stomach —it's a perfect masterpiece! No doubt it is or will be written also on principle, namely that art must be an aim in itself. It is characteristic of the time we live in: even the authors of *The Racans* cannot do without "principles" and up-to-date problems nowadays. But to business. We would like to ask what foreigners could possibly make of us if they judged us by these gentlemen? But, I will be told, surely it was not only such gentlemen who went abroad. Didn't Frenchmen see, for instance, so and so and so and so? But the whole point of my argument is that they have not bothered them so far. And if they had noticed them, they would only have been bewildered again. What, for instance, could they have said to a man who came to their country goodness only knows from where and who suddenly told them that they were behind the times, that the light had already come from the East now, that salvation no longer reposed in the *légion d'honneur,* and so on and so forth in this vein. They would simply have refused to listen to him.

"Yes, you've overlooked a great deal," we would have said to them—I mean, of course, if they had not refused to listen to us. "You know absolutely nothing about us," we would have repeated to them, "in spite of the fact that your Mérimée knows even our ancient history and has written something like a beginning of a drama, *le Faux Démétrius,* from which, though, you can learn as little of Russian history as from Karamzin's *Marfa the Mayoress.* The remarkable thing is that his *le Faux Démétrius* himself is terribly like Alexandre Dumas, not the hero of Alexandre Dumas's novel, but Dumas himself, the real one, the marquis Davis de la Pailletterie. You know absolutely nothing about us or about our history, we would have repeated for the third time, and all you do know so far is that the Geneva native Lefort, etc., etc. This Geneva native Lefort is so indispensable to our knowledge of Russian history that I suppose every Paris concierge knows him, and no doubt at the sight of a Russian demanding *"Le cordon, s'il vous plaît"* at a late hour he mutters to himself: "If the Geneva native Lefort had not been born, you'd still be a barbarian, you wouldn't have come to Paris, *au centre de la civilisation,* you wouldn't wake me up at night shouting at the top of your voice '*Le cordon, s'il vous plait!* '" But in spite of our twice repeated statement that you know nothing about us, we do not blame you at all for knowing only about Lefort. As a matter of fact, we can forgive you your Lefort, for he had saved many of you from being starved to death. Think of the hundreds of tutors—all sorts of Saint Jerômes and Mont-Revèches—who arrived in our country in the old days from the other side of the Rhine to educate Russia, without any knowledge whatsoever except that the Geneva native Lefort, etc., etc., and for that single item of learning, which they purveyed to the children of the Russian boyars, they received money or a social position from us. And, really, why study us at all? Is there any sensible reason for it? For the sake of art perhaps? But you are a businesslike people, a practical people, and you would not waste your time on such nonsense as art for art's sake, though you elected Pansard to the Academy (perhaps for the simple reason that it serves him right). For the sake of science? But then the trouble is that we are not the sort of people that are cut out for any science. That is why, gentlemen, you don't realize even now that if we only had your civilization, we would have felt it to be a little thin and even offensive. We have already had a taste of it and we know it all now from experience.

That is why we know and you do not know that your civilization came to us as a natural fruit, which our soil needed, and not only because there was a Geneva native Lefort, etc., etc. Moreover, your civilization has already completed its circle in our country and we have already gone beyond it; we have taken all that we needed from it and are now freely returning to our native soil. It matters not that the number of civilized people in our country is still not great. It is not a question of numbers, but of the fact that historically the process of European civilization in our country is at an end, that another process is beginning and, what is most important, that this is already generally recognized. It is this realization that matters. We have realized that civilization merely introduces a new element in our national life, without harming it in any way, without forcing it to deviate from its normal way, but, on the contrary, enlarging our mental outlook, making our aims clear to ourselves and arming us with new weapons for further great achievements. Let the number of those who realize this be small; what matters is that they are no longer Racans. We repeat: what matters is not whether the numbers are large or not, but that the process of realization has already been accomplished; you have no idea of the numbers anyway. You, at least, your *vicomtes*, at any rate, are still convinced that Russia consists of only two classes: *les boyards* and their serfs. But for a long time you will remain unconvinced that we have long had a neutral soil, on which all merges into one harmonious and unanimous whole, all classes merge peacefully, harmoniously and fraternally—*les boyards*, whom actually we never had in the sense that you have had them in the West, that is, as conquerors and vanquished, and *les serfs*, whom we did not have, either, in the sense of real *serfs*, as you understand this word. And all this merges so easily, so naturally, so peacefully—above all, peacefully—and it is in this that we differ so much from you, for you had to fight for every step you took, every right you gained, every privilege. If disagreements exist, they are only temporary, accidental, and can be easily eliminated and possess no roots in our soil, and this we realize very well. The beginning of the order of things has been laid long ago, since time immemorial; it has been laid by nature herself in the Russian spirit, in the Russian ideal, and the last obstacle to it is being removed in our time by our all-wise and blessed Czar, blessed of blessed forever for what he is doing for us. We have no class interests because we have no classes in the strict sense of the word. We have neither Gauls nor Franks, we have no qualifications which define in an external way what a man is worth; for we have only one kind of upbringing and only the moral qualities of a man must define what a man is worth; this is generally realized and this has become a matter of general conviction, for the Russian spirit is broader than class enmity, class interests and qualifications. The existence of a new Russia is being gradually felt, it is becoming gradually aware of itself and once again it does not matter that it is not large. It makes up for it, although only unconsciously, by living in the hearts of all Russians, in the aspirations and hopes of all Russians. Our new Russia has understood that there is only one cement, one tie, one soil, on which we can all agree and be reconciled with one another; it is a general, spiritual reconciliation, the basis of which is our upbringing.

This new Russia has already asserted herself by organic and undeniable facts, and not by unsuccessful copies and changes as you think. It has shown itself by the new morality of the younger generation—which is a sign of enormous strength and undeviating aspiration toward a new ideal. Every day her ideal is getting clearer and clearer to her. She knows that she is only at the beginning, but then the beginning is the most important thing; everything depends on the first step; she knows that she has made an end of your European civilization and is now bringing a new, immeasurably broad life. And now, when she is turning to her national roots and wishes to merge with them, she brings science as a gift—the thing she has received from you with veneration and for which she will always remember you. It is not civilization she brings to all the Russians but science, obtained from your civilization, and offers it to the common people as the result of her long voyage away from her native soil to the foreign lands, as her justification to them, and as she hands it over to them, she is willing to wait and see what they will make of this science. Science is, of course, eternal and unchangeable in its fundamental laws, but its grafting and fruit depend upon the national idiosyncracies, that is to say, the soil and national character.

But, we shall be asked, what exactly is your nationality? What exactly are you Russians? You boast that we do not know you, but do you know yourselves? You are on the point of going over to your national roots. You announce it in all the papers and advertise it in pamphlets. Which means that till now you had no idea about your "national roots," and if you did, it was false and you have repudiated it by the very fact of your refusal to go over to it. Now you have thought of it and are shouting about it all over Europe. May we ask you what the hen will do when she lays her egg?

We repeat to our readers that it is the foreigner who is saying all this (let us say, the Frenchman), not a real foreigner but an imaginary one, an incorporeal, fantastic one. We have not seen a single Frenchman when we were writing our article.

"And another thing," he goes on, "in your announcement you express the hope that the Russian idea will in time become the synthesis of all the ideas Europe had so long and so stubbornly cultivated in her separate nationalities. What new idea is this? What do you mean by it?"

"That is," we reply, "you want us to declare plainly and frankly what we believe in?"

"No," cries our Frenchman with a certain alarm, anticipating that he would have to listen to several more pages, "I don't want it at all. All I want is—"

"No, sir," we interrupt him, "you asked for an answer and you are going to listen to our answer."

"He deserves a pinching and will get a pinching," the former German land agent interjects at this point, evidently remembering the time when he managed Buyerakin's estates. Now, anticipating the change in the peasants' social position in the near future, he has retired and is without a job; he hopes, however, to be recalled soon! At the moment he is standing beside me (also in his character of a foreigner), smoking his pipe, as he used to do when going round the estate supervising the work of the peasants, silently, but gravely listening to our conversation, fully convinced that his face expresses a great deal of the most subtle irony.

"We believe," we repeat . . .

But do permit us another digression, gentle reader, permit me to say a few words that have nothing to do with the subject under discussion, not because they are particularly necessary here, but just . . . because they are crying out to be put on paper. Excuse my sincerity.

There are always certain views and convictions in the air which our contemporaries seem to be afraid to acknowledge, repudiating them in public in spite of the fact that they share them in secret. This is particularly true of certain epochs, so much so that even an outside observer cannot help becoming aware of it. We realize that there are some valid excuses for this sort of thing: one can, for example, be afraid of truth, of its success; one can be afraid of compromising it by expressing it at the wrong time. One can be honorably fastidious and mistrustful. All this happens. But often, and indeed mostly, we like to pass over things in silence because of some inner Jesuitism that lies hidden inside us, and the main-switch lever of our pride is raised to a point where it becomes indistinguishable from vanity. A certain skeptic has said that our century is a century of exasperated pride. To accuse the whole world is going too far; but it is impossible not to agree that some modern man will put up with everything in the world, with any sort of dishonor, even with being called a scoundrel, swindler and thief, if these abusive words are expressed in a less precise form, cloaked, as it were, in a milder, more well-bred form. The only thing he will neither put up with nor forgive and never forget is a sneer at his intelligence and he will revenge himself for it at the first favorable opportunity. Let us make our meaning clear. I am speaking of *some*, not all, of my contemporaries. Perhaps this happens just because in our time everyone is beginning to feel more and more and to realize a little that, first of all, every man is right to demand to be respected and, second, that a man deserves to be respected as much as any other man just because he too is a man, for the sake of his human dignity. And that is why he is beginning to demand respect for himself from the professors of humanism and from society at large. But since the power of a man's intelligence is the only incontestable and incontrovertible sign of superiority of one man over another, no one desires to give in to this superiority until those endowed with it stop boasting about it and no longer regard lack of intelligence as something shameful and worthy of caustic derision. This is why no one wants to be a fool and commit the mistake of injuring his own human dignity. A fool should be the last man to blush for his stupidity, because it is not his fault that nature has made him a fool. But the initiative should really be taken by the privileged clever fellows; a fool can be forgiven for not being more intelligent than intelligent people. I know, for instance, one man . . . an industrialist, shall I say? (Today even literature has become an industry and, besides, "industrialist" is such a general, inoffensive, almost abstract term.) Now, if anyone were to ask this industrialist what he would rather be called, a scoundrel or a fool, he would, I am quite sure, immediately agree to be called a scoundrel, in spite of the fact that, though he actually is a scoundrel, he is even more of a fool, and knows it himself and is sure that others know it too. That is why people are today sometimes a little too timid when it comes to expressing certain convictions, even dearly held convictions. They are afraid of being called unintelligent and backward. Intellect, intellect, the fear for one's intellect—that is the chief trouble! By passing over their convictions in silence, they gladly and quite furiously approve of what they do not believe in, at which they laugh surreptitiously, and all because it is in fashion, it is generally accepted, established by the pillars of society and by the authorities. How can one go against the authorities? And yet he who is sincerely convinced ought to respect his convictions; and he who respects his convictions ought to do something for them. Every honest man is in duty bound, etc., etc. Ah well, the reader will say, these are already copybook maxims and I expect to stop reading.

Indeed, the moment you wish to tell the truth according to your convictions you are at once accused of uttering copybook maxims! How extraordinary! Why are so many modern truths uttered in a tone that is just a little pompous at once characterized as copybook maxims? Why is it that if in our age we feel the need to tell the truth we have more and more to resort to humor or satire or irony in order to sweeten truth as if it were a bitter pill, or to present one's convictions to the public while pretending to be a shade haughtily indifferent to them or even with a certain shade of disrespect for them—in short, with some mean little concession? In our view, an honest man ought not to blush for his convictions even if they were out of copybooks, especially if he believes in them. We say *especially,* for there are convinced people who do not believe in their own convictions and, while trying to convince others, keep asking themselves: are you sure you're not telling lies, my dear fellow? And yet they defend these convictions furiously and quite often not at all because they want to deceive people. I used to know a man, one of these convinced fellows, who told me so himself. He belonged to that category of incontestably intelligent people who commit nothing but stupidities all their lives. Incidentally, people of limited mental capacities as a rule commit many fewer stupidities than intelligent people. Why is this, I wonder. When we began asking the gentleman in question why he was trying to convince others if he did not believe in what he was preaching himself, and where he gets this enthusiasm, this fury of conviction from if he himself was in doubt about his words, he replied that the reason why he was so excited was that he was trying to convince himself all the time. This is what falling in love with an idea externally means, getting attached to it out of sheer predilection for it, without proving to oneself (and even *afraid* of proving to oneself) whether the idea is true or not. And who knows, perhaps it is true that some people fly into a passion all their lives, even to the point of foaming at the mouth, in an attempt to convince others solely because they are anxious to convince themselves, and they die unconvinced. . . . But enough. We have convinced ourselves definitely. Let people think that we are carried away by an idea that is neither true nor sound, that we are exaggerating, that we have too much youthful enthusiasm or perhaps even senile feeble-mindedness, that we have little tactfulness, etc., etc. Let them think! For we are sure that we can do no harm to anyone by telling people frankly what we believe in. Why not tell it? Why must we be silent?

59

3.

Yes, we believe that the Russian nation is an unusual phenomenon in the entire history of mankind. The character of the Russian people is so unlike those of all contemporary European peoples that the Europeans still do not understand it and, conversely, understand everything about it. All Europeans try to attain one and the same goal, one and the same ideal; this is quite incontestable. But they all differ among themselves so far as their own national interests are concerned, they are so exclusive of one another that there can be no question of reconciliation, and more and more they follow different ways, deviating from the straight road. It seems that every nation is anxious to discover the universally human ideal in its own country, by its own efforts, and this is why they do harm to themselves and their idea. We repeat now seriously what we have said above in jest: the Englishman cannot to this day acknowledge that the Frenchman has any sense and vice versa, and this is not only the opinion of them all, an instinctive feeling of the whole nation, but can be observed even among their leading men, the statesmen of both nations. An Englishman laughs at his neighbor on any and every occasion and regards his national idiosyncrasies with implacable hatred. Their rivalry at last robs them of their impartiality. They cease to understand one another; they look at life differently, their beliefs are different and they consider it to be the greatest possible merit so far as they are concerned. They separate themselves from one another more and more stubbornly by their rules, their morality, their views of the whole of God's world. The one and the other see only themselves in the whole world and regard the rest as a personal obstacle, and each one separately wishes to achieve in his country what can be achieved only by all nations acting in concert. Well, then, are these only the remnants of ancient rivalries? Must we look for the reasons of this disunity in the times of Joan of Arc or the Crusades? Is civilization so impotent that it could not get the better of these hatreds to this day? Should we not look for them rather in the soil itself and not in all sorts of accidents, in the blood, in the entire spirit of the two peoples? All European nations are alike in this respect. The ideal of universal humanity becomes more and more obliterated among them. It means something different to every one of them, it grows dimmer, assumes a different form in their consciousness. The Christian connection which had hitherto united them loses its force with every day that passes. Even science is unable to unite the nations who drift more and more apart. Let us admit that they are to a certain extent right in claiming that it is this exclusiveness, this mutual rivalry, this keeping of oneself to oneself, this proud reliance on oneself alone that gives each of them his tremendous strength in his struggle against the obstacles in his way. But that in itself leads to a multiplication and steady increase of these obstacles. That is why the Europeans cannot understand the Russians at all and why they have defined the greatest peculiarity of their character as a lack of individuality. We agree that we say all this without any proof. It is not the aim of this article to supply this proof. But at least everyone will agree with us that the Russian national character is sharply differentiated from the European, that it possesses a distinct peculiarity of its own, that it is chiefly remarkable for its highly synthetic ability, its talent for universal reconciliation, universal humanity. The Russian character does not possess the European angularity, impenetrability, inflexibility. He gets on with everybody and gets used to everybody. The Russian sympathizes with humanity at large without distinction of nationality, blood or soil. He finds and at once assumes the presence of good sense in everything of universal human interest, be it ever so little. He has an instinct for universal humanity. He guesses by instinct the universally human feature even among most sharply differentiated peoples. He at once makes them agree and reconciles them to his idea, finds a place for them in the conclusions he draws from it and quite often discovers the point of unity and reconciliation in completely contrary and rival ideas of two different European nations, ideas that, unhappily, they can find no way of reconciling at home, in their own countries, and that will perhaps never be reconciled. At the same time the Russian displays a talent for completely sound self-criticism, a completely sober view of himself and the absence of any self-exaltation, which is so harmful to the freedom of action. We speak, of course, of the Russian in general terms, collectively, in the sense of the entire nation. Even in his physical abilities a Russian is unlike a European. Every Russian can speak all languages and study the spirit of every foreign language with all its fine points just as if it were his own native Russian tongue—which does not occur among European nations *in the sense of a general national ability*. Doesn't this prove something? Is it just an accidental, random phenomenon? Is it really impossible to grasp and to a certain extent divine from such facts at least something of the future development of our people so far as their aspirations and aims are concerned? And it was this nation, overpowered by circumstances, that regarded Europe inimically for so many centuries and refused obstinately to have anything to do with it, little suspecting its own future! Peter the Great instinctively felt the presence of a new power within him and realized the need for broadening the ideas and the field of action of all the Russians—a need concealed in their unconscious and struggling to escape, which was in their blood even in their Slav days. It is said that Peter merely wished to make Russia into another Holland. We don't know; Peter's personality, in spite of all the historical interpretations and researches of recent times, is still a great mystery to us. We understand one thing only: that it had to be very original for a Moscow Czar to think of it—not only to love but to go to Holland. Is it possible that the Geneva Lefort was really responsible for all that? At any rate, in Peter's person we see an example of the sort of thing a Russian can make up his mind to do when he decides that the time has come to put his plans into execution and when he feels the upsurge of new forces within him. And it is terrifying to think how free in spirit a Russian can be and how powerful his will can be! Never has anyone torn himself away from his native soil as he had to do sometimes or, in following his convictions, turned so sharply from his usual course. And who knows, dear foreigners, perhaps Russia was meant to wait until you have finished, so as to have time to grasp your ideas, to understand your ideals and aims and the character of your aspirations; to reconcile your ideas, to give them a universal meaning and, finally, free in spirit and free of all outside class or national interests, to move on to a wide new activity unknown to history, starting from where you have finished and carry you all along with her. Didn't our poet Lermontov compare Russia to the legendary Ilya Muromets, who had sat in one place for thirty years and then suddenly set off, having become conscious of the gigantic power within him? For what other reasons have the Russians been endowed with such rich and original faculties? Surely not to sit around and do nothing. Perhaps we will be asked, where do you get all this boastfulness, all this arrogance from? Where is your ability for self-criticism, where is that sober outlook you were so proud of? But, we will reply, since we began by indulging in so much self-criticism for so long a time, we can now indulge in something that is equally true though it may be entirely contrary to self-criticism. We can still remember how we used to abuse ourselves for being Slavs and for being unable to become Europeans. Is it really impossible to admit now that we talked a lot of nonsense then? We do not deny the importance of the faculty of self-criticism, we love it just because we recognize it to be the best aspect of the Russian nature, as its peculiarity, as something that you lack completely. We know that we will have to go on practicing self-criticism a very long time yet, indeed, perhaps more and more as we advance. But try to touch a

Frenchman on his sore spot, let us say, by questioning his
bravery or saying something derogatory about his *légion
d'honneur*, etc. Try to touch an Englishman on one of his
sore spots by questioning the wisdom of some of his domestic habits, and you will see what they will say to you. Why
then should we be afraid to boast of the fact that the Russians do not possess such fastidiousness and susceptibility
to offense, with the exception, perhaps, of some of our
literary generals. We believe in the power of the Russian
spirit no less than anyone else. Will it not be able to stand
up to praise? No, dear Europeans! Do not as yet expect
from us any proofs of our opinion of you and of ourselves
and try instead to know us better, if you can spare the
time for it. Now, you are convinced that we rejoiced at
your failures, that we were superciliously glad of them
and spat at your efforts when you rushed so bravely and
magnanimously along the new path of progress. No, no,
dear elder brothers, we did not rejoice, we were not happy
at your failures. Sometimes we even wept with you. You
will, of course, be immediately surprised and ask, what
did you weep for? It was none of your business. You had
nothing to do with any of it. Why, gentlemen, we will reply to you, of course we had nothing to do with any of it,
and yet we did sympathize with you. That's where the
whole mystery is. You, for instance, seem to believe for
some strange reason that we are fanatics, that is to say,
that our soldiers are being infected with fanaticism. Good
Lord, if only you knew how ridiculous it is! If there is a
human being in the world who is completely immune to
fanaticism it is the Russian soldier. Those of us who lived
with the Russian soldiers know it only too well. If only you
knew what dear, charming, sympathetic types they are!
If only you took the trouble to read Tolstoy's stories; there
you get something that is so true, so well and sympathetically delineated! But quite apart from that, do you
really think that the Russian defended Sevastopol out of
religious fanaticism? I should think your brave Zouaves
had made the acquaintance of our soldiers and know

them very well. Had they seen a great deal of hatred from them? And how well you know our army officers! You seem to have got the idea into your heads that we have only two classes: *les boyards* and *les serfs. Boyards,* indeed! Let us assume that our classes are well defined, but there are more points of contact than separation between our different classes, and that is what's so important. This is a pledge of our general peace, calm, fraternal love and future prosperity. Every Russian is above all a Russian and only after that a member of some social class. It is not so with you and we are sorry for you. In your countries completely the contrary is true. A whole nation sometimes falls a victim to class interest. This happened quite recently and indeed it sometimes happens even now and I would not be surprised to see it happen many times. Which of course means that your classes and all sorts of corporations are still very strong. You ask with surprise, but where is your much praised development, what does your progress amount to? You can't see anything of it, can you? Oh, yes, you can, we reply, but *you* don't see it, you are not looking in the right direction. It is enough that it exists in spirit and in the needs of the entire people; it is enough even if a small minority of our people is beginning to agree with one another even if only in general matters. Do not call us supercilious and short-sighted or accuse us of having reached maturity too quickly. No, we have been looking into things very carefully for a long time, we have been analyzing everything, we have been asking ourselves questions, we worry ourselves sick in trying to find an answer for them. It is only quite recently that we began to indulge in analysis, but so far as we are concerned it is a long time ago and today we are even getting sick and tired of it. You see, we too have lived a great deal and we have experienced a great deal. Incidentally, would you like me to tell you our *own* story, the story of our development, of our growth? We will not, of course, start with Peter the Great; we will start from more recent times, from the time when our entire educated classes suddenly began to be imbued with analysis. Indeed, there were moments when we, that is, the civilized ones, did not believe even in ourselves. We still read Paul de Kock at the time but rejected with contempt Alexandre Dumas and all his company. We fell upon George Sand and, good Lord, how we devoured her books! Andrey Alexandrovich and Mr. Dudyshkin, who had taken up their abode at the *Home Annals* after Belinsky, still remember George Sand; read the announcement in their journal for 1861. At that time we meekly listened to your verdicts about us and expressed our humble agreement with you. Yes, we did so, and the fact is, we did not know what to do. It was because we had nothing else to do that we had founded the natural school just then. And how many talented natures appeared in our country! Not talented writers—those are a different matter—but natures that were talented in every possible respect. Court Councilor Shchedrin knows the meaning of this expression. And the airs those talented natures gave themselves, how they minced and grimaced before us, while we looked them up and down, told scandalous stories about them, ridiculed them to their faces and made them laugh at themselves. And they did laugh at themselves, somehow not on principle but with a kind of horrible concealed malice. In those days everything was done on principle; we lived on principle and were terribly afraid to do something that was not in accordance with the new ideas. It was then, too, that we experienced a sort of exaggerated mood of self-accusation and self-exposure, while at the same time everyone vied with one another in denouncing and exposing one another; and, dear Lord, the slanderous stories they used to tell! And all this was mostly sincere. Of course, there were also businessmen among them; but there were most sincere men among them, too, completely carried away by their beautiful feelings. It sometimes happened that one fine evening some sincere gentleman would suddenly burst into the soul of another sincere gentleman and begin to tell him the story of his misspent days and "what a horrible scoundrel I am." The other gentleman too would become emotional and start telling his friend the same things. And so they would vie with one another and even tell slanderous stories about themselves in an excess of enthusiasm just as if they were boasting about them. And they would tell so many horrible things about themselves to each other that they would be ashamed to meet the next day and would keep avoiding each other. We also had Byronic natures. They mostly sat about twiddling their thumbs and—even stopped uttering curses! All they did was to occasionally bare their teeth lazily. They even laughed at Byron because he had wept too much and been angry, which was utterly unbecoming to a lord. They used to say that it was not worth while being angry and uttering curses, that things were so bad that it was a waste of time even to move a finger and that a good dinner was best of all. And when they said that, we listened to their words with veneration, thinking that their opinion of a good dinner concealed some mysterious, highly subtle and most venomous irony. But they ate their dinners with relish in the best restaurants and put on weight before your very eyes. And what wonderful complexions some of them had! Some did not stop at the irony of a fat dinner but went much further: they filled their pockets and played havoc with those of their neighbors. Many turned into cardsharps afterward. And we gazed at them with veneration, gaping in astonishment. Well, we told each other, they too do everything on principle; after all, one must take from life what life can give. And when they picked handkerchiefs out of pockets before our very eyes, we saw even in that a kind of refined Byronism, a further development of it that even Byron himself did not know of. We sighed and shook our heads sadly. "See," we said, "what despair can reduce people to. A man is burning with goodness, he is overflowing with most honorable indignation, he is seething with the desire to act, but he is not allowed to; he is hemmed in on all sides, and there he is cheating at cards with demonic laughter and picking handkerchiefs from pockets." And how pure of heart and bright of soul many of us emerged from all that shameful business. Many? Why, almost all, except, of course, the Byrons. There were among us also those who were loftily pure of heart, who did succeed in uttering an ardent, convincing word. Oh, *they* did not complain of not being allowed to express themselves, of being hemmed in on all sides, of being exploited by entrepreneurs; that is, they may have complained, but they did not sit around twiddling their thumbs; they were active as much as they could be and they did do something. In fact, they did a great deal. They were innocent and artless, like children, and all their lives they did not understand their Byronic collaborators, and they died naïve martyrs. May they rest in peace! There were also demons among us, real demons. Two of them, and how we loved them, how we love and value them still! One of them kept laughing all the time; he laughed at himself and at us all his life, and we all laughed with him, we laughed so much that at last we began crying with laughter. He grasped the meaning of Lieutenant Pirogov; he made a terrible tragedy out of a civil servant's lost overcoat. In three lines he told us all about the Ryazan lieutenant—to the last trait of his character. He put before us a whole gallery of moneymakers, kulaks, robbers and all sorts of assessors. He had only to point a finger at them and an indelible mark was branded on their foreheads, and we knew who they were without having to be told, and, above all, what their real names were. Oh, he was a colossal demon such as you have never had in Europe and whom perhaps you would never have allowed to live among you. The other demon . . . But the other one we loved perhaps even more. How many excellent poems he wrote for us; he wrote in albums, but even Griboyedov himself would have been ashamed of calling him an album poet. He cursed and tormented himself, tormented himself in good earnest. He avenged himself and he forgave, he wrote and laughed aloud—he was generous and ridiculous. He liked to whisper strange fairytales in the ear of a sleeping young girl, disturbing her virginal blood and drawing strange visions before her, which she really shouldn't have dreamed about, considering the highly moral upbringing she had received. He told us the story of his life, his love adventures: he seemed generally to mystify us; we never knew whether he was talking seriously or laughing at us. Our civil servants knew him by heart, and all of a sudden they all began to pose as Mephistopheles the moment they left their departments. We did not always agree with him; we felt depressed and sad and vexed and sorry for someone and we were filled with resentment. At last he got tired of us; he could not get on with anyone anywhere; he cursed us and ridiculed us "with the ridicule of a bitterly deceived son of a father who had squandered his money at cards" and flew away from us.

> And over the mountains of the Caucasus
> Flew the exile from paradise.

We followed his fortunes for a long time, but at last he perished somewhere, aimlessly, capriciously and even ridiculously. But we did not laugh. We did not feel like laughing at the time. Now it is a different matter. Now the good Lord has sent us beneficent freedom of speech and suddenly we all feel much more cheerful. Suddenly we somehow realize that we had adopted all that Mephistophelean business, all those demonic principles, a little too soon, that it was too early for us to curse ourselves and despair, in spite of the fact that only a short while ago Mr. Lamansky told us in public that we have not matured yet. Dear me, how offended we were! Mr. Pogodin came galloping from Moscow posthaste, out of breath, and began at once to comfort us, also in public, and, of course, at once convinced us (without even taking much trouble) that we are completely mature. Since then we are so proud. We have Shchedrin, Rosenheim . . . We remember Shchedrin's appearance in the *Russian Messenger*. Oh, it was such a joyful time, a time full of hopes. Mr.

Shchedrin certainly chose the right time in which to appear. I am told the *Russian Messenger* suddenly got so many new subscribers that it was impossible to count them, in spite of the fact that this worthy journal had started talking about Cavour even then, as well as about English lords and farm management. With what eagerness did we read about all sorts of mischievous fellows and talented natures and were surprised at their appearance. Where have they been, we asked ourselves, where have they been hiding till now? Of course, the real scoundrels merely chuckled to themselves. But what really amazed us was that no sooner did Mr. Shchedrin leave the northern capital (the Northern Palmira, as Mr. Bulgarin—may he rest in peace—invariably called it) than all sorts of poor, unhappy Arinushkas and hermits appeared from his pen . . . just as though as soon as you left Palmira you simply had to notice at once all those Arinushkas and start singing a different song, forgetting all about George Sand and Mr. Panaev and everybody . . . everybody. Rosenheim's lyre tinkled loudly, Mr. Gromeka's deep, loud voice resounded, the brothers Meleants flashed by, numbers of X's and Y's swarmed all over in newspapers and periodicals with complaints against one another; poets and prose writers appeared, all of them anxious to expose something or other. Such poets and prose writers never would have made an appearance but for the kind of literature that specialized in exposing things. Oh, do not imagine, my dear Europeans, that we have forgotten Ostrovsky. There is no place for him in that kind of literature. We know his right place. We have said many times that we believe in his new message and that we know that he, as an artist, has divined what we had not dreamed of even at the time of demonic principles and self-accusations, even when we read the immortal adventures of Chichikov. We dreamed and yearned for it as one does for rain in a drought. We were even afraid to say what we longed for. But Mr. Ostrovsky was not afraid. But about Ostrovsky later. We did not intend to talk of him now; we merely wanted to talk about the beneficent freedom of expression. Oh, do not think, do not think, my dear, honored foreigners, that we are afraid of the beneficent freedom of expression, that as soon as we introduced it we got frightened of it and are hiding from it. Most of all, I beseech you, do not believe *Home Annals*, which confuses freedom of expression with literary scandals. This only proves that we still have many people who, like men whose flesh is torn, feel pain at the slightest puff of wind; that we still have people who like to read about others but who are afraid of other people reading about them. Yes, we love freedom of expression and cherish it like a newborn babe. We like this little demon who has only just cut his strong and healthy little teeth. Sometimes he bites when he shouldn't, but he really does not yet know how to bite. Quite often he does not know whom to bite. But we laugh at his mischievous pranks, his childish mistakes, and we laugh lovingly. Ah well, he's only a baby, it's excusable. . . . No, we are not afraid of the freedom of expression, we are not disturbed by it. It is all a symptom of health, it is all a matter of inexperienced strength, which is in full swing and anxious to get out into the open! They are all, all good symptoms.

4.

But why talk of freedom of expression? In every society, there is always the so-called golden mediocrity that claim first place in it. These are terribly ambitious. They regard everyone who is still unknown with annihilating contempt and arrogant impertinence. It is they who are the first to throw stones at every innovator. And how vicious they are! how obtuse in their persecution of every new idea that has not yet had time to enter into the consciousness of society as a whole. But afterward, when the idea gains a predominant place in society, how they shout, what zealous and, at the same time, obtuse followers of the same idea they turn out to be in spite of the fact that they persecuted it at first. No doubt they will ultimately understand the new idea, but they will do so always after everybody else and always crudely and in its narrow sense, and they will never take into consideration the fact that if the idea is right, it is capable of development, and that if it is capable of development, it must in time give way to another idea that has emerged from it and that supplements it but that already corresponds to the new requirements of the new generation. But mediocrities do not understand the need for new requirements, and as for the new generation, they invariably hate it and look down on it. This is their most distinctive feature. Among these golden mediocrities there are always a great number of "businessmen" who make use of the fashionable phrase. It is they who vulgarize every new idea and at once transform it into a fashionable phrase. They vulgarize everything they happen to touch. Every living idea becomes a piece of carrion in their mouths. But they are the first to profit from it on the very next day after the funeral of the man of genius who had proclaimed it and whom they had persecuted. Some of them are so limited in their mental faculties that they quite seriously believe that the man of genius has done nothing, but that it is they who have done it all. Their vanity is beyond belief. We have already said that they are extremely obtuse and clumsy, though the mob believes them to be clever. They succeed most by dint of strident and passionate phrases; they run to extremes without grasping the meaning or the spiritual form of the idea and in this way harm it even while sincerely sharing it. For instance, should thinkers and philanthropists raise the matter of the woman question, of the amelioration of woman's position in society, of granting her equality of rights, of a husband's despotism, etc., the golden mediocrities are quite certain to understand it to mean that matrimony must *immediately* be abolished—above all, immediately. Moreover, every married woman not only could but *should* be unfaithful to her husband and it is therein that the true moral meaning of the idea lies. It is most amusing to observe these gentlemen when, for example, society is divided into two different camps at some troublesome, transitory period. It is then that they do not know whom or what to join, and yet they are all too often regarded as authorities whose opinions are necessary. What should they do? After a great deal of shilly-shallying, the golden mediocrity make up their minds and always inopportunely. This is invariably so. This, too, is the chief trait of the golden mediocrity. And they will commit some ridiculous, idiotic blunder, so that it often happened that some of their decisions passed to posterity as classical examples of stupidity. But we have digressed from our subject. It is not freedom of expression alone that is being persecuted nowadays. Literacy too is being persecuted, and even by those who at the time seemed to us to be, if not advanced, then at any rate not retrograde, and, above all, *terribly* reasonable. We say *terribly* because many of them looked so authoritatively and haughtily upon ignorant people and were so proud of their common sense and their so-called clear and *practical* understanding of things that one felt uneasy even in the same room with them. One simply longed to go into the next room. Such a gentleman forces himself to share the company of well-meaning and progressive people and is considered to be a progressive himself until he suddenly blurts out something so utterly unexpected that Gogol's Korobochka alone could have said something of the kind if, for instance, she had been asked to give a decision in some European financial crisis. But I am afraid we are digressing again. To business, then. We have mentioned literacy.

It is a well-known fact that the literate among the common people fill the jails. The immediate conclusion drawn from this is that literacy is a bad thing. Is this logical? A knife can cut, so a knife is a bad thing. No, we will be told that a knife is not a bad thing but that it must be given only to those who know how to use it and will not cut themselves. Very well. So it follows, according to you, that literacy should be made into a kind of privilege. But would it not be much better, gentlemen, first to consider the circumstances that accompany literacy among the common people and see whether it may not be possible to remove them without depriving the entire people of their spiritual bread. We agree with you that the literate among the common people fill the jails. But consider why and how it happens. Let us tell you this as we have understood it ourselves after a careful observation of prison life over many years. To begin with, there are so few literates among our common people that sometimes literacy really gives one an advantage by imparting greater prestige and importance to him and thus raising him above his ordinary environment. The common people do not consider a literate man better than themselves in any way; they merely regard him as more powerful than they, as a man who can deal with many troublesome matters of everyday life more efficiently—in short, they recognize the usefulness of literacy in life. A literate person cannot be cheated by a document or fooled by anything else. For his part, a literate person is somehow involuntarily inclined to regard himself superior to the ignorant and illiterate people of his environment. More or less, of course. And regarding himself superior, he cannot treat the people among whom he lives fairly. It occurs to him quite naturally that he could not and should not be treated the same as those ignorant people: "They're an ignorant bunch, and we can read and write." He therefore feels an irresistible urge to get out at the first favorable opportunity. Besides, he is nearly always treated with a certain respect, sometimes with great respect, especially if he knows how to conduct himself—that is to say, how to carry himself sedately; he is eloquent, pompous, a bit of a pedant, is contemptuously silent when others speak, and is careful to start talking only when everybody else falls silent, not knowing what more to say; in short, he behaves as some of our clever fellows and some of our thinkers, our progressive practical men, and some of our literary generals behave —those whom you know so well. The same naïveté, the same absurdly impatient tricks. In short, it is the same thing in all the classes of society, except that in every class it takes its own particular form. The need to assert oneself, to distinguish oneself, to be above average is a law of nature for every person; it is his right, his essence, the law of his existence, which in a primitive, unsettled condition of society takes a rather crude and even wild form and in a developed society the form of a morally humane, conscious and completely free submission to the interest of the society as a whole and vice versa, society's continual concern for every person and the least possible constraint of every person's rights. The basis is therefore the same, the difference being only in the use of one's rights. Look at the so-called examiners among the Old Believers and see what an enormous, despotic influence they have on their co-religionists. Society itself, in fact, contains a sort of instinctive need to bring forward out of its own ranks some kind of exceptional personality, to set it up as an exception, as something outside the ordinary customs and accepted rules, to recognize it as something extraordinary and to worship it. It is thus that we get the Ivan Yakovelviches, the saintly beggar women, etc. Let us now take quite a different example. Have a look at some footman or house serf. Though so far as his social position is concerned he is below an ordinary peasant who tills the soil, he deems himself superior, and because his frock coat, white tie and gloves make him look a much nobler person than a peasant, he despises the peasant. And don't tell me that this is a disgusting, contemptible trait peculiar only to the common people, that I mean to repudiate your own folk and neglect them the moment your fortunes have changed for the better. It certainly is a contemptible trait, but no one can be blamed for it. A footman is not to be blamed if in his ignorance he regards the foreign cut of his clothes a sign of superiority to the mere country yokel. The important thing so far as he is concerned is that he has come into contact with gentlemen— that is, with superior beings; he apes their manners and their mannerisms; his clothes distinguish him from his former environment. In the same way literacy, as something that is very rare among the common people, considers itself also as something privileged and different, and a literate person often despises an illiterate one. He can't help wishing to show what a fine fellow he is. He becomes presumptuous, impatient, and is transformed into a kind of little despot. No doubt it sometimes seems to him that he shouldn't be treated like the others, the illiterate ones. He is impatient, he talks arrogantly, he feels that he shouldn't have to put up with the sort of things that all the rest are putting up with—especially when others are present; he is supercilious. Superciliousness gives rise to thoughtlessness, and thoughtlessness to arrogance. At times he relies a little too much on himself; he tries to do things that are beyond his capacity and, suddenly, gets into trouble, sometimes quite by accident, because, for instance, his own people were looking at him at a critical moment, people before whom he was showing off and who were waiting to see how he would act at that particular moment. So he showed them—and landed in jail. Naturally we are not talking of all literate peasants. We are talking theoretically, and it would indeed be ridiculous to claim that a peasant has only to become literate to land in jail. All we wished to show was how literacy as a kind of privilege can give rise to arrogance and presumptuousness and lack of respect for one's own environment and for one's social position, especially if it is not a particularly pleasant one. We were talking theoretically and we are sorry that it is outside the scope of our article to present a few examples of how it all happens in practice, how it develops and what it may lead to. Let me repeat: we were not speaking about all literate peasants; of the literates only those land in jail who are destined by nature to do so under certain circumstances—that is, people who are by nature obstinate, passionate, nervous and impressionable. Literacy has such a baneful effect upon

them because of its privileged inconveniences, just because it is a privilege in our country.

"And what about it?" we will be asked. "You have
proved yourself that literacy is harmful and that our common people are not mature enough for it."

"On the contrary," we reply, "instead of making literacy a privilege and an exception, do away with its exclusiveness. Make it the possession of everyone as much as
possible and it will not under any circumstances give rise
to arrogance or presumption in anyone. There will not
be anyone to presume upon—everyone will be literate.
Hence, in order to abolish the harmful consequences of
literacy, one must spread it as much and as far as possible: this is the only remedy. All the more so since by
their own system (that is, by preventing the spread of
literacy) the opponents of literacy will not achieve their
aim, but will act against their own interests. For by seek-
ing to restrain the spread of literacy they will never destroy it completely. The government would be the first to
oppose their desperate efforts and protect the people
against their kind of philanthropy. Therefore there will
still be literate people among the peasants and, this being
so, they will still fill the jails, so that the opponents of
literacy will have achieved nothing and will have cured
no one. Moreover, the jails will be filled all the more, because the less literacy there is, the more it will have assumed the nature of a privilege. Besides, there can hardly
be any disagreement about literacy being the first step toward education, for how is one to obtain an education
without this first step? And it is impossible seriously to
claim that the opponents of literacy intend to keep the
common people in ignorance and let them indulge in a
life of depravity and dissipation—in short, to corrupt and
kill their souls. Or is that too part of their system? I am
afraid it is. There is no more stubborn, no more harmful
man than the armchair philanthropist. But enough. For
our part we are absolutely convinced that literacy will im-

77

prove the common people morally and imbue them with a feeling of personal dignity which will in turn put an end to many malpractices and disorders, make an end even to the possibility of their recurrence. Everything depends upon circumstances and everything in the world changes only in conformity to circumstances. The moment a direct and urgent need makes its appearance in society, the moment the consciousness of such a need makes itself felt, it instantaneously finds the way in which it can be satisfied. On the other hand, no real improvement will be accepted by the masses as an improvement, but rather as an act of oppression, unless, however unconsciously, the desire for such an improvement has arisen in the masses. This is true of literacy, too. The common people are ripe for it, they want it and they search for a way to achieve it, and that is why it must and will spread in spite of all the efforts of the philanthropists. Look at the Sunday schools. Children are only too anxious to go there even against their masters' wishes. The parents themselves take their children to the teachers. I am afraid that though we have been studying the common people for a great many years and though many of our writers have devoted their talents and their leisure to this study, we still are far from knowing them thoroughly. We are quite certain that ten or twelve years ago many progressive people of those days would not have believed that the common people themselves would have demanded the foundation of temperance societies and gone in crowds to the Sunday schools. We say it seriously because some might take our opinion for a joke. But our civilized society will at last reach the point when it will understand the common people—this unriddled Sphinx, as one of our poets put it recently. It will understand the underlying truths of the common people and will be imbued with them. It is already aware of the fact that this is necessary as the foundation of our future progress and development: it realizes that it has to take the first step and . . . it will at last find a way of taking this step.

5.

And so everything now depends on the first step, everything depends on finding some way of taking this first step, of uttering the first word, so that the common people will hear us and turn their ears and mistrustful faces to us. I have no doubt that there will be a great number of people who will burst out laughing at our words. What are we to reply to them? We know perfectly well that the number of such gentlemen is legion, but then we do not really have any business with them. By the way, someone seems to have spread the story that we —that is, our journal—undertake to bring about a reconciliation between civilization and the national principle. We consider this story nothing but a charming joke. It is not for one man alone to utter this unknown word or solve this problem. In the program of our journal we have merely formulated the main idea that should guide us. We will look for the solution of the problem together with everyone else. But we certainly intend to repeat ceaselessly as well as to prove that it is necessary to—search; we will keep an eye on events, examine and discuss them, put forward arguments and pass on the result to the public. This is all our future activity will consist of. A word uttered at the right moment is useful; it, too, is the same activity, with us more than anywhere else. That is why we hope that we will be useful. Our journal is intended for perusal by educated people, for it is educated society that still has to utter the first word and that still has to take the first step to every kind of activity. We know that nothing as yet has been done to provide reading matter for the common people. If only they had something to read, for what there is, is inaccessible to them. We will welcome joyfully every attempt to do away with this inaccessibility. But, we repeat, we have not the slightest intention of making our journal into an organ for supplying reading matter to the common people. But enough of explanations; let us turn to our business. We consider it the duty of the educated classes to take the first step to this new activity because they were the first to shy away from the people. Approaching the people will not be an easy matter; we all realize that, though we are only dimly aware of the difficulties. The main thing is to remove misunderstandings. Every misunderstanding can be removed by complete frankness. We are beginning to realize that the interests of our class are inseparable from the interests of the common people, and vice versa. Such a realization, were it to become general, would be a guarantee of success. But if such a realization does not as yet exist, there are signs that it is beginning, and that is sufficient. A man may err. We know for our part that no one can be accused of hypocrisy because of an error of judgment. But it is not a question of errors. Let those who want such a rapprochement with the common people commit thousands of errors, the main thing is that the common people should see and divine this desire, that they should understand and value it—that is all that is needed. At least the idea on which it is all based remains as firm as a rock. If we do not succeed in one thing we will succeed in another. Everything depends on the rightness and directness of one's motive, everything depends on love. Love is the basis of one's motive, the pledge of its strength. Love conquers cities. Without it no one can conquer anything, except by force, but then there are things that cannot be taken by force. Love is more comprehensible than anything, than any stratagems or diplomatic subtleties. It can be recognized and distinguished at once. The common people are quick to catch on and they are grateful; they know who loves them. Only those who love them remain in the memory of the common people. The example of this rapprochement was given us by the Monarch himself, who has virtually removed the last obstacles to it, and there is nothing higher or more sacred than his work during the thousand years of Russia's history. And though for a century and a half we had trained the common people to mistrust us, remember

Five Articles

the fable: it was not the rain or the wind that pulled the cloak off the traveler, but the sun. A great deal of unhappiness in the world has been caused by bewilderment and the failure to say the right word at the right time. A word that is not uttered at the right time is harmful and always has been so. Why should one class of the population be afraid to be frank with another? What are they afraid of? The common people will lovingly appreciate the work done by their teachers and instructors from the educated classes, they will recognize us as their real friends, will value us not as hirelings but as shepherds and respect us. We must at long last deserve their respect. And think what immense powers will emerge then! How everything will grow, gain in strength and renew itself! How our views will change as well as the so-called final conclusions! What then will become of our "talented natures" who could find no place for themselves, our indolent Byrons who took up much too much space because, one can only suppose, they put on too much weight while at leisure. No doubt you too, my dear Byrons, did not live in vain and did not put on weight in vain. You lived and protested, you formulated your desires. We looked at your sorrowful faces and asked ourselves, "What are they sorrowing for? What do they want? What are they looking for?" You were therefore instrumental in arousing our curiosity; our curiosity led us to look for an answer and we found an answer. And so you were useful, though only in a negative sense, by the very fact that you lived among us. But the time has come for you too to stop being miserable: try to do something yourselves too. You keep on saying that there is nothing for you to do. Try and see if you can find something to do now. Teach one little boy at least to read and write—there's plenty of work for you. But no. You turn away indignantly. "What kind of activity is this for us?" you say, smiling spitefully. "Immense powers lie buried in our breasts. We want to and we can move mountains. A spring of the purest love for all humanity issues from our hearts. We would like to

81

embrace all of humanity at once. We want work that corresponds to our powers. That is the kind of activity we desire and we perish in inactivity. You can't expect us to stride an inch instead of seven miles. Should a giant waste his time teaching a small boy how to read and write?" You are quite right, gentlemen. But if you are going to do nothing, you will die doing nothing. And here is just a tiny bit of a first step, an atom, but still better than nothing. You crave immense activity. Would you like us to give you one that exceeds all your desires? It is even easier to move mountains than to carry out this kind of activity. Here it is: sacrifice all your gigantic power to the general welfare. Stride one inch instead of seven miles. Realize once and for all that if you can't stride further than an inch, an inch is still better than nothing. Sacrifice everything—your great talents and your great ideas, remembering that it is all for the general good. Step down, step down to the little boy. It will be an enormous sacrifice. Moreover, you are intelligent and talented men, and if you sacrifice yourselves, if you step down to the ordinary affairs of life, to the small things of life, you will perhaps find from the very first step some other activity, a greater one, and then a still greater one, and so on. The whole thing depends on making a start. Make a start. Come on, make a start. Well? But perhaps this is more than can be expected of you. You may be able to sacrifice your life, but such an effort is beyond you.

Of course, we shall have to contribute only a tenth of the total efforts; the common people themselves will contribute the rest. But, we shall be asked, what do you intend to do with your education? What are you going to achieve? You want to go back to the national source and bring education to the people, that is, the same kind of European civilization which you yourselves have acknowledged to be unsuitable for us. Do you want to *Europeanize* the common people? But, we reply, is it possible that the European idea should bring the same results on a soil foreign to it? Everything in our country is so different, so unlike anything in Europe in every respect, internal as well as external, that it is quite impossible to obtain European results on our soil. We repeat: what suits us will remain, what does not suit us will die a natural death. Can you make Germans out of our people? Compared with the common people, we constitute the tiniest minority of independent forces and we possess fewer means than those possessed by the enormous masses of the common people. Why, we had been with the Germans for a hundred and fifty years and we did not succumb to European influence, we did not become Germans. Which means that in spite of the fact that we constitute the tiniest minority and in spite of the little strength we possess and our quite exceptional position so far as the common people are concerned, we still preserved the great Russian principles of the universality of mankind and of universal conciliation and we have not lost them. We are conscious of them and we realized that we could not become Germans and of our own free will we wished to return to our national source. We became ashamed of our inactivity, our own immobility amid the immense activity of the European tribes, and we understood that there was nothing for us to do in Europe. Don't worry, science will not shackle our people; it will merely widen their powers and it will speak its own word with their help. Till now, science had found it difficult to strike roots in our country, where it was like some expensive hothouse flower. Our society did not show any particular scientific activity, neither theoretical nor practical, because it was separated from its native soil and was too weak to do anything by itself. It was the treasury that built bridges and roads, and that too mostly with the aid of foreign engineers.

But science too will at last strike roots in our country. All this may well happen when we are no longer here. We cannot even guess what things will be like then, but we know that they will not be so bad. The honor of taking the first step and uttering the first word was left to our generation. It is not for the first time that a new idea has been expressed in a Russian utterance. We are beginning to study its former expressions and discover in our former literary efforts facts that have hitherto escaped us but that fully confirm this idea. Pushkin's immense significance is becoming more and more obvious to us in spite of some odd literary opinions about him that have recently found expression in two of our journals. Yes, it is in Pushkin that we find the confirmation of the whole of our idea. His influence on Russian intellectual development is profoundly significant. To all Russians he is a living indication, in all its artistic completeness, of the true nature of the Russian spirit, of the direction in which the Russian forces are moving forward and of what really is the Russian's ideal. The fact that Pushkin existed is proof that the tree of civilization has already matured and is capable of producing fruit and that this fruit is not rotten, but excellent, golden fruit. Everything we could possibly have learned from our acquaintance with Europeans about ourselves we have learned; everything that civilization could clarify for us we have clarified for ourselves, and this knowledge was revealed to us in the most harmonious way in Pushkin. It was he who made us understand that the Russian ideal is complete integrity, complete universality and complete reconciliation. The fact that Pushkin existed makes clear to us even what our future activity is to be. The Russian spirit, the Russian idea found expression not in Pushkin alone, but it is only in him that they have appeared to us in all their fullness as a complete, undeniable fact.

We shall say much more about Pushkin in our next article, in which we hope to develop our thought more conclusively. In the next article too we shall take up the subject of Russian literature, we shall discuss its present position, its importance in our society today, we shall discuss some of the misunderstandings, arguments and questions in connection with it. We should like, in particular, to say a few words about the very strange question that has divided our literature for several years into different parties and in this way paralyzed its strength. I mean the famous question of art for art's sake, etc.—everyone knows about it. We must admit in advance that what surprises us most is that the public did not get sick and tired of this question long ago and that it is still willing to read whole tracts about it. But we shall not try to write about it in the form of a tract.

II. Mr. —bov and the Question of Art

In the announcement of our journal we said that our Russian criticism today is becoming pettier and increasingly vulgar. We said this more in sorrow than in anger and we do not withdraw it: we are profoundly convinced of this. Many of the more widely read Russian journals expressed almost the same view in their autumn announcements at the beginning of the present 1861 subscription year. At least many of them promised to pay particular attention to this section in the coming year, which means that they agree that it has been far from perfect so far. They will do well to carry out their promise. I do not think that we can be accused of boastfulness or arrogance, or just because we have found that our criticism has become petty should we be accused of showing off as the heralds of new truths, proclaimers of new ideas, etc., etc. We do not wish to assume such a role. All we know is that we love our work and set about it with enthusiasm and with respect. It is impossible not to admit that our criticism has suffered from a sort of general apathy for a long time, with perhaps only one exception —*Home Annals*. That journal has gone so far as to declare without the slightest hesitation or remorse that Belinsky's entire brilliant activity was, it is true, brilliant, but—how shall we put it?—somewhat superficial (*entre nous soit dit*) and that the real, immense and salutary activity of Russian criticism began after Belinsky had left that journal. We recall that at about that time (that is, when Belinsky had left that journal) Mr. Dudyshkin's article on Fonvizin appeared in *Home Annals*. Is it from its appearance that *Home Annals* started the new era of Russian criticism? It is true that immediately after Belinsky the section devoted to criticism in *Home Annals* was taken over by Valerian Nikolaevich Maykov, brother of the universally known and esteemed poet Apollon Nikolaevich Maykov. Valerian Maykov threw himself into the work ardently, brilliantly, with great conviction and with the first ardor of youth. But he had no time to make his mark. He died during the first year of his appointment. He showed great promise and perhaps we did lose a great deal by his death. Mr. Dudyshkin succeeded him at *Home Annals* and we have some foundation for believing that it is with him that the yellow journal begins its new brilliant era of activity. *Home Annals,* indeed, seems to think that it is to be especially commended for the fact that after Belinsky its criticism assumed chiefly a historic character and that Belinsky, who overthrew the authorities and was preoccupied with George Sand (the remarks about Geroge Sand in *Home Annals'* announcement are the height of perfection—they are so much to the point!), scarcely dealt with the historic aspect of Russian literature. To begin with, this is unjust, but even if it were just, there is more of the historic aspects of Russian literature in two pages of Belinsky's writings than in the whole of *Home Annals* from the very beginning of its publication in 1848 to this day. And since Mr. Dudyshkin's article on Fonvizin is considered by *Home Annals* to be the beginning of its celebrated historic activity, then one must suppose that this activity began with Mr. Dudyshkin. It is true that the article on Fonvizin was quite a sensible one, though rather dull. But since its publication *Home Annals* has been going through such a period of drought that one is simply terrified to think of this time even when compared with the article on Fonvizin. *Home Annals,* however, describes this period as the most brilliant epoch of its activity and, indeed, of the whole of Russian literature. It asserts that during this time the journal became a truly national one. We can only remember one article in *Home Annals* about the broom, the shovel and the oven prongs and their significance in Russian mythology. The information supplied by the author of that article was, of course, very useful, but, surely, it is not in that kind of article that *Home Annals* sees its conversion to our national traditions? If that is so, then its idea of our national traditions is rather original. Original too is another opinion expressed in the *Home Annals* announcement with terrifying frankness, namely that everything that is right-thinking and going forward toward some goal in our society today, everything—inasmuch as there is any sense or consciousness in it—has been due to *Home Annals* and is the fruit of its labors. As that journal itself is beginning to look down a little on Belinsky, it is permissible to conclude that it ascribes all those brilliant results to its subsequent activities, that is to say, beginning with the article on Fonvizin and the article about the shovel and ending with the monstrous article on Pushkin published in the April number of *Home Annals* of last year (1860). Last year's announcement about the forthcoming publication of *Home Annals* really belongs to the history of Russian literature. It will not die; it is eternal, monumental. We think it belongs to the literature of Russian scandals and to the scandals in Russian literature.

But we are digressing. In starting our article, we did not intend to comment on *Home Annals* and its announcements and remembered it quite accidentally, though we did wish to say a few words about the literary criticisms published in Russian journals last year. We say "a few words" because we do not undertake to write a full account of the entire critical literature of last year and indeed consider such a work to a certain extent a gigantic undertaking. It is true that in such an account we should

Five Articles

have had to point out certain rather pleasant facts in our critical writings. But though we do not intend to undertake this *gigantic* work, we realize that we shall have to say something about a certain question in this article, about one of the most important representatives of contemporary criticism who—we must be frank about it—is the only critic who is read today. Indeed, with the exception of three or four critical articles that appeared sporadically in different periodicals last year and some others the public noticed, the rest have gone without leaving a trace behind them. People read Mr. —bov, who has made people read him, and for that alone he deserves attention. However, it is really because of the following circumstance that we want to talk about Mr. —bov on this occasion.

In the January number of our journal, in concluding our introduction to "A Series of Articles on Russian Literature," we promised to talk about contemporary literary tendencies and questions. One of the most important literary questions today we consider the question about art. This question divides many of our contemporary writers into two hostile camps. In this way forces become disconnected. We need not expatiate on the harm such a hostile difference of opinion entails. And the matter has already reached a point of open hostility.

To examine this hostility and its causes, to explain the controversy and express our opinion in regard to it would be entirely in conformity with the aims of our journal and the duties we have undertaken in respect of the public. But first of all let us make clear that if we get involved in this controversy it is not because we lay claim to be the final judges in this matter. Besides, we can't think of any case in which one party would at any time submit to any other party in any of our literary controversies or would agree with it voluntarily or by conviction. With us, every literary argument ends either because we all get sick and tired of it or because it drags on too long or because one of the parties to the dispute gets so much the better of the other that it forces it to fall silent, but only because it is too exhausted to keep up the argument. It falls silent but it does not agree. Somehow we cannot remember any agreements. If there were any, they were so rare as to be hardly worth remembering.

For this reason we do not undertake to make peace or seek an agreement among the parties to the present controversy. Besides, it is not exactly a pleasant task. Recently Mr. Voskoboynikov imagined that Russian writers are too fond of fighting among themselves (in a literary way, naturally) and he dashed off a rather amusing article: "Stop Fighting, Writers." The result was that anyone who did not choose to ignore this article launched an attack on Mr. Voskoboynikov. Whatever else they may have disagreed about, they all agreed about this. We simply consider the present question about art to be extremely important and therefore, as a new journal, we wish to express our opinion also, namely how we understand this question and which particular shade of opinion concerning its solution we support. In this way we shall express our convictions frankly and indicate our leanings, more especially as we have been asked to do so. And as we cannot express our convictions without first explaining where the argument stands today in our literature, we shall define the contemporary character of this controversy by first examining the contentions of the two parties, to which this article is devoted. One of the chief representatives of these contentions is undoubtedly Mr. —bov, who publishes his articles in the *Contemporary*. That is why we entitled our article "Mr. —bov and the Question of Art."

One more remark:

We are told and we ourselves have read in one of our most popular magazines that there are no parties in Russian literature. We suppose that magazine used the word "parties" in the sense of personal feuds, which is really no concern of literature. We should like quite naturally to do our best to take this magazine's word for it: if there aren't, all the better. But parties in the sense of dissenting opinions do exist in our literature. We have Askochenskys, Chernoknizhnikovs, —bovs, and even the most excellent Kuzma Prutkov can, strictly speaking, also be considered a representative of a peculiar literary party of his own. Generally speaking, every journal of ours adheres to certain opinions. Completely colorless journals do not last in our country and die a quiet and peaceful death. No doubt our literary parties have rather vague and indistinct outlines. From some it is quite impossible to obtain a clear definition of their views; some get off with some vague hints; others express themselves as though to order and yet do not seem to have any faith in themselves; others still retire into the misty regions of frowning phrases, bewildering phrases, gibberish—interpret it as you will. It is of course impossible to blame them for it. But so far as the question of art is concerned, some of our journals have taken up quite definite positions, especially more recently. Among them the first place is occupied by Mr. —bov's last year's articles in the *Contemporary*.

After these introductory remarks, to business.

To begin with, we should like to point out that we do not adhere to any existing opinions and declare frankly that in our view the whole question is at present wrongly formulated, just because the controversy is so heated and just because it has reached a point of almost open hostility. We hope to prove it.

But let us consider the very essence of the question: what kind of question is it and what exactly does it imply?

Some declare and teach that art is an aim by itself and must find its justification in its inner content and that consequently there cannot be any question of the usefulness of art in the real meaning of the word. Creation is the fundamental principle of all art and it is an unbroken organic quality of human nature and has a right to exist and develop, if only for the reason that it is a necessary accessory of the human spirit. It is as legitimate in man as intellect and as all moral qualities of man, as legitimate, in fact, as two arms and two legs, as a stomach. It is inseparable from man and forms one whole with him. Intellect, of course, is useful and in the same sense man finds a pair of legs and arms useful. In the same sense art too is useful to man.

But as something integral, organic, creative art develops out of itself, it is not subject to anything and it demands full development. Above all, it demands absolute freedom in its development. For that reason any constraint, any subjection, any outside purpose, any exceptional aim put before it would be both illegitimate and unreasonable. If creative art were to be restricted or if man were forbidden to satisfy his creative and artistic needs by—shall we say?—by giving expression to certain sensations, if man were forbidden any creative occupations that certain natural phenomena would arouse in him, such as sunrise, a storm at sea, etc., then all this would have been an absurd, ridiculous and illegitimate constraint of the human spirit in its development and activity.

This is what one party maintains, the party defending the freedom and the fullest independence of art.

"Of course that would have been an absurd constraint," reply the utilitarians (the other party, which teaches that art must serve man by its direct, immediate, practical usefulness, which may even depend on circumstances), "of course such a constraint without any reasonable aim but simply at someone's whim is a wicked and savage piece of stupidity. But you must surely agree (they could add) that for instance, if you found yourself in the midst of a battle and instead of assisting your comrades you, an artist at heart, suddenly felt that you must preserve a picture of the battle as a whole and so you threw down your arms, took out a pencil and paper and began making a sketch of the battlefield: would you be doing right? No doubt you would be entitled to give yourself over to your inspirations, but would your artistic activity be reasonable at such a moment?

92

"In short," they conclude, "we do not reject your theory about the freedom of artistic development, but this freedom must at least be reasonable."

At the beginning of his interesting reminiscences (the *Contemporary*, 1861, Book 1) Mr. Panaev recalls that when he was a young man, certain Petersburg writers held the view that men of letters, poets, artists and actors must not occupy themselves with anything of current interest, neither with politics nor with the social life of the circle to which they belonged nor with any question that might be of great importance to their nation as a whole, but must devote themselves entirely to *high art*. For to be engaged in anything except art means to abase it, to bring it down from its heights, to scoff at it. According to such teaching, one had to cut the very ground from under one's feet voluntarily, the ground on which all stand and by which all live and, therefore, one was obliged to fly farther and farther toward the stars and there, of course, evaporate somehow or other, for there was nothing else one could do. This theory would mean that, for instance, during the 1812 campaign when the entire Russian people were engaged only in saving their country, men of letters and poets would have been much better occupied in, say, compiling a Greek anthology. In the literary and artistic circle Mr. Panaev is describing, they did act like that: they did not engage in any social questions. One of the most important members of that circle spent his time in those days writing dramas about the lives of Italian artists.

Let us take another example:

Let us imagine that we are in the eighteenth century in Lisbon on the day of the great earthquake. Half of Lisbon's inhabitants are perishing; the houses are collapsing and crashing down; fortunes are lost; every survivor has lost something—his family or his fortune. The inhabitants rush through the streets in despair, thunderstruck and terrified out of their wits. At that particular time a famous Portuguese poet was living in Lisbon. The next morning the *Lisbon Mercury* (in those days all newspapers were *Mercuries*) appears. A paper published at such a moment naturally arouses a certain feeling of curiosity among the unhappy citizens of Lisbon in spite of the fact that at that particular time they could hardly be expected to take any interest in papers. They hope the paper has been published to give them some news of the dead, the missing, etc. And suddenly on the most prominent place on the page they find a poem describing "the whisper, timid breath and warbling of the nightingale," the "silvery gleam and heaving of the sleepy brook," "nocturnal shadows," the "magic changes of the face of the beloved," the "purple of the rose in the smoky clouds," "kisses and tears" and "the sunrise, the sunrise." And as if this was not enough, there is a prose afterword to the poem, repeating the well-known poetic rule that anyone who is not able to jump out of a window on the fourth floor is not a real poet (why? I never could understand this, but let this be so in the case of a poet, I do not want to argue the point). I don't know for certain how the Lisbon inhabitants would have reacted to this poem, but it seems to me that they would have lynched their famous poet there and then in the city square, and not because he had written a poem without a verb, but because instead of the warbling of the nightingale they had heard quite a different kind of warbling under the ground the night before, and the heaving of the brook appeared at a moment when quite a different kind of heaving of the whole city deprived the poor Lisbon citizens of any desire to observe "the purple in the smoky clouds," and the action of their poet, singing of such trivial things at such a moment, seemed much too insulting and unfriendly. No doubt, having lynched their poet (also an unfriendly action), they would most certainly have rushed to some Dr. Pangloss for some clever advice and Dr. Pangloss would at once and without much difficulty have assured them all that it was a good thing they had suffered such a calamity and that since they had suffered such a calamity it was all for the best. And no one would have torn Dr. Pangloss to pieces; on the contrary, they would have granted him a pension and proclaimed him to be a friend of humanity. This is the way things happen in this world, is it not? Let us observe, though, that even if the Lisbon citizens had lynched their favorite poet, the poem that had made them so angry (even if it was about roses and the sunrise) might have been excellent so far as its artistic perfection went. And not only that. They would have lynched the poet, but fifty years later they would have erected a monument to commemorate his wonderful poems in general and "the purple of the rose" in particular. It therefore follows that it was not art that was to blame on the day of the Lisbon earthquake. The poem, for which the poet has been lynched, was perhaps of great benefit to the Lisbon people as a memorial of the perfection of language and poetry, for it aroused in them afterward an esthetic enthusiasm and a feeling of beauty, and lay as a beneficent dew on the soul of the younger generation. Therefore, again, it was not art that was to blame, but the poet who abused art at a moment when the people were not in the mood for it. He sang and danced at the coffin of a dead man. . . . This was of course very bad and extremely silly on his part; but, again, it was not art that was to blame but the poet.

In short, the utilitarians demanded of art direct and immediate usefulness, which should take account of prevailing circumstances and be subject to them to such a degree that if, for instance, society were to be preoccupied at a given time with the solution of a certain problem, then art (according to the teachings of some utilitarians) should have no other aim than the solution of the same problem. If one were to regard this idea of usefulness not as a demand but only as a wish, it might in our view be even praiseworthy, though we are aware that such an idea is not quite right all the same. If, for instance, the entire society were preoccupied with the solution of some important internal problem, it would of course be agreeable to wish that all the forces of that society be directed toward the attainment of that aim and, therefore, that art too be inspired by the same idea and serve the general cause. Suppose that a certain society is on the brink of disaster; everyone possessing any intelligence, any feeling, any willpower, anyone conscious of his being a man and a citizen, is preoccupied with one single problem, one common cause. Is it only poets and writers who need not have any intelligence, any feeling, any love for their country and sympathy with the general well-being of their people? But even if, as the poet contends, the service of the Muses cannot tolerate world-mindedness, it would not be a bad idea if poets, for instance, were not to seek refuge in the empyrean and look down from there on the rest of us mortals. For though a Greek anthology is an excellent thing, it is sometimes quite out of place and it would be much more agreeable to see in its place something more suitable to the business at hand and something more helpful to it. Besides, art can be of help to some cause by rendering assistance to it, for it comprises enormous means and great powers. We repeat: one can only wish it, one cannot demand it, if only because one demands mostly when one wishes to compel by force, and the first law of art is freedom of inspiration and creation. Everything that has been imposed from above, everything that has been obtained by force from time immemorial to our own day has never succeeded and, instead of being beneficial, has been only harmful. The defenders of "art for art's sake" are chiefly against the utilitarians because by prescribing certain aims for art, they destroy it, for they encroach on its freedom, and since they destroy art so easily, they cannot possibly value it and, therefore, cannot even understand what it could be useful for; they are first of all concerned about its usefulness. Therefore, say the defenders of art, if the utilitarians had any idea of the great usefulness of art to the whole of mankind, they would value it more and would not treat it with such disrespect. And indeed, they continue, even if one were to look at art from your point of view, that is to say, consider it only in the aspect of its usefulness, then it must be stated that the normal historical process of usefulness of art to mankind is still unknown. It is difficult to measure the whole mass of usefulness that has been and still is being brought to the whole of mankind by, for example, the *Iliad* or the *Apollo Belvedere,* things that are apparently quite unnecessary today. Suppose, for example, that a certain man when still in his youth, at a time of life when "all impressions of life are still new and fresh," had a look at the *Apollo Belvedere* and the god had imprinted himself in the young man's soul by his majestic and infinitely beautiful image. A seemingly unimportant fact: he stopped for a couple of minutes to admire the beautiful statue and went away. But this kind of admiration is quite unlike the admiration, for instance, of an elegant dress. "This marble is god," and spit at it as much as you like, you will not rob it of its divinity. Such an attempt to rob it has been made before, but nothing came of it. And therefore the young man's impression may have been an ardent and nerve-racking one, an impression that sent a cold shiver down his spine; who knows, perhaps a kind of internal change takes place in man at the impact of such beauty, at such a nervous shock, a kind of movement of particles or galvanic current that in one moment transforms what has been before into something different, a piece of ordinary iron into a magnet. There are, of course, thousands of impressions in the world, but, surely, it is not for nothing that this sort of impression is a special one, the impression of a god. It is surely not for nothing that such impressions remain for the rest of one's life. And who knows? When twenty or thirty years later this young man came to the fore during some great social event in which he had taken a prominent part by acting in one way rather than another, who knows whether among the many reasons that made him act one way and not another there was, unconsciously, his impression of the *Apollo Belvedere* he had seen twenty years earlier? You laugh? Indeed, it does sound rather like the ravings of a lunatic. But, first of all, about these facts, in spite of their explicitness, you do not know anything positive yourself. Perhaps you will know about them in the future (we believe in science), but for the time being you do not know. Second, there are historic indications, certain historic facts, which seem to confirm our belief that our dreams are not altogether absurd. Who, for example, could have imagined that Corneille and Racine would have exerted an influence on such unusual and decisive moments of the historic life of a whole people when at first it would have seemed unthinkable that such old dodderers as Corneille and Racine could have anything to do at such a period. It would seem however that souls do not die. If, therefore, one were to define the aims of art beforehand and determine what it ought to be useful for, one could make a terrible mistake and, instead of doing good, only do harm and, therefore, act against oneself, for utilitarians demand usefulness and not harmfulness. And since art demands full freedom first of all and freedom cannot exist without tranquillity (any kind of disturbance is no longer freedom), it must function quietly and serenely, without haste, without being carried away by extraneous matters, having itself as its aim and believing that every activity will in time confer incontestable benefits upon humanity.

This is what the advocates of art for art's sake say to their opponents the utilitarians.

There is of course nothing new in any of this; the controversy is an old one, but what is new is that while the leaders of the two parties speak like that, in practice they act diametrically contrary to what they are saying. They have indulged in their arguments a little too long. Without expatiating too much, here is an example:

The literature whose chief aim is to expose what it believes to be the evils of our time arouses the indignation of the advocates of pure art. On the one hand, it has a certain justification, because for the most part the works of this kind of literature are so bad that they are more harmful than useful to the general cause, and if we for our part admit that the attacks on these works are partly justified, it is only in that sense. But the trouble is that the attacks on them are not made in that sense at all. The indignation of the opponents of the utilitarians goes much further; Mr. Shchedrin, the father of the literature of exposure, is himself accused in spite of the fact that Court Councilor Shchedrin is a real artist in many of his works. Moreover, the entire genre of the literature of exposure is being persecuted as though no true artist, no genius, no poet could even appear among the writers of this genre, since his specialty would consist of exposure. Because of their hostility toward their opponents, the advocates of pure art, therefore, are spoiling their own chances, are against their own principles, namely, they are destroying freedom of choice of one's inspiration. And it is for this freedom that they should be fighting.

On the other hand, the utilitarians, without openly attacking the high artistic value of any work, do not specifically recognize its necessity. "It is sufficient that the idea of the work should be clear, that only the aim for which it is written should be discernible, its artistic value is of no importance, it is something that is quite unnecessary." This is what the utilitarians think. But as an inartistic work never under any circumstances attains its aim and, in fact, harms rather than helps the cause, the utilitarians are harming their own cause by refusing to recognize the artistic value of a work and, therefore, are spoiling their own chances, for what they are looking for is usefulness and not harmfulness.

We shall be told that we have invented the whole thing ourselves and that the utilitarians have never thought of attacking the high artistic value of any work. On the contrary, they not only attack it, but we have observed that it seems to give them great pleasure to be vexed with some literary work if its chief merit is its high artistic value. They hate Pushkin, for instance, and call all his inspired works pretentious affectation and cheap tricks and his small poems album gewgaws. They even consider the very fact of Pushkin's appearance in our literature as something illegitimate. We are not at all exaggerating. All this is quite clearly expressed by Mr. —bov in some of his critical articles of last year. It is also noticeable that Mr. —bov is beginning to express himself with particular dislike about Mr. Turgenev also, the most artistic of our contemporary Russian writers. In his article "Characteristic Features of the Russian Common People" (*Contemporary*, 1860, N.IX), in an analysis of Marko-Vovchok's short stories, Mr. —bov admits frankly that the author has written it inartistically and maintains immediately after that statement that the author has achieved what she had set out to do with her story by proving conclusively that a certain fact existed among the Russian common people. And yet this fact (a very important one) is not only not proved by this story but remains highly doubtful just because of the inartistic nature of the author. The characters of the story brought forward by the author to prove her main idea have lost under her pen all their significance as Russians and the reader would be inclined to call them Scots, Italians and Northern Americans rather than Russian peasants. How, then, could they prove that this fact exists among the Russian peasants when they themselves, the characters themselves, bear no resemblance to the Russian peasants? But Mr. —bov is not in the least concerned about it: provided the idea, the aim of the story is clear, it does not matter if all the threads and springs are crudely exposed. Of what use, then, is the artistic quality of a literary work? And, come to think of it, why write short stories at all? Why not simply write that a certain fact exists among the common people for this or that reason—it is much briefer, much clearer and much more impressive. Why waste your time telling tales? Have you nothing better to do?

Let us, incidentally, make one more observation. How does one recognize the high artistic quality of a work of art? By the fact that we see the fullest possible harmony between the artistic idea and the form in which it is embodied? Let us put it a little more clearly: the high artistic quality of, let us say, a novelist is his ability to express the idea of his novel in the characters and images of his novel so that after reading it the reader understands the writer's idea as well as the novelist has understood it himself when creating his work. In simple words, then, it means that the artistic quality of a writer is his ability to write well. Therefore, those who claim that the artistic quality of a literary work is of no account admit that it is permissible to write badly, and if they go as far as to agree that it is *permissible,* it is not far from saying quite simply that it is *necessary* to write badly. In fact, they practically say that.

In this article we intend to follow the critical analysis of Marko-Vovchok's works published by Mr. —bov in the ninth number of the *Contemporary* of last year. We do so especially because that analysis illuminates the character of Mr. —bov's literary views together with his view on art. And Mr. —bov, as we have already said, is one of the leaders of the utilitarians. Therefore, by studying even to a certain extent Mr. —bov, we shall understand how the question of art in our literature is treated at the present moment.

The whole Russian reading public knows that Marko-Vovchok is the author of two volumes of stories dealing with the life of the Russian and Ukrainian common people. Mr. —bov analyzes only the Russian stories that have appeared in a Russian translation from the Ukrainian. All the stories are analyzed by him in extraordinary detail on nearly five printed pages of small type. This analysis is especially interesting in that it reveals how Mr. —bov understands the aim and purpose of literature, what he demands of it and what qualities, what means and powers he thinks it possesses so far as its influence on society is concerned. We shall, however, limit ourselves to his analysis of the first story; this is quite enough to get a clear understanding of Mr. —bov's convictions. We do not intend to talk in detail about Marko-Vovchok herself in this article. We shall merely say that we are ready to acknowledge that the author possesses great intelligence and excellent motives, but that we doubt very much whether she possesses any great literary talent. We are very sorry to express this opinion without proving it. We are even sorrier that, as though on purpose, we are compelled to discuss the analysis of her first story, *Masha*, the weakest, we must confess, of all her stories. But in his analysis of this story Mr. —bov has expressed the views to which we should like our reader to pay particular attention.

We do not of course intend to analyze *all* of Mr. —bov's views, though Mr. —bov, in our opinion, deserves such a detailed analysis. In many things we are in complete disagreement with him, and, indeed, his direct opponent; but the very fact that he made the public read him, that the critical articles in the *Contemporary* since Mr. —bov became one of its contributors are the first to be read at a time when hardly anyone bothers to read critical articles clearly testifies to Mr. —bov's literary talent. His talent possesses the power of conviction. Mr. —bov is not so much a critic as a publicist. The fundamental principle of his conditions is just and arouses the sympathy of the public; but the ideas with which this fundamental principle is expressed are often paradoxical and suffer from one important fault—bookishness. Mr. —bov is a theoretician, sometimes even a dreamer, and in many cases has a weak knowledge of reality; he sometimes treats reality a little too unceremoniously, he bends it one way and another just as he wants to, so long as he can treat it in a way that it will prove his idea. Mr. —bov writes in a simple, clear style, though it is said of him that he likes to chew a phrase a little too much before he is ready to put it into his reader's mouth. He always seems to be afraid that he will not be understood. Still, this is not a great fault. The clarity and simplicity of his style deserve special attention and praise at present when in some journals the writers deem it to be a special honor to write in a style that is unclear, heavy and florid, no doubt under the impression that all this is conducive to profundity of thought. Someone even assured me that if one of our critics wanted to have a drink of water, he would never say simply "Let me have a drink of water," but something of this kind:

"Please, bring me that essential element of moisture which serves for the softening of the hard substances deposited in my stomach."

This joke certainly bears some resemblance to truth.

But to business. Almost at the very beginning of his analysis, Mr. —bov says:

"In the Ukrainian stories we saw the abuses of landowners' powers and these abuses are sometimes extremely severe. This, it is said, has even given a well-known Russian critic a reason for stating that Marko-Vovchok's works were 'loathsomely disgusting pictures' and, having ranked them with the works of the literature of exposure, he denies that their author possesses 'any literary talent.' We have not read the articles of this severe critic because we have long given up being interested in his literary verdicts; but nonetheless *we understand the process* by means of which he has come to his conclusion. *He is an adherent of the theory of art for art's sake;* Marko-Vovchok's stories found admirers also among the adherents of this theory. *You can imagine what exactly such admirers like about these stories.* We ourselves have heard two artistic connoisseurs express their admiration for the extraordinary charm and poetic nature of one passage which I believe runs as follows: 'Oh, oh, far away in the field a cross can be seen over his grave.' The severe critic, who has censured Marko-Vovchok, *seems to have been a little more sensible than such connoisseurs,* for he realized that 'Oh, oh, far away in the field' is not yet the height of artistic talent. *But that he was not able to understand anything in 'The Folk Tales' is again very natural and indeed a man would have to be very strange to expect such an under-*

*standing from him. For then he would have had to re-
nounce the theory of 'art for art's sake'; but can he renounce it? What could he do without it? What would he
be fit for?"*

Let us stop here. This passage in Mr. —bov's article is
the best possible justification of our remarks about the
mutually sweet relations between the two literary parties,
that is to say, the utilitarians and the advocates of art for
art's sake. Hostility, predetermined misunderstandings,
wild accusations—those are the things we see in the
above quotation. At first Mr. —bov accuses the *artistic*
critic with the idea that, because of their informative
tendencies, Marko-Vovchok's stories be called "loathsomely disgusting pictures" and, having ranked them
among the works of the literature of exposure, it should
be *denied as a result of this* that the author had any literary talent. Though this accusation is rather harsh, we are
almost inclined to take Mr. —bov's word for it, because we
did not read the article of the *artistic* critic. It is true that
this critic could have denied the author any literary talent
not merely because these stories expose the evils of our
times; we think that in this case he might have based his
judgment on other facts. But Mr. —bov absolutely con-
firms our contention that the advocates of art for art's
sake not only reject the entire literature of exposure without exception because of their hatred of the utilitarian
movement, but also reject the possibility of the appearance
of a man of great talent in this type of literature. We repeat, it is possible to believe it. But, on the other hand,
Mr. —bov himself for his part commits the gross error of
stating that if the artistic critic could have understood
anything in Marko-Vovchok's stories he would have been
untrue to himself because he would have had to immediately renounce *the theory of art for art's sake.*

Some of the advocates of the theory of art for art's
sake could be accused of blindness and spite and hence
also of injustice, but that the theory of art for art's sake
itself possessed a kind of inherent quality of turning its

104

advocates into stupid fools and intelligent men into obtuse people of limited intelligence is already unjust. What
does it matter to what an extreme some theory or party or
doctrine can run at any given moment? One cannot accept any deviation for a general rule.

But let us continue with our quotations.

"But the verdicts of the artistic critic do not really matter: why worry about him? As no one takes him seriously,
his artistic amusements are completely harmless. We
have other views and other doctrines in mind and it is
these we consider it desirable to discuss now in connection with Marko-Vovchok's book. These opinions are quite
widely held by a certain section of our society, which considers itself to be educated, and yet they display a strange
lack of understanding of the matter under discussion, as
well as thoughtlessness. The views we have in mind concern the characterization of the peasant and his attitude
to serfdom. Serfdom is approaching its end. But facts that
have existed for centuries do not pass away without leaving any trace behind them. A kind of order of precedence
is still observed in our people's customs two centuries
after its abolition by law. How, then, can it be expected
that the relationships that are the result of serfdom should
be suddenly changed? That is too much to expect and for
a long time to come the consequences of serfdom will be
felt in books, in high-society conversations and in the
whole organization of the relationships between the different classes of the population. The ideas not only of the
older generation, not only of the generation that is active
at present, but also of the one that is about to enter our
social life have been formed, if not directly on the basis of
serfdom, then, at any rate, not without its strong influence. The principle of serfdom had been legalized and accepted by the state. Now this principle has been rejected,
so that the ideas and demands bred and produced by it
form the subject of discussion among those who formerly
defended them. Now the business of literature is to expose the remnants of serfdom in social life and to root out

the ideas it had produced. In her simple and *truthful* stories Marko-Vovchok appears as almost the first and *a very skillful fighter in this field.* In her last stories she does not even attempt to exhibit before us what is usually described as 'the abuse of the landowners' powers.' Why talk of abuse of something that is in itself evil? Why talk of things which serfdom has given rise to but which it could occasionally dispense with? No, our author now takes the present normal position of the peasant of a landowner who does *not* abuse his rights, and gently, without anger, without bitterness, describes his position to us. And from these sketches, *in which everyone who has had any dealings with the Russian common people will recognize familiar features, from these sketches there arises before us the character of the Russian peasant,* who has preserved his original features amid a relationship that tended to deprive a man of his individuality and to which he had been subjected for several centuries. To some traits of this character we should now like to turn our attention."

We have quoted this extract because it serves as an introduction to Mr. —bov's critique of Marko-Vovchok. He partly states his view of Marko-Vovchok. Consider the lines we put in italics. Mr. —bov owns that Marko-Vovchok's stories are *simple* and *truthful,* that in them she appears as *a very skillful fighter in this field* and that from these sketches, in which everyone *who has had any dealings with the Russian common people will recognize familiar features, from these sketches there arises before us the character of the Russian peasant.* Make a note of these words of Mr. —bov. It is clear from them that he thinks that, in addition to intelligence and knowledge, Marko-Vovchok also possesses *the ability to convey her knowledge and observations*—in short, he thinks that she possesses literary talent.

Then there follow a few excellent pages in which Mr. —bov expounds the different views and theories that are current today among certain gentlemen in regard to the

Five Articles

Russian peasants. This splendid passage (not one of the best by any means in Mr. —bov's article) could have made those of our readers who have no conception of Mr. —bov's talent realize the reason why this writer has made the public read him. We do not quote this passage (though we should like to have quoted it in full) because we are not analyzing Mr. —bov's writings but only his views of art. Passages like that would have destroyed the unity of our article. But we should like to draw attention to the passage we are about to quote. Here Mr. —bov examines Marko-Vovchok partly also as an artist, declares that he does not think that she really possesses any artistic talent, but goes on to assert that it is obvious that she has a thorough knowledge of the life she is depicting and that this is why he likes her stories so much. Moreover, Mr. —bov allows himself to be carried away: as an intelligent man he could have discovered the springs and noticed the hints and intentions of the author; he could even have concluded from certain confused and incoherent observations made by her that she was referring or wished to refer to certain matters, and, overjoyed that those matters are being referred to, he felt so grateful to her that he was ready to find in her stories the presence of the Russian spirit, familiar characteristics (of the Russian peasant), etc., etc., all of which are already signs of an artistic quality which he himself admits the author does not possess. The important thing is that Mr. —bov is quite satisfied with the absence of artistic qualities so long as the right things are discussed. This last wish is of course praiseworthy, but it would be more agreeable if the right things had been discussed well and not just anyhow.*

* Let me make myself clear. In expressing this opinion about Marko-Vovchok's works, we have in view only the first of her stories from the Russian volume—*Masha*. We cannot but agree that there are many talented pages in her other stories, though as a whole, not one of her stories is satisfactory from the literary point of view. Reality is often idealized and lacks conviction, and

But here is this passage from the article.

"We must first of all observe that these characters have not been reproduced in all their artistic amplitude, but are merely outlined in Marko-Vovchok's little stories. We cannot look for an epic of Russian life in them—that would have been a little too much to expect. Such an epic we might expect in the future, but for the time being we need not even think of it. The consciousness of our common people has not yet reached the period in which it could express itself wholly in a poetic form; the writers of the educated classes have till now almost all dealt with the common people as though they were a curious kind of toy, without attempting to regard them seriously. The realization of the importance of the common people is only just dawning on us and next to this hazy realization there appear observations of the life and character of the common people which are of a serious nature and are made with love and sincerity. Among these observations an honorable, if not the most honorable, place belongs to Marko-Vovchok's sketches. There is a great deal that is scrappy and unfinished and sometimes a fact is taken that is purely accidental, referring to one particular case, and we are told about it without any explanation of its internal or external causes, a fact that does not tie up with ordinary life in a way that would seem inevitable. But, we repeat, we cannot as yet demand an all-round perfection from our stories of peasant life, for it does not as yet reveal itself to us in all its fullness, and even what is revealed to us we cannot always find a satisfactory expression for. We still do not know how to find it. *So far as we are concerned, it suffices* that we see in Marko-Vovchok's stories a desire and an ability to pay close attention to the life of the common people; *we feel in them the presence of the Russian spirit, we meet familiar images,* we learn

---

yet you know that, though lacking conviction, everything might have happened in real life and you can't help feeling vexed that it is not convincing. We are, however, only referring to the Russian stories and not to the stories of Ukrainian life.

to know the logic, the feelings that we observed before sometime or other but did not pay any attention to. *That is why these stories are dear to us, that is why we have so high an opinion of their author.* We find profound attention and lively sympathy in her as well as a deep understanding of the life that is regarded so lightly and that is understood so narrowly and so inadequately by many of the highly educated of our economists, Slav scholars, jurists, novelists, etc., etc."

And now after this extract we shall pass to Mr. —bov's analysis of Marko-Vovchok's first story—*Masha.* We should like to quote this extract in full. We should like our readers to get to know this story in spite of the fact that it is Mr. —bov himself who tells it and makes extracts from it—the advocate, admirer and defender of Marko-Vovchok's talent.

"We remember the first appearance of this story," says Mr. —bov. "People who still believed in the inviolability of serfdom were horrified by it. A peasant girl's natural and indestructible development of love for independence and horror at slavery are revealed in it. As you can see, there is nothing criminal here; but upon the adherents of serfdom such a story must really have produced a shattering impression. It reached their last refuge, which they thought to be unassailable. You see, as human and enlightened people, they agree that serfdom is absolutely incompatible with the progress of modern education. But, having acknowledged this, they at once remark that the peasant has not yet reached that stage at which he could be truly independent, that he does not think about it at all and does not want it and that his position as a serf is not at all a burden to him—except perhaps where forced labor is very severe and the landowner's agent very stern. 'Why, where on earth could a peasant get an idea of freedom? He reads no books, he knows no writers, he has plenty of work and has no time for inventing all sorts of utopias. He lives as his fathers and forefathers lived, and if one wants to free him now it is simply a matter of kindness and magnanimity. . . . And, believe me, it will take a peasant a long time to come to realize what it is he is given and why it is given to him. Many, a great many of them will live to regret their former life. . . .' This is what intelligent and educated men asserted and they thought there was no denying it. And suddenly, just think of it, the reality of the fact they rely on so much is being contested. They are told of a case that proves that love of free labor and independent life is natural among the peasants and that the development of this feeling stands in no need of assistance from literature. This is the *simple* case they are told about.

"An old peasant woman is bringing up two orphans: her niece Masha and her nephew Fedya. Fedya is a boy like any other boy, cheerful, quiet, acquiescent; but Masha displays great independence of character from an early age. She is not satisfied with listening to an order, but demands to be told why and wherefore; she lends an attentive ear to everything, she watches everything closely and very early displays an inclination to form her own opinion. If the girl had been living with her father and mother, they would, of course, have knocked the nonsense out of her head at once, as usually happens to thousands of boys and girls in our country who display too great an inquisitiveness, which is considered a misplaced desire for a premature exercise of their brains. But by Masha's luck or ill-luck, her aunt was a simple and kindly woman who not only refused to punish Masha for her nimbleness of mind but yielded to it herself and was very upset when she could not answer her niece's questions or get the better of her arguments. Thus Masha got the convictions that she had a right to think, to ask questions and raise objections. That was enough. When she was seven years old something happened that gave a special turn to all her thoughts. Her aunt and Fedya had gone to town and Masha was left alone to keep an eye on the cottage. She was sitting on the mound in front of the cottage and playing with other children. Suddenly the wife of the

Five Articles

owner of the estate walked past, stopped, and, looking at
Masha, said, 'What are you making such a noise for?
Don't you know your mistress? Eh? Whose are you?'
Masha must have become frightened, for she did not reply, and the lady scolded her for it: 'You're growing up a
fool. You can't talk properly.' Masha burst into tears. The
lady felt sorry for her. 'Come, come to me, you silly little
girl,' she said. But Masha would not come. The lady told
the children to bring Masha to her, but Masha ran away
and did not return home. When her aunt and Fedya
came back from town they did not find Masha at home.
They went to look for her, but could not find her. It was on
their way back home that she suddenly rushed out of a
hemp field and ran up to them. Her aunt wanted to take
her home, but she would not go. 'The lady will take me
away,' she said. 'I won't go back.' Her aunt calmed her at
last and told her that one had to obey the lady of the
manor, however sternly she might give her orders.

" 'And what if I do not obey her?' asked Masha.

" 'Then you will be in real trouble, darling. You
wouldn't like to be punished, would you?'

"Even Fedya looked frightened and just stared at her
in silence.

" 'I could run away,' said Masha. 'Far away. Like the
Trostyansk peasants who ran away last summer.'

" 'But they were caught, Masha. And some of them
died on the way.'

" 'And when they caught them they put them in prison
and tortured them,' said Fedya.

" 'Yes, child,' said the aunt, 'they had to put up with a
lot of suffering and shame.'

" 'But,' Masha insisted, 'why is everybody standing up
for the lady?'

" 'She is a lady,' her aunt kept telling her. 'She has the
right to do what she likes. She has lots of money. That's
how it's always been.'

" 'I see,' said the little girl, 'and who is standing up for
us?'

III

"The old woman and Fedya exchanged glances. What was the matter with her?

" 'You're just a silly little thing,' her aunt said.

" 'Who's for us?' the little girl kept asking.

" 'We're for ourselves,' her aunt replied. 'God is for us.'

"After that day Masha never stopped talking about the lady. 'Who has given us to her? Why? When? There is only one lady and there are so many of us,' she said. 'If we went away from her, what could she do?' Her old aunt could not of course satisfy Masha, and the little girl had to find out the answer to her questions herself. Meanwhile, she soon had to put her ideas into practice. The lady remembered Masha and ordered the elder of the village to send her to work in the orchard. Masha refused to go. Her aunt was sorry for her and told the elder that Masha was ill. The little girl snatched at the excuse: every time she had to go to work for her mistress, she pretended to be ill. The mistress summoned her to the big house and asked her where it hurt her. 'It hurts me all over,' Masha replied. The mistress scolded her, threatened to punish her and sent her back to her cottage. Next time the same thing happened.

"However much her cousin tried to persuade her and however much her aunt implored her to do as their mistress demanded, Masha kept refusing to work and behaved as though she had a right to refuse and as though she did what she had to do. She would not agree, for instance, to go and ask their mistress to let her off work. 'All you have to do,' her aunt told her, 'is to bow to her and ask her, and she would let you off.' But our Masha was made of sterner stuff. She would not even raise her eyes to her mistress and one could hardly hear what she said, so husky did her voice sound. And the way of the lord of the manor is of course well known: you've deceived me . . . bow down to the ground, you're wicked . . . be respectful, beg, implore: it's in your power to forgive or to punish . . . forgive me! . . . and everything will be for-

given you; but if you allow your heart to rebel ever so little, if a bitter word escapes from your lips—however
honest and truthful you may be, there will be no mercy
for you . . . you're a ruffian! Our lady had the reputation of a kindly and compassionate woman, but how she
used to plague Masha. 'Wait,' she would threaten, 'I'll
teach you a lesson!' Though she did ɾɔt punish her as yet,
those promises of hers did not make the time pass very
cheerfully.

"Meanwhile, Masha's aversion to doing any work for
her mistress reached such a point of bitterness that it
roused her to *an act of unconscious, insane heroism.* One
day her cousin reproached her for refusing to work by
pleading illness but always being the first in the village
games and dances. 'Don't you think our mistress will find
it out sooner or later? It's bad. You will make our mistress
angry with us all.' After that, Masha was never seen in
the street again. She felt bored, she looked wistfully out of
the window at the games of the village girls, a tear rolling
down her cheek, but refused to leave the cottage. Her
aunt began sending her to visit her friends, her cousin began begging her not to be angry with him for having reproached her. 'I'm not angry, Fedya,' she said, 'only do not
ask me to go out, for I won't go out.' And she didn't go out;
neither did she sleep at night, walking about in the
kitchen gardens all alone without telling anyone about it.
Only one night her aunt caught her going out. 'What's the
matter, Masha?' she said. 'Why don't you try to live as
other people do? Do your work for your mistress and you
won't have to be afraid of anything, and stop doing as
you're doing now: walking about at night and not daring
to go out in the daytime.' 'I can't,' Masha whispered, 'I
can't. Kill me, but I won't do it!' And so they let her be.

"Meanwhile, Masha grew up into a beautiful girl and
it was time for her to get married. Her aunt was beginning
to talk about it and to predict a happy marriage for her.
But this too Masha did not seem to like. 'It will be the same
thing when I am married,' she declared. 'A happy mar-

riage, indeed!' Her aunt told her that not everything in the world was sorrow, that there was happiness in the world too. 'There is,' Masha replied, 'but not for us.' Listening to her, Fedya too was beginning to wonder, but he had no time to indulge in such thoughts, for he had to do his share of work for their mistress. Masha, however, still stubbornly refused to do any work. The villagers began to wonder at her and to murmur against her idleness, and the mistress got so angry one day that she ordered Masha to be brought before her by force. They brought her, and the mistress rushed at her, scolding her and thrusting a sickle into her hands. 'Go and cut the grass in my flower garden! Cut it at once!' she shouted. Masha raised the sickle and, as she brandished it, cut her own arm. Blood spurted out, and the mistress got frightened: 'Take her home at once. Here, take this handkerchief and bandage her arm!' That was the end of the matter. Masha did not even appreciate her mistress's kindness: as soon as she got home, she tore the mistress's handkerchief off her arm and flung it aside.

"Masha's obstinate refusal to do any work for their mistress, her misery, her strange questions had a bad effect on her cousin. He, too, grew sad and lost all his interest in work. Their old aunt thought that it was time to marry the lad off and began talking to him about the girls he might wish to marry. 'If you don't like any of the girls of our village,' she said, 'you'd better go to Dernovka. There are some nice girls there.' 'The Dernovka girls are all free,' said Masha. 'What does it matter if they are free?' The old aunt tried to make them listen to reason. 'Don't free girls marry men who belong to some landowner? They do if they like the lad.' 'If I had been free,' said Masha, trembling all over with agitation, 'I'd sooner put my head on the executioner's block.' Fedya was very upset by such an opinion. 'You're much too hard on us, Masha,' he said, changing countenance. 'We too are God's people, only we're unlucky.' And having said this, he went out. The aunt began, as was her wont, to try to persuade Masha, saying that by tears and sorrow one could not change things but only die before one's time. But Masha replied that she would rather be dead. 'What's there to keep me in this world?' she said.

"So the poor family went on living, suffering from the young girl's questions and demands that were both out of place and unlawful. A bad woman landowner or a stern land agent would of course have soon put an end to such nonsense. But the story shows us a good, gentle woman landowner, a woman of liberal ideas. She decided to give her peasants permission to buy their freedom. You can imagine how this news affected Masha and Fedya. But we cannot restrain ourselves from quoting in full two small chapters, concluding Marko-Vovchok's story.

"Fedya was getting gloomier and gloomier, whilst Masha was pining away slowly. One day her aunt was sitting next to her—she seemed to be thinking hard. Suddenly Fedya came into the room, looking cheerful and in the best of spirits. 'Masha,' he said, 'you are getting ready to die, but don't you think you're a bit too young to die?'

"He was smiling to himself, but Masha made no answer.

" 'Come on, Masha,' he said, 'cheer up, I've brought you some news!'

" 'I don't want your news, Fedya,' Masha replied. 'You can be happy if you want to, but leave me alone.'

" 'What's the news, Fedya?' the aunt asked.

" 'Listen,' said Fedya, embracing and kissing her warmly, and seizing Masha's hand, he raised her from the floor. 'The mistress told us that anyone who wanted to be free could buy his freedom.'

"Masha uttered a joyful cry and sank at her cousin's feet. She kissed him, burst out crying, trembling all over. 'Buy me my freedom, Fedya,' she said in a shaking voice. 'May the Lord bless you, darling. Buy me my freedom! Help us! Help us!'

"Fedya himself could not restrain his tears. Their aunt alone did not seem to share their emotion as she looked at them.

" 'Wait, Masha!' said Fedya. 'Let's talk it over first. We must think it over properly.'

" 'There's nothing to think about, Fedya. Let's buy our freedom quickly, quickly, Fedya.'

" 'There are difficulties, Masha,' said the aunt. 'I expect we shall have to sell everything we have. How shall we live then?'

" 'I shall work, I shall work my fingers to the bone, Fedya! I shall beg people to give me work. I shall work day and night, only buy me out! Please, darling. I'm pining away, I don't even remember the time I was cheerful, I have not had a good night's sleep for years. Have pity on my youth! Buy me out! Go, go to *her!*'

"She made him put on his coat and hurried him out of the cottage, imploring him and crying all the while. Then she kept pacing the room, wringing her hands, but when she saw him coming back, she burst into tears, while he shouted from a distance: 'Thank God!' Masha just collapsed on the bench and wept for a long, long time. They tried to calm her, but she said, 'Let me have a good cry, I feel as happy as though I were being born again. Now you must get me work. There is nothing wrong with me. I am strong. I am much stronger than you think!'

"So they bought their freedom. They sold their cottage, everything they possessed. The aunt was sorry to leave the cottage, and Fedya too did not look too happy to leave the place where he had planted things and watched them grow for so many years. Masha alone looked gay and cheerful. She did not shed a single tear. Why, she looked as though she had been brought back to life. Her eyes were shining, her cheeks were covered by a healthy flush, every vein in her body seemed to tremble with joy. She worked with a will. 'Have a rest, Masha!' 'A rest? I want to work!' she replied, laughing merrily. It was only then that people discovered what a ringing laugh she had. Before,

Five Articles

Masha was considered too lazy to do anything, but now everyone had to admit that she was very clever with her needle, that she was a first-class worker. Crowds of men were eager to make her their wife. Her former mistress was very angry. 'Good heavens,' her neighbors taunted her, 'the stupid serf girl pulled the wool over your eyes, didn't she? You must have let her go for next to nothing!' And, of course, it was quite true that the mistress did not value her very greatly.

"They rented an old, dilapidated cottage in town and began to work. The Lord helped them and soon they built themselves a new cottage. Fedya got married. Then Masha, too, wed. Her mother-in-law doted upon her. 'She is like my own daughter to me. What a happy soul! What a good worker! And she has never been ill since her marriage!' "

It is to this first story that Mr. —bov has written a brief introduction. But you have read it already. Mr. —bov asserts that after the appearance of this story, people who still believed in the inviolability of serfdom were greatly shocked and that the story tells about the "natural and indestructible development of love for independence and horror at slavery" in a young girl. We can't help feeling strange when we hear about people believing in the inviolability of serfdom being shocked, etc. We don't understand what kind of people Mr. —bov has in mind and how many such people he has seen. And though this remark of ours has no direct bearing on the literary question dealt with in our article, we cannot refrain from making it. Anyone who has the slightest idea of Russian reality must admit that in Russia absolutely everyone, the civilized and uncivilized, the educated and uneducated, with perhaps very few exceptions, has known for a very long time all about the degree of the development the author is talking about, quite apart from the comic nature of the suggestion that a short story could shock such a great mass of people and even horrify them. "They are told of a case," Mr. —bov states, "that proves that love for free labor and independent life is natural among the peasants and that the development of this feeling stands in no need of assistance from literature. This is the *simple* case they are told about."

To tell about such cases and to tell it with talent and with proper knowledge is always useful, in spite of the fact that such cases have been known for a long time. Talent is given to a writer for the sole purpose of creating an impression. One can know a fact, one can see it a hundred times oneself and still fail to get the same impression as when someone else, a man with special gifts, stands beside you and points out that fact to you, explains it to you in his own words and makes you look at it through his eyes. A real talent is recognized by this sort of influence he exerts. But if one is to tell now, at this very moment, about love for free labor and tell it in order to prove that such a fact exists, then it is the same as if someone tried to prove that a man has to eat and drink. Now we should like to ask the reader to consider the story itself, this *simple* case, as Mr. —bov expresses it. Have you ever read anything more improbable, more crude, more muddle-headed than this story? What kind of people are they? Are they human beings at all? Where is it taking place: in Sweden, in India, on the Sandwich Islands, in Scotland, on the moon? They speak and act at first as though they were in Russia; the heroine is a peasant girl; there is her aunt, her mistress, her cousin Fedya. But what is it? This heroine, this Masha—why, she is a kind of Christopher Columbus who is not allowed to discover America. The whole ground, the whole reality is snatched away from under your feet. Distaste for serfdom could of course develop in a peasant girl, but would it reveal itself in this form? Why, she is a kind of side-show heroine, a kind of bookish invention and not a woman. All this is so artificial, so thought-out, so pretentious that in some places (especially when Masha rushes up to her cousin and shouts: "Buy me off!") we just could not help bursting out laughing. But is that the impression that this passage in the

story should create? You will say that one must show respect for certain situations and forgive the failure to express an idea properly. We quite agree and we assure you
that we do not laugh at things that are sacred, but you too
must admit that there is no idea and no fact that could not
be vulgarized or shown in a ridiculous light. One can, to
be sure, restrain oneself for a long time, but in the end you
just can't help bursting out laughing. Now, let us suppose
that all defenders of serfdom do not, as Mr. —bov assures
us, believe that a peasant wants to gain his freedom.
Would this kind of story convince any of them that they
are mistaken? "But," they'd cry, "this is quite improbable!" But let us hear what Mr. —bov himself has to say.

" 'A fantasy! An idyll! Dreams of a golden age!' the
practical people of humane views but with a secret sympathy for serfdom shouted on reading this story. 'Who has
ever heard of a consciousness of one's individuality being
developed to such a degree in a simple peasant nature?
If something of the kind had ever happened, it would
have been an exceptional case that had arisen because of
some quite exceptional circumstances. The story of Masha is not a true picture of Russian life; it is simply an
absurd invention. The author has not treated an ordinary type of Russian woman but an exceptional case, and
that is why her story is false and lacks any artistic merit.
It is the duty of a work of art to embody . . .' and so on.

"Here the worthy orators embarked on a discussion of
the qualities of creative art and felt themselves in their
element.

"But people who have no personal interest in serfdom
would never dream of protesting against the normality
of the fact which is told in *Masha*. On the contrary, it
seems normal to everyone who is acquainted with peasant life. And, indeed, is it possible to deny that something
we consider a necessary quality of the human mind in
every man exists in the peasant? That would be a little too
much. . . .

"But argue as you will, such facts will prove to you

that people like Masha and Fedya are far from being exceptions among the mass of the Russian people."

Let the worthy author argue about it and try to prove that a peasant can really feel the need for independence and realize that freedom is better than serfdom (which no one has ever doubted), let him waste his gifts of eloquence on these proofs as though it really is necessary to prove to anyone that a peasant is able to think, and let him, in his enthusiasm, even prove that a character like Masha is normal, since she can observe things, reason, dream, feel and, finally, realize her position. All this is just, Mr. —bov. Without your having to exercise your eloquence to prove it, we believe that all this is just: a peasant girl really can reason and suspect and be conscious of things and feel aversion, etc., etc. But is all this to be revealed as it is presented in the story? Isn't everything presented in such a way that the probable becomes improbable and doesn't one get the impression that it is all taking place on the Sandwich Islands and not in Russia? You say:

"Yes, we agree that *Masha* does not tell of an exceptional case, as the landowners and the artistic critics seem to think. On the contrary, the desire that is characteristic of the whole mass of the Russian people has been embodied in Masha's personality. And if the need for reasserting the independence of one's personality exists, it will become apparent in the life of the common people."

One moment, Mr. —bov. If we decided to make such long extracts from your article, it was not at all because we wanted to talk about Marko-Vovchok and the problems she deals with in her stories. We have observed at the very beginning of our article that nowhere else do you, the leading spirit of utilitarian ideas in literature, express your ideas of art so clearly as in this article of yours. Now we have reached the point for which we have been making these long extracts. It was our intention to show that by despising art and high artistic values and by refusing to put them in the forefront of literary excellence, the

Five Articles

utilitarians are simply spoiling their own chances. Moreover, they are actually harming the cause they serve, and
we shall prove it.

Look, you maintain that art for art's sake makes a
man incapable of understanding the need for a sensible
tendency in literature; you said it yourself to the artistic
critic. Moreover, affecting to talk for the artists, all of
whom (mark you, *all*) you put on the same level as the
serf owners, you shout, as though using their own words,
after reading *Masha:* "A fantasy! An idyll! Dreams of a
golden age! Who has ever heard of a consciousness of
one's individuality being developed to such a degree in a
simple peasant nature?" We reply: In a simple peasant
nature much bigger things have developed and not as an
exception, either, but almost at every step; we know all
this and we believe all this. But we can also see that you
yourself feel the whole absurdity of the way in which the
question is dealt with in Marko-Vovchok's story, otherwise
you would not have indulged in so heated a defense of the
story and in affecting to talk for the artists, whom you
abuse as serf owners. Now, you'd better listen to us—not
to our advice or our verdicts, but simply to our arguments
in this case. We have not taken part in the old controversy
on art, we have so far not been a member of any literary
clique, we are at least impartial, having only just arrived
on the scene. Therefore, be so good as to listen:

To begin with, we should like first of all to assure you
that notwithstanding our love for artistic values and for
pure art, we ourselves hunger and thirst for a good point
of view and hold it in high esteem. And therefore please
try to understand the main thing we are concerned with:
we are not attacking Marko-Vovchok because she writes
with a point of view; on the contrary, we laud her for it
and would be glad to rejoice in her activity. The reason
why we attack the author of these stories dealing with the
life of the common people is that she was unable to do her
work well, because she made a mess of it and, by doing so,
harmed the cause she had set out to benefit. Please under-

stand us—we do not want to be misunderstood or de-
famed. What is it that makes you so happy about these
stories? That they express sensible ideas, that they show
intelligence and a right, truthful view about things? Is
that so? But even supposing that you are right and that
the defenders of the present position of the peasants, as
you say, believe that the peasant does not want to be a
free man, will you, we repeat, convince him by this story?
You say yourself that this story "finds its way into their
refuge," therefore you believe in its *usefulness*. And yet
your opponents will say in reply to you: "You assert that
this case is universal and get into a frenzy in order to
prove it; but the trouble is that it is told in such a way that
we are made clearly aware of its exceptional nature
which runs to an absurdity that is almost unbelievable.
If in order to prove your idea you found no way of expressing it in accordance with the Russian spirit and with Russian characters, then you must admit that it is permissible
to conclude that such a fact does not exist and is quite
impossible in real life in Russia." This is the answer you
will get, which of course means that instead of leaving a
sensible and serious impression, the story will merely pro-
voke laughter and remind us of the fable of the bear and
the hermit. "With your idea you could not even imagine
a Russia," your opponents will add. "When you had to
show how your idea has been realized in life, the Russian
slipped through your fingers. You were forced to put Russian caftans and *sarafans* on some Swiss ballet dancers;
these are shepherds and shepherdesses and not peasants.
The ground sank from under your feet the moment you
took the first step to prove your absurd paradox. And after
that you want us to believe you when you yourselves, the
defenders of your idea, are quite unable to imagine such a
thing among Russians! No, unpractical dreamers, since
you cannot deceive us although you deceive yourselves,
you'd better leave us alone." That is what they will tell you
and they will be right according to their lights. And yet the

Five Articles

idea of the author is right enough. Just imagine if, instead
of the side-show puppet Masha, the author of these stories
had depicted a strikingly true character so that you could
have at once seen in real life what you were arguing so
heatedly about—would you have rejected the story simply because it was artistic? Why, such a story would have
been a thousand times more useful. The truth is that you
despise poetry and true art; all you are concerned about
is your cause, you are practical men. The whole point is
that, so far as the masses are concerned, art is the best,
the most persuasive, the most incontestable and the most
intelligible method of presenting in images the very cause
about which you are so concerned, the most businesslike
way, if you like, you who are so keen on putting everything on a businesslike basis. Therefore art is useful to
the highest degree and useful from *your* point of view.
Why, then, do you despise and persecute it when it should
really be put first before any other demands? "Not before
any other demands," you say, "because the business we
are after is of the first importance"; but of business one
must talk in a businesslike manner, like experts. Even a
businessman is of little use if he cannot express himself.
It is just as if you had under your command a platoon of
soldiers, all of them good and reliable fellows. Suddenly
there is an alarm: everyone jumps to his feet and starts
putting on his pack, his ammunition, and snatching up
his rifle. "Quick, quick!" you command. "Throw away your
haversacks and your cartridges. You don't want them. We
shall only be late with all this unnecessary delay. We don't
want any arms, either—off you go with what you have
had time to pick up!" And you really are in time to get to
the new position and to occupy it, but then your soldiers
are without arms and without ammunition, so of what
use are they? You did your business all right, but it was
not well done, was it? Or, to take another example, you
find yourself before a fortress. You have to attack it, and
as an indispensable condition you demand that all your

123

soldiers should be cripples. A writer without talent is the same as a soldier who is a cripple. Would you really prefer a stutterer to express your idea?

But you smile, you find it amusing to hear that you are being taught what you know so excellently yourself and what you have explained in its proper place a long time ago. In one of your articles you say: "All right, let a literary work be artistic, but it must also be contemporary." And in another article: "If you want to exert any influence on me in a forceful way, if you want to make me love beauty, then be able to catch this general meaning in it, this breath of life, be able to point it out and explain it to me; only then will you achieve your aim." To put it in a nutshell: you do not reject artistic excellence, but you demand that the artist should talk about things that are important, should serve the general cause, should be true to contemporary reality, its needs and its ideals. An excellent wish. But such a wish which becomes a *demand* is, in our view, already a misunderstanding of the fundamental laws of art and its nature—freedom of inspiration. It means simply a refusal to recognize art as an organic whole. Therein lies the whole mistake in this confused question, which has resulted in misconceptions, disagreements and, what is worse, in extremes. You seem to think that by itself art has no standards, no laws of its own, that it can be ordered about just as you please, that inspiration is something everyone has in his pocket and can be fetched out on demand, that it serves this and that and follows the road you want it to follow. While we believe that art has an independent, inseparable, organic life of its own and hence also fundamental and unalterable laws for this life. Art is as much a necessity for man as eating and drinking. The need for beauty and creation embodying it is inseparable from man and without it man would perhaps have refused to live in the world. Man craves it, finds and accepts beauty *without any conditions* just because it is beauty and worships it with veneration without asking what it is useful for or what one can buy

124

with it. And perhaps it is in this that the greatest secret of creative art lies, namely that the image of beauty created by art at once becomes something to be worshiped *without any conditions.* And why does it become an object of worship? Because the need for beauty is felt more strongly when men are at variance with reality, in a state of disharmony, in conflict, that is to say, when they are *most of all alive,* for men are most of all alive when they are searching for something and trying to obtain it; it is then that they are overcome by a most natural desire for everything that is harmonious and for tranquillity, since in beauty there is both harmony and tranquillity. When they find what they are looking for, life itself seems to slow down for a time, and we even know of examples of men who have attained the ideal of their desires and, not knowing what else to strive for, are completely satisfied, lapse into a kind of depression, even do their best to aggravate it, search for another ideal in life and, surfeited, no longer appreciate the things they had taken pleasure in; they even deviate from the straight path deliberately, stimulating in themselves all sorts of unhealthy, sharp, inharmonious and sometimes quite monstrous tastes, losing all sense of tact and esthetic flair for healthy beauty and instead demanding all sorts of exceptions. Beauty is therefore inherent in everything that is healthy, that is to say, everything that is most of all alive and is a necessity of the human organism. It is harmony; it holds the promise of tranquillity; it is the embodiment of man's and mankind's ideals. "But," we shall be told, "what ideals are you talking about? We want reality, life, the modern trends of life. For instance, our entire society is at the moment engaged in solving some contemporary question, it is striving to find an answer to the ideal which it set for itself. For this ideal the poets too should strive. But instead of embodying this ideal and making society understand it, you suddenly burst into song about Diana the Huntress or some Laura." All this is incontestable and just. But before answering this, let us say something that has an indirect bearing on the matter under discussion so as to finish once and for all with it and then pass on to the main answer to your excellent and extremely just remark.

We have already said at the beginning of our article that the normal and natural ways of usefulness are not altogether known, at least that they have not been calculated with any accuracy. How, indeed, is one to determine clearly and incontestably what one has to do in order to approach the ideal of all our desires and of all that mankind desires and strives for? One can make a guess, one can invent, conjecture, study, dream and calculate, but it is impossible to calculate every future step of the whole of mankind as one does a calendar. Therefore how is one to determine *absolutely correctly* what is harmful and useful? And this is true not only of the future; we cannot have precise and positive knowledge of all the ways and deviations, in short, of the whole normal progress of the useful even in our past. We study those ways, we make guesses, we build systems, we draw conclusions, but, all the same, we cannot draw up a calendar even here, and to this day history cannot be regarded as an *exact* science, though we have practically all the facts before us. And therefore how can you possibly determine, measure and weigh the benefit the *Iliad* has conferred on humanity as a whole? Where, when, in what particular cases has it been useful, what influence did it have on certain nations at a certain period of their development and how much of this influence has there been (well, let us say, in pounds, tons, yards, miles, degrees, etc.)? And if we cannot determine even this, then it is quite possible that we can err even now when we tell people sternly and categorically what each of them has to do and point out to art its normal ways of usefulness and its true purpose. But the moment you agree that one can make a mistake, then perhaps Laura too can be of some use. Beauty, it is true, is always useful; but we shall say nothing about it now (though we warn you beforehand that we might say something that is quite unheard of and shamelessly impudent, but do not be embarrassed, for all we say is mere surmise); what we are going to say is what if the *Iliad* is much more useful than the works of Marko-Vovchok, and not only in the past but even today, when we are dealing with contemporary questions, more useful as a means for attaining certain aims, of dealing with these same questions, of solving the urgent problems of today? For even today the *Iliad* sends a thrill through a man's soul. For it is an epic of so great and full a life, so high a moment of national life and, let us observe too, a life of so great a people, that in our time, a time full of aspirations, struggle, vacillations and faith (because our time is a time of faith), in short, because our time is a time of highly active life—that in our time too this eternal harmony which is embodied in the *Iliad* can most decidedly have an active influence on the soul. Our spirit is more receptive now, the influence of beauty, harmony and strength can have a great and beneficial influence on it, a *useful* influence, infuse energy, maintain our strength. The strong loves strength; he who believes is strong, and we believe and, above all, want to believe. What exactly is so odious about the study of the *Iliad* and its imitation in art at our time according to the views of the opponents of pure art? What is so odious about it is that we, just as though we were dead, just as if we had experienced everything or just as if we were cowards who are afraid of our future, and finally, just as if we were indifferent traitors to those of us in whom there still remains the life force and who are striving to go forward—that we fling ourselves into the epoch of the *Iliad* in a kind of despair and in this way create for ourselves an artificial life, a life we have not created or lived through, an empty and seductive dream, and, like the contemptible people that we are, borrow or steal our life from a time that has passed long ago and turn sour in our enjoyment of art as worthless imitators! You must admit that the arguments of the utilitarians are, from the point of view of these and similar criticisms, to the highest degree noble and lofty. That is why we sympathize with them so much; that is why we are so anxious to respect them. The trouble is that these arguments and criticisms are all wrong. Even disregarding the fact that we have been talking of the necessity of beauty and that mankind already has a pretty good idea of what its eternal ideals are (so that all this has already become part of universal history and is bound indissolubly and forever with the present and the future by these universal ideas of mankind), even disregarding this, we shall remark to the utilitarians that it is possible to look upon the past and the ideals of the past not naïvely but historically. In his search for beauty, man has lived and suffered. If we understood his past ideal and what this ideal had cost him, we would first of all be showing great respect for humanity as a whole, we would be ennobling ourselves by our sympathy with him, we would be aware that this sympathy with and understanding of the past was making it certain that we too would possess humanity, vitality and ability for progress and development. Besides, our attitude toward the past could also be a so-called Byronic one. In the pangs of life and creation there are moments not so much of despair as of boundless anguish, a kind of deeply felt emotion for the past, so mightily and majestically brought to an end by the destiny of vanished mankind. In this enthusiam (Byronic enthusiasm, as we call it) for the ideals of beauty created by the past and left to us as an everlasting inheritance, we often pour out all our anguish of the present, and it is not because of our impotence before our own life, but, on the contrary, because of our ardent thirst for life and because of our longing for the ideal, which we try to achieve with so much suffering. We know a poem that can be considered the very embodiment of this enthusiasm, a passionate call, a supplication before the perfection of past beauty and a concealed longing for the same kind of beauty for which the soul is searching, but for which it will have to search for a long time and have to suffer for a long time in the pangs of birth in order to find it. . . . The last two lines of this poem are

128

full of such passionate vitality, such yearning, such significance that we do not know of anything more powerful or vital in all our Russian literature. It is something that belongs to the past but that has come to life in the poet's soul, has come to life with such force after two thousand years that he waits and believes, in supplication and enthusiasm, that the goddess Diana would descend from her pedestal and pass by before him "her milky white body appearing and disappearing between the trees. . . ." But the goddess does not come to life and it is quite unnecessary for her to come to life, for she has already arrived at the highest point of her life: she is in eternity, time has already stopped for her; this is her highest point of life after which life ceases and in its place comes Olympian calm. Only the future is infinite, the future that calls forever, that is forever new, and there too a highest point exists which has to be sought and sought forever, and this eternal search is called life, and how much tormenting sorrow is there in the poet's enthusiasm! What anguish for the present is there in this enthusiasm for the past!

Without doubt, we agree that there may exist a nasty little worm who has utterly lost his feeling for reality, who does not realize that he too has to cope with life, who has moved over into the past and lives there browsing among the ancient poets of Greece and Rome without suspecting that he too has a life of his own with its own problems and torments. But in the first place a worm too must live and, second, are these innumerable crowds of cheap progressives better than he, with their ready-made convictions, with their jeers at something that is infinitely above them, with their miserable little minds, they who get hold of some phrase and keep on flogging it? But what's to be done about it? Both have to live. Real life is extremely various. What is one to do about it?

Now let us turn to our chief and final reply to your just question of why the ideals of art do not always agree with the general and contemporary ideal, or, in other words, why art is not always true to reality.

Our reply to this question is ready.

We have already said that, in our opinion, the question of art is not properly formulated today, that it has gone to extremes and got hopelessly confused as a result of the mutual bitterness of either party to the dispute. No, the question has not been formulated properly and there is really no need to argue about it at all, for:

Art has always been contemporary and real, it has never been different and, above all, it can never be different.

Now we shall try to reply to all the objections.

To begin with, if it sometimes seems to us that art deviates from reality and does not serve useful causes, it is only because we do not know for certain the ways in which art is useful (about which we have already talked), and also because we are much too keen to obtain direct and immediate use, being unable to subdue the ardor of our desires, that is to say, because of our all too ardent sympathy for the general weal. Such desires are, of course, praiseworthy but sometimes unreasonable and like the demand of a child who, having seen the sun for the first time, thinks it should be taken from the sky and given to him.

Second, it sometimes seems to us that art deviates from reality because there really are mad poets and prose writers who sever all relations with reality, who are really dead to anything that has to do with the present, turn themselves into some sorts of ancient Greeks or medieval knights and devote themselves entirely to ancient Greek poetry or medieval legends.

Such a transformation is possible; but a poet artist who acts like that is an absolute madman. There are only a few of these.

Third, our poets and artists really can deviate from the true path either because they do not understand their civic duties or because they lack the flair for social life or because their social interests are divided or because of their immaturity and their lack of understanding of real-

130

ity, or because of some historical reasons, because of the fact that society as a whole is still not sufficiently developed, because many go one way and many another, and that is why Mr. —bov's reproaches, explanations and appeals are from this point of view entirely justified. But Mr. —bov goes much too far. The things he calls toys and album trifles we, from another point of view, acknowledge to be both normal and useful, and hence not all poets who admire ancient Greek poetry are mad (as Mr. —bov thinks), but only those of them who have completely renounced contemporary reality, like many of our grand ladies who spend all their lives in Paris and who have lost the use of the Russian language (which, of course, they are at liberty to do). In our view "toys" are useful because, both in our historic life and in our inner spiritual life, we are bound up with our historic past and with universal humanity. What can be done about it? Nothing, for it is impossible to get along without it; it is a law of nature. Indeed, we think that the more a man can respond to the historic and the universal, the broader is his nature, the richer is his life and the more able is such a man to cope with progress and mental development. You cannot possibly satisfy a man who has a certain need for something by telling him, "Oh, no, I don't want you to do that, I want you to live like this and not like that!" For whatever reasons you may advance, no one is going to listen to you. And do you know what else? We are convinced that in Russian society this call for what is universally human and therefore also the response made by all its creative abilities to all that is of historic and universal importance and, in general, to all these various subjects would be a sign of its most normal condition, at least to this day and perhaps even for all times. Furthermore, it seems to us that this universally human response is even stronger in the Russian people than in all other nations and is its highest and best characteristic. As a result of the Petrine reform, as a result of our sudden intensive experience of a great variety of different kinds of lives, as a result of our instinct for adapting ourselves to human experience in every shape or form, our creative genius too ought to become apparent in so characteristic and so special a form as in no other nation. For what you are rising in rebellion against is really the normal condition of our people. All the literatures of the European peoples were almost our own and they had the same effect on Russian life as on the lives of their own peoples. You, too, Mr. —bov, must remember that you have been educated in the same way. You must agree that a poet such as Zhukovsky is impossible among the French, let alone a poet like Pushkin. Would any of the greatest European poets respond to the idea of the universality of man as readily and as fully as the representative of our poetry, Pushkin, has done? That is partly why we regard Pushkin as our greatest national poet (and, in the future, of the common people too, in the literal sense of the word), because he gives the fullest possible expression to the trends, instincts and needs of the Russian spirit at any given historic moment. For he is to a large extent a contemporary type of Russian, at least so far as his historic and universally human aspirations go. It is absurd to say (because this may be the opinion of some bookish scholar) that all these aspirations of the Russian spirit are useless, foolish and unlawful. And do you really think that, for instance, the marquis of Posa, Faust, etc., etc., were of no use whatever to the development of our Russian society and will be of no use in the future? We did not wander off above the clouds with them, but came to the problems of contemporary life, and who knows? perhaps they had greatly contributed to this. That is why, for instance, all these ancient poems, the *Iliad*, Diana the Huntress, Venus and Jupiter, Madonna and Dante, Shakespeare, Venice, Paris and London—all have perhaps existed lawfully with us and have had to exist, first, according to the laws of universal human life, from which we cannot separate ourselves, and, second, in accordance with our own special Russian life.

Five Articles

"What are you trying to teach us?" the utilitarians will say to us. "We know all this perfectly well without you, we know how much our connection with Europe was useful to us when we were moving toward the universal human life; we know it very well because we ourselves have emerged from it all. But for the time being we no longer want any universal humanity or any historical laws. We have to do our own washing now, our dirty linen is being rinsed out and washed white; now we have washtubs everywhere, the splashing of water, the smell of soap, wet floors. Now we have to write not about the marquis of Posa but about our own affairs, about well-known questions, about freedom of speech, about usefulness, about Krutogorsk, about the realm of darkness. Our answer to this is as follows: first of all, it is very difficult to define what is needed and what is not needed in weight and figures; one can make guesses, calculations, and it is right and proper to carry out tests in practice: will our calculations prove to be right if we do this or that? To wish, to convince and to admonish is lawful and useful to the highest degree. But to write decrees in the *Contemporary*, to demand, to order people to write only about this and not about that is both mistaken and useless, if only because they won't listen to you. (No doubt we have lots of timid people and some of them are terrified of criticism. There is, besides, their *amour-propre:* they hate to lag behind the *avant-garde,* so they write in accordance with the advanced ideas of the time, and since they do not write as the spirit moves them, the result is rubbish; but the despotic reign of our critics will pass; people will again start writing what they want to write about, they will be more themselves and then they will perhaps write something very good even in the form of exposure. God grant it be so!) Besides, one may make a mistake. Perhaps what our *avant-garde* intellects consider to be uncontemporary and useless is contemporary and useful. A patient cannot be the doctor and the patient at one and the same time. One can be aware that one is

133

ill, one can be aware of the fact that one has to take some medicine, but it is certainly unwise to make a prescription for oneself. And if poetry, the word, literature is also a medicine, there is at least some measuring rod to determine what is good in poetry and what is inappropriate for it. The measuring rod is simple: the more sympathy a poet arouses in the masses, the more he justifies his appearance as a poet. Here, too, no doubt great mistakes can be made. There have been examples of it: the masses may not know at a given moment what they want, what they ought to love or sympathize with. But these deviations soon pass away by themselves and society can always find the right way by itself. The important thing is that art is always true to reality to the highest degree—its deviations are transient and pass away quickly; it is not only always true to reality but it cannot possibly be untrue to contemporary reality. This is the mark of true art: it is always contemporary, vital and useful. If it shows an interest in ancient poetry it means that it *needs* ancient poetry; mistakes and deviations, we repeat, may happen but they are not permanent. Art which is not contemporary and which is not in line with modern requirements cannot even exist. If it does exist, it is not art; it degenerates and loses all force and all artistic qualities. In this respect we go even further than Mr. —bov in his idea: he still recognizes that there is such a thing as useless art, pure art that is neither contemporary nor vital, and he declares war on it. But we do not recognize the existence of such an art at all and therefore we keep quite calm—there is nothing to declare war on. And even if deviations exist, there is nothing to get excited about: they will pass away by themselves and quite soon, too.

"But," we shall be asked, "be so good as to explain on what you base your conviction that true art cannot possibly be uncontemporary and untrue to modern requirements?"

We reply:

First of all, according to all historic facts, from the

beginning of the world to the present day, art has always been inseparable from man, has always responded to his needs and ideals, has always helped him in finding these ideals; it was born with man, it developed next to his historic life and died together with his historic life.

Second (and above all), creative ability, the foundation of all art, may be inherent in man as only part of his total nature, but it is inseparable from man. Therefore man's creative ability can have aspirations other than those to which man himself aspires. If it had gone another way, it would have become separated from him, and, consequently, would have been false to the laws of nature (generally speaking). There is therefore no need to be worried about art, for it will never be false to its purpose. It will always live with man his own real life: it can do nothing else. It will therefore always remain true to reality.

No doubt man can deviate from normal reality, from the laws of nature, during his life; art too will deviate with him. But it is this that proves its close and indissoluble connection with man, its constant loyalty to man and to his interests.

But, all the same, art will be true to man only if its freedom of development is not hampered.

It is therefore our first duty not to hamper art by all sorts of aims, not to prescribe laws for it, not to confuse it, for, as it is, it has to deal with many underwater rocks, many temptations and deviations, inseparable from man's historic life. The more freely it develops, the more normal the development of its true and *useful* path will be and the more quickly it will find it. And as its interests and aims are the same as those of man, whom it serves and with whom it is inseparably united, then the freer its development will be and the more benefit it will be to humanity.

Please, understand us: we want art always to correspond to man's aims and not to be against his interests, and if we want the greatest possible freedom for art, it is because we believe that the freer it is in its development the more useful it will be to man's interests. You must not prescribe aims and preferences to art. Why prescribe anything for it; why doubt it when it is a normal development and even without your prescriptions and according to the law of nature cannot possibly do anything that is not in the interests of man? It will never get lost or lose its way. It was always true to reality and always walked in line with man's progress and development. The ideal of beauty and normality cannot perish in a healthy society; and for this reason you ought to let art go its own way and be sure that it will not go astray. If it did go astray, *it would immediately retrace its steps,* respond to man's first need. Beauty is normality, health. Beauty is useful because it is beauty, because a constant need for beauty and its highest ideal resides in mankind. If the ideal of beauty and the need for it is preserved in a people, it means that the need for health and norm also exists, and this, therefore, is itself a guarantee of the highest development of that people. A single man cannot divine fully the eternal and universal ideal, were he Shakespeare himself, and therefore he cannot prescribe either the ways or the aims for art. Divine, wish for, prove, ask people to follow you, by all means—it is all permissible; but to prescribe is not permissible; to be a despot is not permissible; and yet you, Mr. —bov, treated Mr. Nikitin almost despotically. "Write about your needs, describe the needs and the requirements of the common people, to hell with Pushkin, don't you dare admire him, but admire this and that and describe this and that." "But," Mr. Nikitin cries (and we echo him), "Pushkin was my banner, my beacon, my development. I belong to the artisan class; he held out his hand to me from where there was light, where offensive prejudices do not oppress the spirit as they do in my environment at least; he was my spiritual bread." "You don't want him! Nonsense! Write about your needs." "But," Mr. Nikitin objects, "I am not in need of physical bread, what I need is spiritual bread. Please, don't take this bread away from me while wishing it for everybody else. You wish it for everybody else, but when it comes to putting your wish into effect, you take it away from me first. You want me to describe my needs, my way of life. Well, I may do that too. But now please let me live the higher life. You do not think it is higher, you despise it, but to me it is still very tempting!" For our part, we vouch for Mr. Nikitin, we add our plea. Let him live as he likes. Pushkin is everything to him now. Well, we too had to go through Pushkin before we came to deal with contemporary questions. For Mr. Nikitin he is more than kith and kin. Pushkin is the banner, the point of junction for all who thirst for education and mental development; for he is the most artistic of all our poets and therefore the most simple one, the most fascinating one, the most intelligible one. It is because he is intelligible that he is a national poet. Having gone through Pushkin, Mr. Nikitin, if he really has got talent, will, believe me, Mr. —bov, pass on to contemporary questions, as we have done, and will write with a definite aim in view. But to demand that he should do it now, why it is . . . it is—how shall we put it?—a leap in the void. . . .

But enough! We have not the honor of knowing Mr. Nikitin or his social position. All we know is that he belongs to the artisan class, a fact he himself announced on the publication of his works. If Mr. Nikitin is not in the position in which we have placed him, we readily offer him our apologies. In that case we shall put an abstract Mr. N. in his place.

III. Pedantry and Literacy

Read, read, and then — he's gone!
Famusov, *The Misfortune of Being Clever*

First Article

THIS YEAR AND LAST there was a lot of talk in literature and society about the need for reading matter for the common people. Attempts were made to publish such a book, proposals were made, a prize was almost offered, *Home Annals* published in its February issue a proposal for the publication of a "reader"—that is to say, a book specially written for the common people—and addressed to our writers almost reproachfully: "We have published a proposal for a *Reader*, but who will do something for this proposal? Why does not even one writer tell us what he thinks of it?" Well, we now wish to do so. But first let us say something about this interesting social phenomenon, namely about the appearance of similar projects and of the general desire of the upper classes to educate the lower classes. We say "general" because the really high, that is, progressive society has always carried along the majority of all the higher classes of Russian society and therefore if there still are some people who are against the education of the common people, there will not be many of them left soon: they will all be carried along behind the progressive majority and those few who remain will be too feeble to protest.

We speak of it as *certain* because society has at last realized the absolute need for general education of the masses. It has been realized because society itself has at last accepted the idea as necessary, seen in it an element of its own life, a condition of its own further development. We are glad of it. We mentioned it in the announcement of our journal: "Literacy," we wrote, "before everything else, greater literacy and better education—this is the only salvation, the only progressive step which still remains and which must now be taken. Moreover, even if other steps have to be taken, literacy and education still remain the *first* step which *must* and ought to be taken." We made a promise to stand up particularly for literacy because its spread alone can bring about our union with our native soil, with the very source of our national heritage. We have realized the necessity for such a union because we cannot exist without it; we feel that we have wasted all our strength in a life that is separated from the common people, wasted and fouled the air we breathe, that we are gasping for breath and are like fish out of water. We shall say more about it later. First let us draw attention to the fact that is most startling and significant, a fact that also is of profound historic importance in Russian life, which has struck us a long time ago but which is particularly prominent now. We have spoken of this fact before. Now we can see it as a striking proof that we have not been mistaken about its existence.

This fact is the immense depth of the chasm that divides our civilized and "Europeanized" society from the common people. You can see for yourselves that as soon as something has to be done we don't even know how to approach the common people. The idea of general education was followed by the idea of the need for a book of popular reading and we seem to be completely at a loss what to do about it. The problem is how to compose such a book. What should the common people be given to read? It need not perhaps be even mentioned that for some reason all of us silently and without any unnecessary words realized at once that all that has been written by us, the whole of our modern and old literature, is no good as reading matter for the common people. Whether this is true or not is another question; what is clear is that we seem to have all agreed that the common people will understand nothing of it. And having agreed about it, we have all silently admitted the fact of our separation from the common people.

"There is nothing particularly striking about this fact," we shall be told. "The thing is self-evident: one class is educated and the other is not. The uneducated class cannot be expected to understand the educated one the first time. This has happened and is happening everywhere, and there is nothing significant about it."

Let us suppose it is so, we do not want to argue about it now. But *we* have all the same failed till now to think of something to give the common people to read. What do you say about that? One must agree that our failures in this case are quite astonishing and most ridiculous. Have a look at all the projects to publish popular "readers" (the very fact that projects are written about it!). They are written by intelligent and conscientious people, and yet one mistake after another. Some of the mistakes are absolutely comic.

And yet, we repeat, all these "readers," all these projects are written by experienced and talented authors. Some of them have acquired fame as experts on the life of the common people. What have they achieved till now?

We shall go further: we, for our part, are absolutely certain that even our best "experts" of the life of the common people still do not realize how *wide* and deep is the gulf that separates us from the common people and they do not realize it for a simple reason: because they never lived with the common people, but lived another, special kind of life. We shall be told that it is absurd to put forward such a reason, that everyone knows it. Yes, we say, everyone knows it, but they know it theoretically. They know, for instance, that they have been living separate lives, but if they had any idea *how* separate their lives had been they would not have believed it. They do not believe it even now. Those who have really studied the life

140

Five Articles

of the common people and even *lived* with the peasants, that is to say, lived with them not in some landowner's country place but next to them, in their cottages, *looked at* their privations, saw all their peculiarities, were acutely conscious of their desires, got to know their views, even their turn of minds, etc., etc. They ate together with the peasants, the peasants' food; others even *drank* with them. Finally, there are even those who worked with them, that is to say, did the same manual work as they. There may not be many of them, but there are some. These people are convinced that they know the common people. They would even laugh at us if we contradicted them, if we said to them, "You, gentlemen, know only the exterior; you are very intelligent and you have noticed a great deal, but real life, the most important part of them, their very heart and soul, you do not know. A peasant may tell you about himself, laugh with you, he may even cry in your presence (though not with you), but he will never look upon you as one of his own people. He will never seriously consider you to be one of his own family, as one of his *homespun* countrymen. And he will never, never trust you. Even if you were to put on homespun clothes (or fate puts them on you), if you were to work with him and share his toil, he would not believe even that. He would disbelieve it unconsciously, that is to say, he would disbelieve even if he wanted to believe, because this mistrust is part of his flesh and blood.

The reason for it is of course, first, the whole of our previous history and, second, the fact that for many years you have got used to regarding one another as strangers as a result of the difference of your interests. We must now try to earn the trust of the common people; we must get to love them, we must transform ourselves completely so as to become indistinguishable from them. Can we do it? Do we know how to do it? Are we equal to it?

Our reply: we are and we shall be. We are optimists. We believe. Russian society must unite with its national soil and must admit its national element. This is a *sine qua non* of its existence, and once a thing has become an absolute necessity, it will, of course, be done.

Yes, indeed, but how?

This year the government has granted new rights to the peasants. It has summoned them to the exercise of great independence and activity—in short, to development. Moreover, it has half filled up the ravine that separated us from the common people; life and the great many conditions that will quite certainly become part of the future life of the common people will do the rest. At the same time, our higher society, having lived through the epoch of its intimacy with Europe, its epoch of civilization, has itself realized the need for turning back to the native soil. This need has been felt for a long time now, and at the first chance of expressing itself, it did so. Both these historic phenomena took place at one and the same time and they will continue to progress parallel with each other.

Incidentally, lately our journals have been talking a great deal about the specific Russian national character. *Home Annals*, especially, preached it with great enthusiasm. The *Russian Herald*, having entered on its new reactionary road, has gone so far as to express doubt of the existence of any Russian nationality, according to *Home Annals*.

And who was so outraged at the views expressed by the *Russian Herald*, who began seriously to defend and vindicate the idea of Russian nationality—that is, prove its existence? *Home Annals*, the same *Home Annals* that refuses to recognize *anything* national in Pushkin. What a comic situation!

Among other things, *Home Annals* states:

". . . The idea expressed by us a year ago (that is, that there is nothing specifically national in Pushkin) was not the result of that violent journalistic exasperation that makes a journal say wild things in order to make people aware of its existence: thank God we have no need to engage in this kind of business."

Good Lord, we believe you, we fully believe you. You have been attacking Pushkin so *good-naturedly* for almost a whole year and are so indignant at literary men for paying no serious attention to your articles that we cannot possibly look upon you as wild Herostratus or someone of the kind. You do not want such glory. You are "learned" men, you value "truth" most. In our opinion you are simply German *Gelehrte* transplanted to Petersburg, looking quite seriously with a lantern in your hands for the specific Russian nationality, which seems to have hidden from you, and unable to see what is happening under your very noses.

And, to cap this comic situation, what if this specific Russian nationality will itself come and find you while you are arguing with the *Russian Herald* and trying to prove to it that a Russian nationality does exist while it, in its turn, declares that it does not exist? What will then become of all the *Russian Herald*'s English theories and English standards the Russian nationality fails to measure up to? I can imagine the surprise of its defender in *Home Annals*, too. He will certainly be taken aback.

"But surely," he will say, looking it in the face, "you are not the Russian nationality?"

"Yes," someone will reply, "it is the Russian nationality."

"H'm, perhaps and perhaps not. Anyway, I don't know it."

"Quite likely, only it happens to be it."

"H'm. Really?"

"Yes, indeed."

"I'm afraid I can't believe it. First of all, has this phenomenon been stipulated for? Does it agree with the well-known and generally accepted scientific principles? Mr. Buslaev, by the way, says in his book . . ."

And so on and so forth. In short, it is a repetition of the case of the "metaphysician."

Yes, they are metaphysicians. We are told (and we heard it said many times) that it is shameful to reply to

Home Annals. Why? What kind of aristocratism is this? We are told that it is impossible to talk to people who do not understand the simplest things, who do not understand Russian, in the same way as it is impossible to talk to blind men about flowers and to the deaf about music.

Granted that it is difficult to speak to the deaf about music, but then it is not at all our intention to try to persuade a *learned* journal to change its opinion. We are saying all this for the public. We admit that we even wish to publish a special article in reply to Mr. Dudyshkin's views. Of course, it is extremely *difficult* to answer Mr. Dudyshkin, but then one can do nothing without some difficulty.

Imagine, for instance, the character of the chronicler in *Boris Godunov.* You are suddenly told that there is nothing Russian in him, not the slightest emergence of the national spirit, because it is a fictitious, invented character; because at the time of the Moscow Czars we never had such solitary independent monk chroniclers, who were dead so far as the world was concerned and for whom, in their unctuous, meekly wise insight, truth was dearer than anything; the chroniclers, we are told, were practically courtiers who loved to engage in intrigues and were always in favor of a certain party. Even if this is so, you exclaim in surprise, does this mean that Pushkin's chronicler, though fictitious, ceases to be a true ancient Russian character? Does he really lack the elements of Russian life and nationality because he is historically untrue? And what about the poetic truth? Is not Achilles a truly Greek type because he perhaps never existed as a person? Is not the *Iliad* a national ancient Greek poem because all the characters in it are quite obviously re-creations of national legends and perhaps even simply invented?

And yet *Home Annals* flaunts such proofs almost on every page. What is one to say to it after that if it does not understand the main point, the heart of the matter?

Onegin, for example, it does not consider to be a national type. There is nothing national about him. He is merely a portrait of a high-society scapegrace of the 1820's.

Try to argue with it.

"How do you mean, 'not national'?" we say, for instance. "But where else and at what other time has Russian life of that particular period been more fully expressed than in Onegin's type? Why, it is a historic type. Expressed in him with blinding vividness are exactly those features that were characteristic of a Russian only at a certain period of his life, namely at the moment when for the first time he became aware of civilization as life and not as an artificial piece of grafting, and at the same time all the misunderstandings, all the strange and, as they then thought, insoluble problems began to beset Russian society on all sides and emerge into his consciousness. We stood bewildered in those days before our European reader; we felt that we could not get off it, as though it were the only true road accepted by us without any hesitation as such, and for the first time, too, we began to be conscious of the fact that we were Russians and felt how hard it was to sever the connection with our native soil and breathe somebody else's air."

"But why do you find it all in Onegin?" the *scholars* interrupt us. "Is all this really in him?"

"Of course it is. Onegin does indeed belong to that epoch of our historical life when almost for the first time we became aware of our agonizing consciousness and our agonizing perplexity, as a result of our consciousness, as we looked around us. Puskhin, too, belongs to the same epoch, and that is why he was the first to speak as an independent and *conscious* Russian. It was then that we all began to see and despise the strange influences in the Russian life around us which did not seem to conform to our so-called European element and at the same time could not make up our minds whether it was good or bad, ugly or beautiful. This was the first beginning of an epoch during which our progressive forces sharply divided into two camps and then started an internecine war. The Slavophiles and the Westerners, too, are a historic phenomenon and a national one to the highest degree. They did not appear out of books, did they? But at the time of Onegin all this was still only very dimly apprehended. At that time—that is, in Onegin's epoch—with surprise and veneration and, on the other hand, almost with a touch of derision, we first began to understand what it meant to be a Russian, and, as the finishing touch to this strange business, all this happened only when we began to be properly conscious of ourselves as Europeans and realized that we too had to enter into the life of universal mankind. Civilization brought its fruits and we began to understand a little what it meant to be a man and what his significance and dignity amounted to, that is, in accordance with the conceptions that Europe had worked out. We realized that we could be Europeans not only because we were wearing European coats and wigs. We realized it and—did not know what to do about it. Gradually we began to understand that we need not do anything. We had no need of any independent action and, having nothing better to do, we flung ourselves into skeptical self-contemplation and self-examination. This skepticism was no longer the cold, external Kantemir and Fonvizin skepticism. From the very outset Onegin's skepticism had something tragic in it that sometimes took the form of spiteful irony. In Onegin, the Russian begins for the first time to be bitterly conscious or at least feel that there is nothing for him to do in the world. He is a European: what can he contribute to Europe and does Europe want any contributions from him? Onegin as a type had to emerge for the first time in our so-called high society, in the society that had severed its ties from the soil most drastically and in which the outward semblance of civilization had reached its highest development. In Pushkin's poem this appears as an extremely true historic feature. In that society we spoke all European languages, toured all over Europe, felt bored in Russia and at the same time were conscious of the fact that they (the Europeans) were busy while we were not, that they were in their own countries while we were no-where.

Onegin is a member of that civilized society, but he no longer respects it. He is already beset with doubts, he hesitates, but at the same time he stops in perplexity before the new phenomena of life, not knowing whether to worship them or laugh at them. His whole life is an expression of this idea, this struggle.

And yet his soul is at bottom thirsting for a new truth. Who knows, perhaps he is ready to go down on his knees before a new conviction and accept it with veneration, eagerly. This man will not be able to resist; he will never be the same man again, the man who had been thought-lessly unconscious of himself and so naïve; but he will not solve anything, either, he will not define his beliefs; he will only suffer. He is the first martyr of Russian conscious life.

Russian life, the Russian countryside overwhelmed him with its irresistible charm. A Russian girl too passed before him, the only type in our entire poetry before which Pushkin's soul bowed down with such affection as before a native Russian creation. Onegin failed to recognize it and, as was to be expected, at first showed off before her, proving himself to be to some extent a good man, and did not know himself whether he had acted well or badly. But he knew perfectly well that he had acted badly in killing Lensky. . . . His torments began, his long agony. His youth slipped by. He was in good health; he felt the need to do something with his powers. But what should he do? What should he undertake? His conscience whispered to him that he led a futile kind of existence; he felt the stirring of spiteful irony within him, but at the same time he knew that he was not a frivolous individual: for could such a man suffer? A frivolous man would have gambled, made money, run after women, swaggered. Why then did he suffer? Because he was idle? No, that kind of suffering belongs to a different epoch. Onegin suffered still only because he did not know what to do, because he did not even know what to respect, though he was firmly convinced that there was something that one had to respect and love. But he had become embittered and respected neither himself nor his ideas and views; he did not respect even the passion for life and truth which was in him; he felt that though it was strong, he had not sacrificed anything for it, and he asks ironically: what could he sacrifice for it and why should he do so? He became an egoist and yet, at the same time, laughed at himself for not being able to be even a good egoist. Oh, if only he could be a real egoist, he would find peace of mind!

What can I expect! Anguish, anguish! exclaims this child of his epoch amid his unresolved doubts, strange hesitations, unelucidated ideals, lost faith in former idols, childish superstitions and indefatigable faith in something new and unknown but certainly existing, something that cannot be destroyed by any skepticism or irony. Yes, indeed. He is a child of his epoch; it is the whole epoch that *for the first time* consciously had a good look at itself. Needless to say, to what a degree of artistic excellence, to what a degree of fascinating beauty all this has been realized—Russian, ours, original, unlike anything European, national. This type at last entered into the consciousness of our society and went on transforming and developing with each new generation. In Pechorin it reached the point of unquenchable, jaundiced spite of a strange and to the highest degree original and Russian contrariness of two heterogeneous elements: egoism to a point of self-adoration and, at the same time, spiteful disrespect of oneself. . . . And still the same craving for truth and activity and still the same fatal *inactivity!* Out of spite and seemingly for fun, Pechorin flings himself into a strange, wild sort of activity which brings him to a stupid, ridiculous and unnecessary death.

And all this is really true, all this has *really* been happening in our life. The laughing mask of Gogol then made its appearance with its terrible power of laughter, a power that has never found the same expression anywhere or in anyone, in any other literature since the creation of the earth. And after this laughter Gogol dies in the sight of us all, having starved himself to death, in sheer inability to create and precisely define the ideal at which he could not laugh. But time goes on and the last stage of our consciousness has arrived. Rudin and Hamlet of Shchigrovsk District no longer laugh at their activity and their convictions: they believe and this belief saves them. It is only occasionally that they laugh at themselves; they are still unable to respect themselves, but they have practically ceased to be egoists. They have suffered a great deal unselfishly. But even the Rudins no longer belong to our time. . . .

"But, good Lord," the learned journal exclaims, "what has all this got to do with our national character?"

"National character?" we say, gaping with astonishment.

"Yes, national character," says Mr. Kraevsky, trying to come to the assistance of Mr. Dudyshkin. "I mean, fairy-tales, folk songs, legends and so on. . . ."

"No, no, not that exactly," Mr. Dudyshkin hastily interrupts his worthy colleague in the field of literary criticism. "What I would like to know is whether the whole of Russia professes the elements of Pushkin's poetry or only ourselves alone, the educated section of the population? A truly national poet must surely express the political, social, religious and domestic convictions of the common people. What kind of a national poet is it when nothing of his poetry has penetrated into the people, the *real* people?"

"Ah, so that's what you are driving at? So you don't even recognize the higher society, the so-called 'educated,' as belonging to the people! What are they, then, in your opinion? Aren't they Russians? *In that case,* what does it matter that the people have been so sharply divided into two parts by a revolution? The difference is only that one half is educated and the other is not. The educated half has proved—hasn't it?—that it is also Russian, that it is the same kind of people, for it has come to accept the idea of union with the rest of the nation. And since this educated part of the nation is more mentally developed and more conscious of the problems facing the nation as a whole, it is from its ranks that our national poet has emerged. Do you want a national poet who should speak in the vernacular before the process of mental development and consciousness of the common people has been accomplished? When and where has that happened? It is difficult to imagine such a poet. If, for instance, the French have their Béranger, would you regard him as the poet of the whole nation? He is only the poet of the Parisians. The great majority of Frenchmen do not know and do not understand him, because they are not sufficiently mentally developed and are unable to understand him and, besides, profess all sorts of other interests. And if Béranger is still not as far removed from the consciousness of that section of the French nation that does not understand him as Pushkin is from our own common people, it is because France has not known such a historic division of the people as we have had in our country. Besides, you seem to equate nationality with the common people. It is therefore not surprising that no one seems to understand you. Why and for what possible reason should national character be the property only of the common people? Does the national character disappear with the development of the people? Are we, the 'educated,' no longer to be regarded as the Russian people? The contrary seems to us to be true: with the development of the people, all their natural gifts develop and grow in strength, all their riches, and their spirit comes to light much more clearly. Were the Greeks no longer Greeks at the time of Pericles as they had been three hundred years earlier? You think we are contradicting ourselves by trying to prove the necessity for a return to our national roots, that is to say, that we are thereby admitting to ourselves that we are Germans and not Russians? Not a bit; we have proved that we are Russians by the very fact that we admit the necessity for returning to our native soil. All we are conscious of is that we have become divided by purely external circumstances. These external circumstances prevented the rest of the nation from following us and in this way engaging in our activity *all* the forces of the Russian national spirit. We are only conscious of the fact that we are an all too secluded minute section of the people, and if the people will not follow us, we shall never be able to express ourselves fully but will express ourselves too one-sidedly, too feebly and even—we can say it boldly— not as we should have expressed ourselves if the whole Russian people had been with us. But this does not mean that we no longer possess the Russian spirit, that we have degenerated. Why *are* we not the people? Why do you deprive us of that honorable title?"

No, you are wrong. You are right only about one thing: we are not the whole people, but only a section of them; but that Pushkin, being part of that section of the people, was at the same time also a national poet is incontestable. You don't understand it? But, we repeat, tell us where you saw a national poet who was just as you imagined him to be? Has he ever existed? Is a poet as you seem to conceive him at all possible? Think: if such a poet were to appear, what would he be talking about? He would express "all the political, social, religious and domestic convictions of the people," you say. Very well. Béranger did express this, but he did so only for a small section of the French people, for those, in fact, who were interested in the political, social, religious and domestic affairs of the nation. The rest of the Frenchmen perhaps never even heard of Béranger, because they had not as yet taken part in any of the nation's affairs. When they take part in them, they will understand their old Béranger, though by that time they will have a new Béranger (of that I am certain), who will say something new, something that the old Béranger never dreamed of. They cannot ignore him: first, he will be of historic importance for them and, second, because he was a national poet, because he expressed all the same views, beliefs and convictions of the French people. The same is true of Pushkin. One part (and the largest part) of the Russian people took practically no part in the activities of the other part and the division between them went on for a very long time. Pushkin was the national poet of the one part; but that part was, first of all, itself a Russian one and, second, it felt that Pushkin was consciously speaking to it in the Russian language for the first time, with Russian images, with Russian views and ideas—it felt the Russian spirit in Pushkin.

It understood very well that the chronicler and Otrepyev and Pugachov and the patriarch and the monks and Belkin and Onegin and Tatyana—that all of it was Russia and Russian. Society did not see in him merely something contemporary, slightly Frenchified and something estranged from the spirit of the Russian people. Society knew that Bulgarin alone could write like this. It is of course ridiculous to answer such questions as, where is the Russian family that Pushkin wanted to depict, what does his Russian spirit consist of, what particularly Russian did he depict? The reply is clear: all one has to have is just a slight comprehension of poetry. Disregard everything of a colossal nature Pushkin has done; take only his songs of the Western Slavs, read his *Vision of a King;* if you are a Russian, you will feel that that is superlatively Russian, that it is not an attempt to imitate a Russian legend but an artistic form of all national legends, a form that has already passed through the poet's consciousness and, above all, is shown to us for the first time by the poet. For the first time—this is no joke! Yes, almost for the first time the whole beauty, the whole mystery and the whole deep significance of a national legend has been grasped by our society. You claim that Pushkin is not appreciated by the common people. Yes, but that is because the common people have made no progress in their development, and they have made no progress because they could not do so. They are illiterate. But the moment education makes any headway among the common people, Pushkin will acquire his national significance for the masses also. Moreover, he will have a historic significance for them and will be for them one of the most important heralds of *universally human* principles, so humanely and so widely developed in Pushkin. It is this that is the most necessary thing of all, for the chief reason for our division into two sections was that one of them went to Europe while the other stayed at home. With this universally human element, for which the Russian people show such a predisposition, the common people, we are certain, will become acquainted through Pushkin.

We shall go even further: we are ready to admit that a national poet may appear out of the ranks of the common people themselves, not a Koltsov, for instance, who was immeasurably superior to his environment intellectually, but a real people's poet. Such a poet would, in the first place, give a poetic expression to his environment without being in any way above it by accepting surrounding reality for the norm, the ideal. His poetry would in that case be almost indistinguishable from folk songs composed somehow spontaneously at the moment of the singing itself. He could appear in a different guise, that is, without accepting his surroundings as the norm but partly disclaiming it, and depict any moment of the life of the common people, any national movement or any popular desire. Such a poet could be very powerful and could express the people truthfully. But he would not in any case be profound and his horizon would be very narrow. Pushkin would in any case be infinitely greater than he. What does it matter if the common people, at their present stage of development, will not understand Pushkin? They will understand him later and will learn to know themselves from his poetry. And why must a national poet necessarily be of an intellectually lower level of development than the higher classes of the people? According to you, it must needs be so. On his level of intellectual development, Pushkin never could have been understood by the common people. Should he, in order that the common people might understand him, have gone halfway to meet them and, speaking in their language (which he could very easily have done), concealed his intellect from them? The common people are almost always right in the fundamental principle of their feelings, desires and aspirations; but their ways are sometimes incorrect, mistaken, and, most lamentable of all, the form of their ideals is often radically opposed to what they aspire to, contrary only for the moment, of course. In such a case Pushkin would have had to conceal his real self, to believe all sorts of prejudices and feel falsely. What a cunning fellow a poet ought to be in your opinion! What a Dresden shepherd!

But let us suppose that it is not necessary to conceal one's intellect and don a mask. That one could tell the common people the truth candidly and without falsehood or prevarication, boldly and honorably. That the common people would understand everything, would be grateful for the truth, and that all one had to do was to speak the truth in a simple language that the people could understand.

Do not let us argue about it. Anyway, such a poet would not have been more powerful than Pushkin, nor would he have expressed everything Pushkin expressed. To do this, Pushkin would have had to give up his real work and his great vocation, never make any use of part of his powers, deliberately narrow his horizon and consciously renounce half of his great activities.

And what did these activities consist of? Again we repeat: to get an idea, one must first of all understand poetry even a little.

The *Russian Herald*, by the way, refused to do honor to Pushkin because he is unknown in Europe, because Shakespeare, Schiller and Goethe made their way everywhere in European literature and contributed a great deal to the European intellectual development, whereas Pushkin did nothing of the kind. What a childish demand.

Quite apart from the fact that such a statement is incorrect, are Schiller and Goethe really known in France? A few French scholars know them, as well as a few serious poets and writers, and that too mostly from translations, not in the original. The same is true of Shakespeare: in Germany alone, and that too only in educated circles, can he be said to be known; in France he is very little known. It is undoubtedly not their fault, for then they had so far done very little for the universal European development but were useful each in their own countries. (I am told reliably that there are writers in Paris who do not know anything about Barbier. Not only have they not read him, they don't even know his name. How should they know Schiller after that?) The *Russian Herald*, it seems, has fallen into an error: it probably judged the universal influence of the above-mentioned great poets from their influence on Russian society. Yes, Schiller undoubtedly got into the blood of Russian society, especially in the last generation and in the generation before the last. We were brought up on him; he is one of us and has left a great mark on our mental development. Even Goethe is known more in our country than in France and perhaps even in England. We also have an incomparably greater knowledge of English literature than the French and perhaps even the Germans. But the *Russian Herald* treats these facts with contempt; it does not regard them as facts because they're not in accord with its views. The fact of the extraordinary aspiration of the Russian tribe for universal human values is pointed out to this journal as well as one of the propagators of this aspiration—Pushkin; it is told that this is an unprecedented and an unparalleled fact among nations; that it can be taken to prove an extremely original trait of the Russian character, and that it is perhaps the chief essence of the Russian nationality. But the *Russian Herald*, far from listening, goes on saying that there is no such thing as a Russian national character. . . .

But, above all, why should Pushkin be blamed because

Europe is still ignorant of him? Surely the important thing is that Europe is still ignorant of Russia, too: it has known it till now from dire necessity. It will be different when the Russian element enters the stream of universal human development: then Europe will come to know Pushkin, too, and will most certainly find in him more than the *Russian Herald* was able to find till now. It will be ashamed before foreigners then!

Russia is still young and is only now beginning to live; but that is not a fault.

In trying to defend the Russian national character against the *Russian Herald, Home Annals* claims as proof of its real existence the fact of the extraordinary development of State organization in Russia.

In our view this alone does not prove the reality and peculiarity of the Russian national character. Its peculiarity consists of the unconscious and extreme steadfastness with which the Russian people cling to their idea, their strong and keen resistance to everything that contradicts it and their everlasting, beneficial and untroubled faith in truth and justice.

Great was the moment in Russian history when the great and entirely Russian will of Peter decided to break the chains that were strangling our development. In Peter's work (we no longer argue about it) there was a great deal of truth. Whether consciously or unconsciously, he divined the universal purpose of the Russian tribe. And yet the form of his activity was, because of its extreme harshness, perhaps mistaken. The form into which he had transformed Russia was undoubtedly mistaken. The fact of the transformation was correct, but its forms were not Russian, not national, and quite often were in direct and fundamental contradiction of the Russian national spirit.

The common people could not see the final purpose of the reform, and it is doubtful that anyone who followed Peter, even any of the so-called "fledglings of Peter's nest,"

156

understood it. They followed the reformer blindly and lent their help to his authority for personal gain. If not all of them, then almost all. And how were the common people at that time to guess where they were being led? Even today only one dirty stream of civilization has reached them. No doubt it is impossible that nothing should have had a fruitful and vivifying effect on the common people, even if only unconsciously. But anything in the reform that was un-Russian, false and mistaken, the people divined at once, the moment they caught sight of it, and—we repeat—as they could not see its good, healthy side, they recoiled from it at once. And how steadfastly and calmly they could protect themselves, how they could die for what they considered to be truth and justice!

But the Petrine idea has been accomplished and has reached its final development in our time. It came to an end with our acceptance of the principle of universal humanity and our realization that we are perhaps destined by fate to bring about a world union of nations. If not all of us have realized it, then many have. But at least all of us are conscious of the fact that civilization has brought us back to our native soil. It did not make us exclusively into Europeans, it has not cast us into a ready-made European form, it has not deprived us of our national character. The *Russian Herald* is completely wrong when it states that "where they argue about the Russian national character, it does not exist" and *Home Annals* is completely right when, in reply, it states:

"The history of literature in Germany and France at the beginning of the nineteenth century gives the right answer to this, for the same kind of controversy is characteristic of a whole period of literature in those countries, only they were known not as arguments about national character but about romanticism. The same arguments were introduced into our country, but much ahead of the time, and we were not ready to accept them or to understand them in all their profundity. The result of this controversy in Western Europe is known: the abrupt swing of European literatures to independence and nationalism. . . ."

Civilization has not helped to develop the social classes in our country, either. On the contrary, it seems to be aiming at smoothing them out and uniting them into one class. The *Russian Herald* may resent it, but we have no English lords; we have no French bourgeoisie, either, and we shall have no proletarians—we are quite sure of that. There can be no question of any class struggle in our country; on the contrary, the classes in our country tend to merge; for the time being everything is still in a state of flux, nothing has become clearly defined as yet, but we can already tell what the future will be like. The ideal of this merging of the classes into one will become clearer when education becomes general among the people as a whole.

Education is already considered a matter of the first importance in our society. Everything makes place for it; all the class privileges disappear in it. Our whole future, our whole independence, our strength, all depend on the quickest possible development of education; it is the only conscious step forward and, what is most important, it is a peaceful step, a step of agreement, a step toward true strength.

The true higher class in our country at present is the educated class. But without true, serious and correct education, there appears at once a phenomenon in society which is harmful and pernicious to the highest degree— *knowledge without knowledge*. Since the desire for knowledge can never be destroyed in society, and least of all in our present society, then in view of the feeble development of true and correct teaching, those who desire to study are driven to study without teachers, without a system, without rules, often choosing the wrong kind of teachers or, what is worse, teachers who have only a one-sided acquaintance with science. In this way, false ideas become established in society, particularly in a young and new society, take root in it and afterward—indeed, sometimes rather quickly—bring about harmful and unpleasant results. Quite the opposite is true with a correct and wide development of education. True science has its own methods, traditions, systems. A true custodian of such a science does not allow a young mind to go astray. He preserves the student from errors because he acts upon him with all the force of science, with all its traditions, with everything man's intellect has accomplished steadfastly and correctly.

It is only with education that we can fill up the deep ravine that separates us now from the native soil. Literacy and its intensified diffusion is the first step to every kind of education.

Some time ago *Home Annals* made cruel fun of us in stating that by claiming that educated society should unite with the common people, we were merely bringing the common people the same kind of European civilization which we reject.

We reply:

We are going back to our soil with the consciously acquired and accepted idea of our all-human destiny. Civilization itself brought us to this idea, but we reject civilization in the sense of an exclusively European creation. Our return shows that civilization could not make a Russian into a German and that a Russian remains a Russian in spite of it. But we have also become conscious of the fact that it is impossible for us to go any further by ourselves alone; we require all the forces of the Russian spirit to help our further development. We bring to our soil our education, reveal openly and frankly what we have attained with it and what it has made us into. Then we shall wait and see what the whole of our nation says after having received learning from us, we shall wait so as to be able to take part in our further national development, a genuinely Russian one, and enter upon the new path with renewed strength gathered from our native soil.

Knowledge does not regenerate a man, it merely

changes him; but it changes him not into one general, conventional form but in accordance with the man's nature. It does not make a Russian into a non-Russian; it did not alter even us, but merely made us go back to our own people. The whole of our nation will, of course, say its new word in life and science much more quickly than a small group of people which composed our society till now. We merely reject the exclusively European form of civilization and maintain that it is not for us.

But let us pass on to the booklets for the common people and particularly to the *Reader*.

IV. PEDANTRY AND LITERACY

Second Article

I SUPPOSE one could compose a whole list of book titles for popular reading. Although we promised in the last article to discuss all these books separately, as the game is hardly worth the candle, we would like to start on an analysis of the *Reader* as the only really serious project for a book for the common people. The reader will be able to see from this analysis our idea about such books; he is therefore deprived only of a long list of worthless booklets for "popular reading." One can find them easily in some bookseller's advertisement, while in the shops they are usually given a separate place, not excepting Mr. Grigorovich's unsatisfactory books and Mr. Pogodin's "Red Egg."

We have still another writer of books for popular reading, Mr. Pogossky, who, it is true, writes mostly for soldiers. But we intend to talk about him later. Mr. Pogossky is quite an exceptional phenomenon in our "popular literature." About the other "popular" books, one can say that there are dozens of them but that one can hardly say a good word for any of them. They merely prove one thing, namely the extraordinary need for books for the common people; but this is also proved by the *Reader* and therefore let us pass on to the *Reader* at once.

The *Reader* is not a book but a project of a book for the common people drawn up by Mr. Shcherbin and offered for the public's consideration by *Home Annals* last February of the present 1861 year. The article is entitled: "An Essay about a Book for the Common People."

The author's views, the integrity of his project, even the tone of his article struck us as very remarkable, first because I know of nothing more intelligent than his project that has been published in our country. *Home Annals* states that a discussion of Mr. Shcherbin's essay would be of great advantage to the writers of books for the common people, and I wholeheartedly agree.

Mr. Shcherbin begins his article by expressing his disappointment with a brochure for popular reading which appeared last year with the title *Primer* at the price of five kopecks in silver. After expressing his satisfaction that the book did not cost more than five kopecks, Mr. Shcherbin remarks that it is "unthinkable" to him that it should have published Pushkin's fairytale *About Kuzma Ostolop* and Krylov's fable *Demyan's Fish Soup*.

However, as we intend to analyze Mr. Shcherbin's plan in its entirety and in detail (as much as we can, of course), let us quote from the beginning of his article this highly indignant tirade against the short-sighted and simple-minded publishers of the *Primer*.

"It is simply unthinkable to us why it should start with Pushkin's fairytale *About Kuzma Ostolop* and Krylov's fable *Demyan's Fish Soup*. We need hardly mention that the title of the book, *Primer,* will be incomprehensible to the common people, but then it might be due to reasons beyond the control of the publishers, but why include Pushkin's fairytale? It has meaning and significance in our circle, but it will strike the common people as *silly* and may to a certain extent compromise the whole idea of learning to read and write. If this booklet were to fall into the hands of a Sunday-school pupil, his master, a sedate saddler, coppersmith or locksmith, would quite likely say with a sigh, 'What do they teach them in them schools! Just wasting their time, they are!'

"A peasant may hear a similar fairytale in the street or in a bar and a peasant boy in his workshop or from some

162

caretaker. A book put together in so haphazard a manner will not inspire respect for literacy and will not impart any serious or useful meaning to it. How, for instance, will *Demyan's Fish Soup* help to spread knowledge among the common people? It can be understood only in literary and artistic circles the existence of which the common people do not even suspect. And what is there in it that the common people might find interesting and instructive? What a great evil is Demyan's good-natured importunity. Is this what the people want? Is this not their scandalously negative side which must be extirpated by satire and mockery expressed in an image? One might think that the *Primer* was published not in Petersburg but somewhere in Arcadia, it is so full of childish ignorance of life, naïve conceptions and bucolic simple-mindedness . . . that you just expect to see on its title page the words 'published by Menalca and Tircis.' It is clear that it is logically impossible to deal with it at length; but its publication nonetheless makes one think of a book for the common people which today more than at any other time seems to be extremely important.

"Experience has shown that books written exclusively for the common people were unsuccessful and found no buyers among them. It is possible that no practical steps were taken for their distribution, but the chief reason is that Russia is still a *terra incognita* to us. It was a kind of *a priori* attitude on our part so far as books for the people were concerned. Direct observation, life with the common people, a true comprehension of their needs—all this was far from us. 'We love,' according to the poet,

> 'In a chamber sumptuously furnished
> Of our poor brothers to argue,
> Talk fervently of goodness . . .'

after which the poet was fully justified to exclaim:

> 'Oh, in the words of an old poet:
> Words, words, words! . . .' "

Noble and strong words; noble indignation, too. Some of these arguments are perhaps quite to the point; the remark that the fairytale *About Kuzma Ostolop* was written for gentlemen and would be received by the common people with scorn is very true, so that even if you had had nothing to do with the noble but short-sighted compilers of the *Primer* you cannot help feeling sorry for them. But we cannot altogether agree with the arguments about *Demyan's Fish Soup*. Actually, what we are concerned about is not Krylov's fable but some of Mr. Shcherbin's views, some of his, so to speak, fundamental ideas. "What a great evil," he declares, "is Demyan's good-natured importunity." "Is this what the people want? Is this not their scandalously negative side which must be extirpated by satire and mockery expressed in an image?"

That is the trouble. *Demyan's Fish Soup* has a particular meaning in Krylov and without this meaning, which is of no interest to the common people, it is not only not interesting, but could be replaced with equally good effect by thousands of other fables. We quite agree, but what is important is not the fable itself but Mr. Shcherbin's conviction that the aim of such a book and, as far as possible, of every item of such a book should be to extirpate "the negative side" of the common people and to persecute them "with satire and mockery expressed in an image." *Demyan's Fish Soup*, on the other hand, does not *persecute* anything, and therefore the *Primer* that found a place for it in its pages is so innocent, is "so full of childish ignorance of life, naïve conceptions and bucolic simple-mindedness . . . that you just expect to see on its title page the words 'published by Menalca and Tircis.'"

We do not at all intend to defend here either *Demyan's Fish Soup* or Menalcas and Tircises, though the latter had been useful and even dear to us once upon a time. What we regard as important is the demand of "satire" and "the extirpation by mockery" of the prejudices current among the common people. We must, so to speak, chastise . . . We must teach, *above all* teach. . . .

Let us repeat once more: the aim is both lofty and ex-cellent and corresponds entirely to the nobility of our spirit. The educated must teach the uneducated. It is their duty, isn't it? But what is rather strange and even bad is that they do not seem able to approach the common people without laughing at them, "without satire" and, above all, without wishing to *teach* them. Can we not even imagine how we are to appear before this aboriginal population without ceremony and not as people who wield authority over them? No doubt we are most anxious to confer benefits by our satires and mockeries (although sometimes we ourselves do not know what it is we find so funny about the common people, but that's between us). We merely wanted to observe humbly that before thinking of any *immediate* benefits conferred by the popular books, before indulging in satiric mockeries, moral admonitions and eradications, it would not be a bad idea to concentrate simply on the spread of reading among the common peo-ple, on trying to arouse in them a desire for reading enter-taining books even without any satirical contents pro-vided they are just a little absorbing and positively *harmless* (I hope it will be understood what we mean by the word *harmless*).

"Ridiculous fault-finding!" the enlighteners will tell us. "Who said we were against entertaining reading and in-deed against the growth of fondness for reading? That's exactly what we do want! Only instead of *Demyan's Fish Soup* one ought to put some extremely entertaining, ex-tremely amusing and, at the same time, extremely useful and extremely derisive thing that would put an end to the 'negative side' of the common people. In this way all the aims would be achieved. How, then, can usefulness be said to be bad? Or are you against usefulness altogether, against the eradication of prejudices and the dispersal of the darkness of ignorance?"

"Not at all," we reply, "God forbid! Who likes igno-rance and prejudices, and not merely ignorance but 'the darkness of ignorance'? Except for one thing: *exclusive* emphasis upon ignorance and prejudices and exclusive anxiety to eradicate them as soon as possible is (in a certain sense, of course) also ignorance and prejudice in our view. We don't know how to express it more clearly. For instance, we know that the common people are prejudiced against us, the masters, so much so that they would listen even to something good from us with mistrust. Well, we, on the other hand, approach them in spite of it as people who exercise power over them, the same as their former masters, in fact, and we cannot, in short, bring ourselves to act otherwise, that is to say, to act more mildly, act in a way that shows that we have tried to find out how to settle this matter in the best possible way. 'The common people are *stupid*, therefore they must be taught'—that is the only thing we seem to have got into our heads, and if we can no longer appear before them as their masters, then at least let us appear as wise men. . . . However, let us interrupt our arguments for a moment. We cannot forego the pleasure of quoting Mr. Shcherbin's opinion of some of our progressives and wiseacres and, generally, the so-called 'experts' of the life of our common people who are getting ready to become their leaders. What golden words!

"Some book seems to have been composed rather cleverly, but it found no favor among the common people because it somehow involuntarily resembled a German or Frenchman disguised as a Russian peasant, while the translations of *Paradise Lost* had a greater effect on the feelings of the common people than the books written by their fellow countrymen for them in their language and whose subject matter was taken out of their history and their life. It is worth while paying attention to this. We were incapable of putting ourselves in their place, to comprehend with our hearts and minds their ideas, tastes and inclinations instinctively, straightforwardly and at the same time practically. Our knowledge, our talents, our European education were of no use to us in this matter and that is because we know Russia least of all, because *our national characteristics remain practically outside the curriculum of our education;* that is why we lack practical ability and independence of thought. Every time we consider ourselves, the data and facts of our own life, we look at them through some kind of colored spectacles we had bought at the Palais-Royal, or the Leipzig Fair or our own flea market.

"Besides, without being aware of it, we ourselves are mostly slaves of our daily routine and, indeed, every brief period of time has its own routine. Let anyone try to treat some fashionable little idea that happens to be the rage of the moment without prejudice and without cringing analysis, and he will be bespattered with mud. On the other hand, if he does let himself go, then even the giants are of no account to him; on the one hand we represent the personification of servility, being in a kind of state of serfdom to any stupid little idea and those who uphold them, and, on the other, the personification of intolerance and despotism: we regard everybody who is of a different opinion from ourselves either as mentally deficient or as unscrupulous. There is no denying that we have a great many noble ideas, quickened by European learning, but what we lack is the knowledge of many conditions, of the minutest data, the spirit and the environment of our national and local life. We are ideologists in practical life and this is partly so because it does not require a great deal of work. We do not grasp knowledge as a whole, organically, we do not start our studies *ab ovo;* we are quite satisfied with the last results of an idea, of the high points of knowledge. The majority of us are no more than 'dogmatists.' In our country it is very easy for anyone to become a clever and progressive person and find oneself among literary or some other public men. We know of only two extremes: either your own home-made 'infallible' judgment or unconditional, servilely dogmatic acceptance of some theory from outside. We still consider to be educated, honorable, up to date and, above all, intelligent a man who has acquired some kind of knowledge in its *abso-*

lute sense and who, possessing the most mediocre mind, formulates it when the occasion arises, using all sorts of fashionable phrases and European platitudes. Besides, these virtues are even personally profitable in our time. We are still far from the conviction that true *intelligence* is possessed by the man who at any given time finds the right word to say and who can understand the *relative aspect and meaning of things*—this whirlpool of ceaselessly revolving, changing and arising facts, who can grasp their invisible connection with the ideal and their connection with each other. It is here that independence is required, independence of thought and solid strength of knowledge. This you cannot obtain by reading. What is to be done about it? This is the general fault of our education, which perhaps doesn't even depend on us."

Truly golden words, golden and noble! Every word is true. The italics in the above quotation are Mr. Shcherbin's. We were inclined to italicize the more telling and true of his remarks, but we did not do so, because every sentence would have had to be italicized. The whole thing is so much to the point and so true that we have seldom read anything more intelligent. It is a pity it is expressed so abstractly, though. We cannot express even such truths in their closer application to reality and, besides, it is *not the done thing* with us. Everything with us turns on a theory, on knowledge in its *absolute* sense, on *the absolute aspect of things*, to use Mr. Shcherbin's own words. Continuing his tirade, Mr. Shcherbin is a little too much carried away by anger. His anger is of course honorable, but not altogether fair, because it is a little too strong. This is what Mr. Shcherbin says:

"Such apparently insignificant facts involuntarily suggest the idea of the need for a radical reorganization of our educational system. Their bankruptcy, emptiness and futility are obvious: they contain no roots of their nationality, self-knowledge or solid and rigorous knowledge. We are still so simple-minded that we mistake the hollowness of modern fashionable phrases for a sign of good education: we are so well-meaning that the word *progress* never leaves our tongue, while actually that word has no meaning whatever in our country. To act, one has to love; to love, one has to know what to love. We do not know. And so all our noble aspirations have become fashionable with us for no rhyme or reason, accepted as dogma because of the general authority with which they are invested, and even the love of our cause is something we have 'put on'. . . ."

Mr. Shcherbin is a little too severe here. It is impossible that we should have "put on" our feeling of love for our cause. We do not believe in the severity of such a verdict. The present movement of ideas will in time have its strict and dispassionate history. The whole thing will perhaps then find its more profound and more gratifying explanation. If we look at the thing not so abstractly but a little more practically, basing ourselves on certain facts, then we shall certainly find among the facts that are contrary to our views some that are in favor of them. Why see only the worst? One can take a dispassionate view of the thing without being a confirmed optimist, a *ridiculous* optimist, for with us, when expressing any opinion, one is terribly afraid of being ridiculous. That is why we have so many people who hold *general* opinions, opinions that are shared by the majority of people. To be like anyone else is the best way of completely escaping ridicule. We do not at all mean to say by this that Mr. Shcherbin, too, is inclined to hold *general opinions,* to be like everybody else. Mr. Shcherbin's views are, as a matter of fact, shared by the *majority* of our people who are most honorable and most progressive, and our progressives cannot for obvious reasons differ very greatly from the views expressed by Lermontov in his *Reflection,* though this poem anticipated us by a quarter of a century. No doubt among our progressives the idea that any progress would take place in our country in twenty-five years is scornfully rejected; but it is hardly possible that there should be no progress at all. We are sure Mr. Shcherbin will not ask us for any nominal fact to prove our views. Let us give him one example, namely the following: wherever Mr. Shcherbin in the tirade we have quoted says: "we don't know . . . we have no idea . . . we do not love . . . we 'put on' our feeling of love . . ." he probably uses the pronoun "we" as a term of courtesy. For surely he does not include himself among those who do not love, who are immature, who cannot love, who pretend to love, etc., etc. Otherwise he would not get so angry, so reproachful, so contemptuous, or give such advice. And if that is so, then there is at least one person who knows how to love, how to appreciate, how to act.

"But," we shall be told, "you don't seem to be very candid: you seem to talk ironically, you seem to be critical. . . . A moment ago you appear to have said that it was not necessary *to teach*, that an exclusive emphasis on ignorance and prejudices and an exclusive anxiety to eradicate them *as soon as possible* from the common people was also a certain kind of ignorance and prejudice. What nonsense you do talk!"

"We merely ventured to observe," we reply, "but now we are even sorry to have made that remark. It is a terribly ticklish business so far as we are concerned. 'Let anyone try to treat some fashionable little idea that happens to be the rage of the moment without prejudice and without cringing analysis, and he will be bespattered with mud.' Those are Mr. Shcherbin's very words and we seem to be in that position now." "What do you mean!" we can hear people shout. "Not to teach the common people, that is, to *spread* prejudices, ignorance and illiteracy among them! Obscurantists! Criminals!"

It is sometimes terribly difficult to make one's meaning clear.

God forbid! We never meant to say that it was *not necessary to teach*. Why, we ourselves shout about nothing else, we never proclaim anything else: literacy! literacy! On the contrary, one must teach. But, in our view, one would have to possess a tremendous amount of self-confidence to imagine that the common people would just gape in astonishment as they listened to us preparing ourselves to teach them. For, after all, the common people are not exactly a herd of cattle. Indeed, we are convinced that they realize, and if they do not realize, that at least they feel that in trying to be their teachers, we, their masters, do not know something ourselves, so that we have first of all to learn something from them, and that this is why they really have no respect for our learning, at least why they dislike it.

Everyone who at any time had any business with the common people can verify this impression on himself. For to make the common people really listen open-mouthed to us, we must first of all deserve such attention from them, that is, win their trust and respect; but our thoughtless conviction that we have only to open our mouths to carry everything before us will never win their trust and least of all their respect. For they understand it all. A man realizes nothing so quickly as the tone in which you address him and the feeling you have for him. Our naïve idea of our great superiority in wisdom and learning will merely seem ridiculous to them and in many cases even insulting. You, Mr. Shcherbin, are apparently convinced that the common people will not be aware of it, that is, of our extraordinary superiority with which we apply ourselves to the composition of a book for them according to your program. You, Mr. Shcherbin, love the common people—we are certain of that—and you work for them because you love them. But, you see, to love is not enough; one must know how to show one's love. You want to show your love by teaching the common people, by praising them for their good deeds and laughing at them for their evil deeds, especially by cracking down on their *negative side* with the help of mockery, etc., etc. Oh, but then they have had and still have lots of teachers already and they have had and still have lots of people who have been and are laughing at them. You can't prove your love for them by this sort of thing, at least you may find it a little inconvenient, and, besides, they will get tired of so many teachers. And what if the common people should find out suddenly (or if not find out then feel) that they could teach us a great many things too, while we don't seem to realize it and even laugh at such an idea and come to them with our orders in a haughty manner. And the common people could teach us a lot, if only, for example, how we are to teach them. For there are sometimes quite amazing teachers among us. One of them, for instance, severed himself from the soil long ago. His great-grandfather had been one of the administrators and had no common interests with the people, deeming it beneath his dignity to have any; his grandson's education had been generally of a high level, scientific and theoretical, dealing with ideal truths—in short, the man himself turned out to be most honorable but extraordinarily like an effaced fifteen-kopeck coin: one can see that it is silver, but there is neither stamp nor date to be seen and it is impossible to say whether it is French, Dutch or Russian. Some of these fellows will suddenly take up a position in the middle of the road, dressed like a fop, and start eradicating prejudices. All these gentlemen are somehow extremely fond of eradicating prejudices, such as hypocrisy, bad treatment of women, idol worship, etc., etc. Many of them have written whole treatises about it; others have studied these questions at the universities, sometimes abroad, with learned professors, using most excellent books. And all of a sudden one of these "social workers" comes face to face with reality and becomes aware of some prejudice. He gets so fired with enthusiasm that he flings himself upon it with loud laughter and hisses, pursues it with mockeries and, in his honorable indignation, spits on this prejudice in full view of the people, forgetting and failing to realize that the particular prejudice is for the time being still dear to them; moreover, the common people would have been truly base and unworthy of the slightest respect if he had given up anything they revered and held dear all too easily, all too *scientifically*, all too *suddenly.* "Don't you laugh and spit, sir," the peasants will tell him. "Don't forget that we have received it from our fathers and our forefathers and that we love and honor it." "Ah," shouts the enlightener, "that's why it is so important that this prejudice should be eradicated as quickly as possible, for it has struck such deep roots in you; that is why I spit on your prejudice, first, because it revolts my noble sentiments, and, second, to prove to you, fools that you are, how little I value it. You'd better look and learn from me!" What is one to do with a man like that? For such a man is not only incapable of looking at things *historically*, in connection with the soil and life, he is even incapable of looking at them in a humane way, for he is humane only theoretically, in a bookish way. As for being more respectful to the common people, it would be a mere waste of words to tell him that. He does not care that the prejudice in question means nothing only to himself, that to others it is a testimony and a sign of their past life and that now, perhaps, it is the *whole* of that life and its banner. But, then, why talk about it? We are convinced that Mr. Shcherbin knows it much better and much more thoroughly than we. How could a man of his intelligence fail to know it? But knowledge alone is not enough; it would certainly be advisable to be more careful. For an all too exclusive and hasty desire to "teach," to "ridicule" and to "attack the negative side" is also a kind of carelessness. Would it not be better to approach the common people on more equal terms? When they realize that you are not *exclusively bent on teaching them*, they might believe you more quickly. To teach is an excellent thing, but not every teacher is popular. And if it comes to that, if it is only a matter of *teaching* and nothing more, then would it not be much better to have said at once quite openly, "Look here, you common people, you are all fools and I am a learned man. I have come to teach you: you'd better listen and do as I tell you!" This would certainly be better. For you are really trying to trick them by concealing that you want *exclu-*

sively to teach them and *nothing more*. You are a little too crafty and you regard the common people as a little too stupid, which, you must admit, is rather offensive. However, you will probably find our words unintelligible and even captious. We ourselves realize that one should not argue something *a priori*. Let us rather proceed to analyze your project. To do this, we have to quote rather large extracts from your article.

"The *Primer* we have mentioned seems to challenge everyone who ever thought about a book for popular reading to explain his own plan for publishing such a book. Such a book, of course, is meant only for a certain period of time and therefore its plan must be regarded as only relative, but, to begin with, let us entitle it:

A Reader

"It is assumed that this book will be widely read by the common people. . . . In compiling the *Reader,* the editor has in view:

1) "Basing himself on *psychological reasons,* he arranges the sections and articles in the book in such a way that one section, developing certain conceptions and exciting the reader's curiosity, should prepare him imperceptibly for the next section, and after having read the second section, the reader will be prepared for the third, and so on. . . .

"Beginning with everyday occurrences in the lives of the common people, expressed in a number of fables, parables, proverbs, etc. (which are closest to their personal life), and passing on to the objects of visible nature that surround them (earth, air, sky), and several other articles of a similar kind, they gradually come to the end of the book, which is devoted to spiritual and moral subjects, let us say, from Krylov's fable *A Peasant in Trouble* to Khomyakov's poem *On Reading a Psalm;*

2) "Basing himself on *practical considerations* and taking into account the radical faults that exist among the common people, faults of a general nature or peculiar

only to our people, the editor chooses the contents of the articles in his book. In addition, he must observe which subjects are of the greatest importance, considering the living conditions of the common people, and which they are particularly interested in. In the latter case he will look for the things mentioned in folk poetry, songs and legends, in ancient Russian literature which should explain to him what the common people like best in a book. . . .

"The subjects of the articles for spiritual and moral development should deal with humanism or should be directed against a life of idleness, soulless self-interest, petty tyranny, lack of social feeling, disrespect for human personality, the rights of another person and all sorts of other things that are observed particularly among our people as a result of historic circumstances beyond their control. All this must as much as possible be expressed in images and not in a didactic or dogmatic way, taking into consideration the fact that our common people are still almost in an epic state.

"It is clear therefore that the whole book must seek to achieve two aims: 1) to provide the common people with the knowledge of a number of subjects that are as necessary as air for every man as well as for the common people; 2) to help the common people to achieve a greater development of their moral and human feelings in strict relationship to the habits, customs, history, environment and daily life of the Russian common people. Besides, the book for the common people should contain everything they want and ask for."

In addition, you add that it is necessary to speak to the common people in a simple, clear and straightforward language and not to try to imitate the style of popular speech: "Every attempt to imitate popular speech," you write, "every buffoonery, every affectation will compromise not only the book but literacy in general. Our common people are intelligent and will at once recognize a crafty intention; this they regard similar to the dressing-up of their masters in peasant clothes in order to collect folk songs or in order to read admonitions to an illiterate peasant, which usually go in one ear and out the other."

Let us pause here. So you see, you yourself are against tricks of any kind and what you say about this is excellent, especially where you mention the gentlemen who dress up as peasants and the admonitions that go in one ear and out the other. You handle theory very well sometimes, but where practice is concerned, you immediately contradict yourself. Don't you really approach the common people with tricks? Isn't what you have just written a kind of deception, beginning with the title of the book? Why *Reader*? Because it is the sort of title that can be met in the literature of the period before Peter the Great? But then all the books bore similar titles, while today the titles are quite different. Why keep the old-fashioned title for the common people, then? This peculiarity may be noticed by the people for whom the book is intended. "So for us they have composed a special kind of book, because their own books are above us!" Such an argument will not make the book popular among the common people, and, besides, those among them who like to read will prefer to read the books read by their superiors, the forbidden fruit, and will respect them a great deal more than your everyday, homespun, *menial* book. The common people will not notice, you say. I doubt it. What if they do? But even if they don't, you must admit that it is quite an unnecessary, petty, labored attempt to make the book fit for the common people even by giving it a special kind of title. It puts its mark on the whole book. From its title we can already tell what it is going to be like—and we are not mistaken. You say that one could not entitle it *A Primer* or *A Book for Sunday Schools and Popular Reading,* since it would both be impractical and show a lack of knowledge of the common people, for they must not be told that they have to read only such a book. So there you are already deceiving the people, though with the best intentions in the world; but without even considering the fact that your unnecessary and petty effort to conceal the deceit will lead the common people to find it out, there is something unpleasant about the whole thing. You say in another place that though the articles on physical nature ought to be lifted from children's books, care must be taken to conceal the fact that they were written for children. "On the one hand," you observe, "the common people are also children." Again, it is too late to decide which subjects are necessary for such a book while compiling it. That ought to be decided much earlier. Besides, the peasant for whom the book is intended may well wonder what sort of special man he is that he ought to have special subjects for reading. "All I want to know," he says, "is what the world is standing on."

"Nonsense," replies his wise guardian. "This is too soon for you to know. You are a peasant and that is why you ought to know something about your own things, the things that have to do with the life of the peasant. So here we have *chosen* them for you. . . ."

The answer is, of course, both just and reasonable, and no doubt the peasant will have to accept it, but, after all, to express it so openly is a little offensive, is it not? It is a well-known fact that people do get offended sometimes. For example, one of Gogol's heroes called someone the son of a priest, and although the man really was the son of a priest, for some obscure reason he got offended. And yet there was no reason for him to be offended at all, was there?

The peasant, it is true, will never suspect anything, and you count on that, don't you? And, indeed, is it necessary to be so overscrupulous, so very careful? It may become a little too noticeable, you know. Too much effort is spent on the *choosing* of the material for the book. If you would try not to be so particularly careful and even a little suspicious, it would be much better, I assure you. You would be less formal, more on an equal footing with your future peasant-pupil. It might occur to him that you have compiled your book for the sake of making money, as a speculative undertaking, and your very choice of material, which would still of course be noticeable but to a lesser degree, would be to your advantage. The common people would say, "Look at the cunning fellows! They are trying to persuade us to buy the book—look how well they have written about everything!" And I hope they will think like that—nothing could be better—for in that case they would certainly buy the book. No doubt they would be wholly ignorant of our generous aspirations, of our self-lessness, of the losses we incurred in order to educate them, but, then, why shouldn't they be? In the first place, it is certainly better to prepare a reward in heaven for oneself, and, second, if the common people were to guess your intentions they would probably not buy your book. The common people, you see, are stupid; for all you know, they may dismiss all your efforts and say, "It's some sort of guardianship!" You see, they too are terribly sensitive. The profit motive is much better: there would be more of a sense of equality and familiarity with them in an uncon-cealed desire to make money out of this transaction, for they like to feel that they are your equal, for they would rather trust one of themselves than some guardian. But your *Reader* is a kind of conspiracy. At any rate, I am ready to take a bet that a book composed according to your program would be a failure, for although it might be distributed in all sorts of charitable ways, the common people would not think very highly of it. Indeed, I cannot help feeling that they would regard it with some fear, especially if it were given to them as a reward for good conduct and diligence with the added information that it did not matter if they tore it or lost it, as you state in your program. But of this later . . .

Now, let us imagine some nursemaid: there she sits on a seat in a park with other nursemaids who are eager to have a talk about their own affairs. To make sure they will not be disturbed by their charges, they first of all tell Petya to play where he can be seen and not to go behind the bushes, for "the devil is sitting there and waiting for you and he will put you in a sack and take you away." The little boy listens and though he is only five years old he knows very well that his nurse is talking a lot of nonsense, that there is no devil behind the bushes, that that's exactly the place where he could have a really good game, and already he is laughing at his nurse in his young mind. If I were a peasant I would certainly resent it very much if I were still regarded as a little boy to be taken care of by a whole secret committee: I assure you I would have imagined it were I in the peasant's place. No doubt there would have been no reason for imagining it. On the contrary, those people would have been genuinely fond of me and wished me to be happy, but I would have thought so all the same at the time. However, I am merely judging by myself, perhaps because I am a bad and ungrateful man. I should have realized, were I in the peasant's place, that I had to learn, that I did not as yet know anything, but the trouble is that any kind of guardianship is a nuisance. You see, everything has been so carefully selected in accordance with my shortcomings and vices; it has even been noted what kinds of subjects I ought to learn and what I am particularly interested in. These things I ought to know and those I ought not to know because I may get hurt. I might add that, in addition to all my bad qualities, I am terribly suspicious and sensitive and I can't think of myself as a peasant without being suspicious and oversensitive. Were I in the peasant's place, I would most certainly have pondered deeply and said to myself, "What if I do get hurt? It is I who will get hurt, not you. It's my look-out." In short, I would have acted in a most ungrateful fashion.

"But it's for your own good, you stupid oaf!" my charitable guardian would have shouted at me.

And, of course, I would have been unable to argue with such a learned man and at once agreed with him about everything. I might even have added, just to be on the safe side, "Give me a flogging, sir. If the peasant misbehaves, you must give him a good flogging." But I would still have refused to buy the book. It would have been of no use to me whatever.

"My master," I would have gone on thinking to myself, "is a kind man, but he's a bit queer. Seems to have grown very fond of me for some reason. Don't know why. Has nothing to do, I suppose, so he just takes it into his head to grow so fond of me that it gives me the shivers. Got out a book for me, he has. Must have given him a lot of trouble, poor fellow! Come on, he says to me, try to learn something so that I can have something to talk to you about, so that we can have some things in common. When you've learned everything in one book, I'll give you another, from which you can also learn everything. It's a Reader, which tells you that you must read it. That's the trouble: the masters have books, but I have only a Reader. This means that I am not yet fit to read real books. And this Reader was composed for me in secret by a whole committee so that I should not find out that they composed it for me on purpose, and to make it more acceptable to me they did a lot of looking around and took into account why I liked *Milord George* and *The Battle between the Russians and the Kabardinians.* See how greatly concerned they were about me, an ordinary peasant! Do I appreciate it? Many thanks to my masters," I continue to think to myself. "It's a good thing I am a stupid country bumpkin and cannot have any idea of it all, for how could I have any idea of it without a university education? I suppose if I did have a university education, I could tell them off good and proper. 'Do you really imagine, my dear orthodox guardians, that if I don't know who Count Cavour is or that there are infusoria in stagnant water I am an utter fool and don't understand anything?' Do you really imagine that the common people won't realize that although you seem terribly anxious to teach them something, you are also terribly anxious to conceal something from them because you think that they are as yet unfit to have that knowledge? Yes, the fact that I did not have a university education is the greatest piece of good luck I have ever had (I continue to think to myself,) and that's why I do not understand anything. For if I had had a university education, I would remind you of a saying by Prince Talleyrand: *Pas de zèle, messieurs, surtout pas de zèle!* But then you know that anecdote better than me, a peasant. . . ."

We have written this down now and we feel frightened: what if the reader should get angry with us and say to us, "You aren't accusing Mr. Shcherbin of indulging in such cunning tricks, are you? You don't mean to imply that he is not anxious to bring genuine education to the common people? Do you really think that the necessary caution with which he approaches this problem is a deliberately ill-intentioned deception? Well, this is the sort of thing that always happens in our literature. The moment a well-intentioned man who is out to do good takes up some useful pursuit, our critics immediately start sharpening their pens and, like bloodhounds, start looking for faults, looking for something to cavil at, something to vent their spleen on, and all this not because they burn with zeal for the promotion of the general good, but simply because their hands are itching, because they wish to deliver themselves of some caustic remarks, to show off their wit, to display their knowledge without actually knowing anything about the matter at hand. *La critique est aisée, mais l'art est difficile.* Why don't you draw up your own project and show us that we are wrong, but not by unsubstantiated critical notices. Then we shall perhaps pay attention to you. . . ."

It is these critics we are afraid of. Above all, we are afraid of being accused of wishing to heap abuse on Mr. Shcherbin's project. Of course, we do not wish to do anything of the kind. We declare with all the sincerity at our command that we have no such intentions so far as Mr. Shcherbin is concerned and, in considering his excellent project, we can feel nothing but gratitude. We have quite involuntarily transported ourselves to the ignorant and suspicious masses of the common people and we *could not help feeling* that by some obscure process it might occur to them to welcome Mr. Shcherbin's book (when he publishes it) not with the sympathy it deserves but perhaps with mistrust. We repeat, *we could not help feeling,* but of course we may be mistaken (which we wish we were in this case). Let us, however, continue after this slight digression with our detailed and circumstantial summary of Mr. Shcherbin's project. The whole of this project is most interesting and quite remarkable when one considers its ultimate aim. What else is there more interesting and remarkable to discuss if this is not interesting? Let us state our opinion beforehand: all this is so cleverly and cunningly contrived, so carefully selected, calculated, thought out, foreseen in such detail that it is quite impossible not to pay tribute to Mr. Shcherbin's conscientious work or to thank him for it or even to admire involuntarily its quite marvelous finish, its consistency and intelligibility. However, we repeat once more: if there is anything in this project that we do not like, if there is anything that disturbs us, it is this unnecessary painstakingness; the fact that it is too clever, quite unnecessarily prefigured and calculated; that is to say, what we do not like about it is that it is much too good: an absurd impression, no doubt, but not unknown in nature. The very psychological foundations of the project seem also carefully measured out by a pair of compasses, just as if a square root has been extracted from the soul of our poor peasant. And all this has been extracted so calmly with such perfect conviction. . . . But to business.

The project is divided into the project proper and preliminary considerations. We have already discussed the first of these considerations, the fundamental views on which the whole edifice of this project rests, as well as the impression this project has made on us. Continuing his considerations, Mr. Shcherbin declares that what the common people expect least of all from the *Reader* is any tomfoolery or buffoonery, such as facetious sayings, jokes, etc., and that the printed word seems to be a kind of holy of holies to them and not a kind of farcical side-show and that, finally, they are very fond of the so-called high-flown sentimental style and this is why *The Battle between the Russians and the Kabardinians* sold in thousands of copies among them. Having made this excellent and quite correct remark (though it is not always so, for a *really* witty joke is appreciated by the common people, who are perfectly able to understand it), Mr. Shcherbin proposes to publish serious and important articles, such as "The Conquest of Kazan" from Karamzin's history, for he argues that 1) the reading matter is important and 2) the common people will at least obtain the knowledge of a historic event concerning their nation. But Mr. Shcherbin comes down very heavily on the fantastic and supernatural. He banishes from his *Reader* everything of a fantastic nature on the ground that the common people have too many superstitions as it is (and, let us add for our part, in spite of the fact that the common people are terribly fond of everything fantastic and read it avidly or listen to others reading it). We think it is all very excellent, but again, as before, we cannot help noticing his quite extraordinary anxiety and fastidiousness about what one must and what one must not include in such a book, his well nigh morbid suspiciousness and apprehensiveness. "Don't come near me, don't come near me," Oblomov cries, "you've just come in from the cold street!" Of course, the common people treat a book as an authority, but even the common people are not such hypochondriacs as Mr. Pisemsky's *hypochondriac*, who is afraid of everything: a slight breeze and immediately death. Naturally we do not want anything fantastic. But Mr. Shcherbin takes much too exaggerated a view of his "book for the common people," as though imagining that in it lies the beginning and the end of the entire future of the people, their only means of education, their university, their happiness for the next thousand years; he imagines that if a peasant were to read it and find a single discordant line, he would be undone forever. Mr. Shcherbin is so fastidious that he does not want to call even Krylov's *Fables* fables and proposes merely to state their bare titles, for example *The Peasant and the Laborer* or *Two Peasants*, and "Krylov" under them. All this on the ground that the common people are supposed to consider a fable something of no account and that this becomes even clearer from the Russian proverb "You can't feed a nightingale with fables" or "old wives' tales." This is certainly going a little too far and, besides, it is not true that fables are held in so little esteem by the common people. Quite a number of them are very popular among the people; some are even full of very witty allusions. The common people certainly understand the meaning of a fable. Though you may *conceal* from them the fact that it is a fable, the rhyme alone will confuse them. This is much more dangerous. And, indeed, if the common people were as easily confused as you think, they would at once object to the rhymes: not written as it is spoken, must be a piece of buffoonery. You even suggest selecting fables in which animals and not people should appear. "Talking animals and trees," you write, "will strike the common people as tomfoolery, as clownishness, and will harm the authority and the credit of the book." Will it? Is not a fable the creation of the common people? The common people will realize that it is an art form, don't worry. They are not as stupid and narrowminded as you think.

Mr. Shcherbin goes on to discuss the inclusion of general subjects in the book, especially those dealing with physical phenomena, but he points out that though the editor of such a book ought to choose his articles from children's books, he must not let his readers notice that the articles were written for children. For, Mr. Shcherbin remarks, "the common people are also children."

How absurdly touchy you suppose the common people to be and how afraid you are of them! What microscopic prudence!

The next section of the book is to be devoted to history.

Beginning with the historical folk song and the chronicles written in easily understood language, there should be a "gradual and consecutive" transition to passages from our national historians.

To begin with, why all this cautious gradualness and consecutiveness? You are not preparing the common people for a university entrance examination, are you? What if they do open the book at random and read the national historians before the chronicles and folk songs? Will they at once be undone or will all your efforts be in vain because of it? Are you to print a warning on the title page that the book should not be read at random? You'd better get the authorities or the rural councils to see to it that the peasants read the book from beginning to end in strict *gradualness* and *consecutiveness,* starting with the *historical* folk songs to the national historians inclusive, etc.

No doubt the common people dislike desultory reading, but why include in the *Reader* verbatim the charter inviting the house of the Romanovs to the Russian throne? If you want to tell the common people about this event, you can tell it in your own words in modern language and not reproduce the *charter* just because it is written "in the language of the people" (what people?) "in a mixture of Church Slavonic which the common people respect." Whatever for? Do the common people hold Church Slavonic in great esteem because they find it unintelligible? But Mr. Shcherbin observes:

"Such a composition of the book is liable to educate the common people in accordance with their positive national and historic character, provide a healthy and organic development and direction for it, which to our regret we who are lighted by the sun from the West lack."

Well, you see, the real trouble is that you are trying to achieve by your *Reader* both the educational enlightenment and the development of the common people at one go—and all this by your book alone. You are not compiling it simply to provide the common people with a pleasant and useful book for reading. You want to achieve almost a university education with it all at once. We are not bringing any false charge against you: it is something that strikes one at first glance. Otherwise you would not be so punctilious, you would not be thinking of *consecutiveness* that would make sure that one thing followed naturally out of what preceded it. You would not be afraid that the common people would read one article before another. No, "popular readers" are not compiled for that kind of purpose, and it is quite inevitable that your desire to achieve that purpose will make your book pedantic, confused and, above all, as dry as dust.

We are not at all against your aspirations: we admire your intelligence and your application sincerely. For instance, you demand that your *Reader* include legal articles for the enlightenment of the common people and even for raising their moral standards, as well as a medical article of "hygienic" contents, on the ground that "great numbers of peasants die and get crippled simply because of the absence of the most ordinary, general and necessary information on hygiene" (from which it follows that, having read the *Reader*, the common people will at once stop dying and getting crippled, for they will already be in possession of hygienic information.) We are not making fun of you. We realize that you yourself do not count on such an immediate effect of your *Reader* on the common people, but you seem to expect such an influence. Such, at any rate, is the impression produced by your *Reader*. You further suggest publishing a calendar, a dictionary of foreign words that are in common usage (at a time when hundreds of Russian words in use by educated people are unknown to the peasants), and, finally, you intend to explain to the common people "what sciences there are," that is, to explain to them at once the nature of all the sciences in the world.

"The concluding section of the book," you write, "will be a section of moral ideas, and to ensure their gradual psychological perception, it will be preceded by a literary

186

section, something in the nature of a popular anthology which for certain practical reasons, however, will not have an exclusively esthetic aim. The stories, passages and extracts included in this section will, under the more or less artistic cover, always include some historic or some other kind of information, fact or humane and spiritually moral idea, which our common people need most of all."

All this is excellent and useful, clever and magnificent; one precedes the other, one follows the other, one section prepares the peasant's soul for the next section, etc. What could be better? There follows the summary of our project. You write:

"In order to give a clear idea of the contents, arrangement and organism of the book, we must here provide a summary of its sections so as to explain as clearly as possible the essential qualities of the logic and the practical and psychological motives which the editor put at the basis of his *Reader*. Here, of course, all the sections will be indicated, as well as some of the articles they will contain."

There follows a summary of the sections:

"The first section. The reality of life. Worldly wisdom. The practice of everyday life as depicted in artistic forms."

Under this high-sounding heading are grouped the fables by Krylov, Khemnitser, Dmitriev and Izmaylov, fairytales about Truth and Falsehood (NB: one could have found something more interesting and more modern), then extracts from the "Memorials of Ancient Russian Literature," by N. Kostomarov, "About Wise Kerim," by Zhukovsky, short stories by Dahl, such as "The Axle and the Linchpin," some anecdotes (the most uncomplicated ones), parables, such as "A Parable about Drunkenness," folk proverbs, the most stereotyped ones (that is, those that the common people know without the *Reader*), riddles to exercise one's brains, sayings, etc.

"This section has been placed at the beginning of the book in order to inveigle the reader at once by the artistic lure of didactic thought, immediately comprehended, by the spontaneous ingenuousness of form, by the entertainment interest, by the clear-cut brevity of the expression of idea and facts, and, at the same time, attempt to drop into the unsophisticated mind the practical and moral rules of life in its everyday manifestations."

Well, what a glorious section! Or is it? The common people will become engrossed reading it! Or will they? To begin with, why so many "memorials" of ancient Russian literature? Something fresher would be much more agreeable. But, of course, when we recall that without these memorials the common people "will not be brought up on the positive and exclusively national basis of their history," we shall realize that they are necessary.

All this is excellent, but even better is Mr. Shcherbin's idea that as soon as the common people have read this first section, the moral and practical rules of life in its everyday manifestations will be dropped into their unsophisticated minds and at the same time prepare them for the second section. It was with this idea in view, as Mr. Shcherbin assures us, that this section was to be placed at the beginning of the book. How is one not to thank him for all this trouble and not wish him success?

Incidentally, we would like to say a few words about "the unsophisticated mind" of the common people. For some reason it has long been assumed that the mind or soul of the common people is something extraordinarily fresh, undefiled and "unsophisticated." We, on the other hand, are of the opinion (that is to say, we are quite certain of it) that the soul or mind of the common people is exposed to so many temptations every minute and has, owing to certain circumstances, been wallowing in dirt for so long a time that it is high time we felt sorry for the poor thing and had a closer look at it from a more Christian point of view and not form our opinion of it from Karamzin's stories and shepherds on china crockery.

All these "sections" are just "methods of approach" and "cunningly devised ways" of inveigling the reader.

The first section is followed by five others, in strict

succession, the one giving rise to the other. For brevity's sake, we shall summarize them in our own words.

The second section deals with *past life,* that is to say, historical events, pictures, stories and articles on geographical subjects. It begins with Russian *historical folk songs,* followed by passages from the chronicles, chronographs, etc. Then *official documents and charters.* (You don't believe it? A university!) Then—what do you think, *The Song of Igor's Campaign* in the translation by Dubensky! This is really the limit! What interest can the common people have *now* in *Igor's Campaign?* It is interesting only to scholars and, perhaps, poets, though it is the ancient form of the poem that might interest the poets. The common people have no idea at all about history: what will they make of *Igor's Campaign?* They will only be bored to tears and find a great many unintelligible and inexplicable things in it. This is what it means to *sacrifice everything* to the *scholarly* education of the common people! For "otherwise they would not have been brought up with their national spirit and history." As though there was not something incomparably more interesting and not so odd for that purpose.

There follow historical poems by Russian poets, such as *A Little Word about the Great* (Peter I), by Benedictov, etc. It seems to us that one should have told the common people something about Peter the Great first before extolling him in song.

Next come historic stories and passages from writers of national history (that is quite good), and biographies: Yermak, Minin, Lomonosov, Kulibin, followed by Russian geographical articles: Petersburg, Moscow, Kiev, Siberia, etc. Finally, stories dealing with universal history and geography (in fewer articles), such as Alexander of Macedon, Napoleon, Columbus, Constantinople.

The third section is devoted to *visible things,* that is to say, everyday life and nature studies.

This section contains articles about the earth, the air, the sky and—infusoria! Why confuse the peasant without rhyme or reason with infusoria? Why all these mysteries of German science dished out prematurely? Why this itch for teaching *quickly* and *everything*? The common people do not like teachers who come to them as educators and enlighteners who know what is good for them. It is this desire of teaching in haste and not so much the infusoria that is the trouble. The common people are *historically* inclined to be distrustful and suspicious; they will never believe in your good intentions and they will never show any goodwill toward you: and it is to win their goodwill that you must try first of all. Dryness, prescriptions, scholarship, system, infusoria—this you must know and that you must not know—that is what your *Reader* is like!

The fourth section—encyclopedia and information. Here we find an enumeration of existing sciences, a vocabulary of foreign words in Russian usage (which, Mr. Shcherbin remarks, is necessary when reading newspapers and in everyday life—for the common people and now?). Then come legal hints a peasant might find useful, hygienic information, calendar—in short, everything possible is done to make the common people ask why other books are not written in the same way, at least it is something they are quite sure to ask themselves.

After the fourth section comes the second part of the book, which is devoted to the moral and spiritual uplift of the common people. It is suggested that it should be printed in a more compact type. It begins with the fifth section—an anthology for the common people which seems to be the best section of the whole book; at least it is more entertaining than the rest. For, you see, unabbreviated stories and passages *from national literature and Russian writers capable of developing and directing the common people humanely* (Mr. Shcherbin's italics) will be arranged in it systematically (most certainly systematically). In short, everything will be arranged artificially, and this section itself has no uniformity of its own but has been arranged so as to "prepare" the reader for the last and final section of the book. This penultimate section will include songs and poems, but mostly prose works, some of which are even mentioned. It is also stated that only those folk songs will be included which "express humanitarian feelings or which *bitterly condemn some characteristic fault in the common people's habits and customs.*" What an approach! Even gay songs are forbidden!

There follow Koltsov's—what do you think?—why, of course, "You sleep, little peasant" or "Oh, why was I wed by force?"

The songs are of course very excellent, full of the freshest poetry, Koltsov's immortal creations. But, then, it is not the songs that we are criticizing here.

Then, of course, poems by Nikitin, Count A. Tolstoy, Tsyganov, Shevtsov and Nekrasov—all chosen with the same theme, as well as "poems of the same kind" by Pushkin, Yazykov, Maykov, Mey, Berg and so on, and Lermontov's *Song of the Merchant Kalashnikov* is considered "necessary"—have you guessed why?—because in it "you find the expression of the idea of honor in relation to a wife, *which our peasants ordinarily lack.*"

There follow translations of poems by various Serbian, Bulgarian and other Slav poets, next prose: Slav folk stories and legends from Borichevsky's book, from ancient Russian literature of Kostomarov, anecdotes from the lives of Peter the Great, Suvorov, Napoleon; extracts from novels by Zagoskin, Lazhechnikov, and stories by Leo Tolstoy.

This, of course, is excellent.

Next comes the transition to the sixth and final section. This section contains "reading for indispensable spiritual requirements and higher mental development (specially selected for the common people)." It is composed of "dogmatic," "historic," "practical-moral" parts, including, for example, the following things:

Symbol of faith, the Lord's Prayer and the Ten Commandments. (Must be printed in the Church-Slavonic type to acquaint the common people with the Church-Slavonic type and "to give the book greater authority and weight".)

There follow stories from the holy writ, from *The Book of the Wisdom of Jesus, Son of Sirach,* passages from the New Testament, translated into Russian, the last days of Jesus Christ from the book by Innokenty, passages from the exegesis of the liturgy, from Gogol's works and works by other writers, from Kochetov's "Enumeration of Christian Duties," the sermons of Irodion Putyatin, and the Sermon on Drunkenness of Tikhon Zadonsky. Next follow "church-historical and secret-geographical" articles, such as *The Conversion of Constantine the Great, The Adoption of Christianity in Russia* by Vladimir, the lives of a number of martyrs, the life of St. Olga, Cyril and Methodius and the chronicler Nestor. Descriptions of the Holy Places—Jerusalem, Bethlehem, Athos—extracts from Barsky's travels and the travels of the monk Parfeny, Muravyov, etc. Next religious-moral poems and even Derzhavin's ode *God.*

Again we repeat: all this is of course excellent and most excellently *chosen.* The author says in conclusion:

"This is how the writer of these lines imagines to be the contents and form of a book for the common people and Sunday schools. Everything written here has been taken from direct observation and experience of the life of the common people and from the great variety of relative facts and phenomena of present-day practical life, and formulated into an idea which may perhaps be far from present requirements but which has been expressed in accordance with our understanding and conviction. No one can cut himself off entirely from his environment, his education, and therefore this article probably has its own peculiar faults."

What can we say to this? I believe we have already said everything we think. Let us, however, recall the few words said about the *Reader* by one of our writers in the

May issue of our journal. We feel that these words may serve as a good concluding observation to our article.

". . . From the mixture of two old lives we may get a new one. Open up your lives to the peasants and study their lives and this, no doubt, will make the wished-for reconciliation nearer and bring about an end of our divided social classes more quickly; but tell the secrets of our life to the common people without concealing anything and leave them to choose between the good and the bad, and then they will become reconciled to you because they will believe you: otherwise they will become aware of our superior attitude toward them and this will make the position worse than ever. One must show respect for the taste and the curiosity of the common people; they must be given what they ask, what they want, and must not be irritated by articles on economic subjects about labor, co-operative workers' groups, housekeeping. . . . If we cannot make our own wives interested in such articles, how can we hope to make the peasants take an interest in them, the peasants who regard work with distaste because of certain historical memories? Let reading be at first nothing but an entertainment for them, something they can enjoy; they will realize the usefulness of it all later. Freedom first of all. Why thrust something upon the people against their will?"

But do you know? I have not finished my article after all. I suddenly imagine that I am compiling a "reader" for the common people and so many ideas occur to me that I feel I simply have to communicate them to any future compilers of similar "readers." No doubt these are only *certain* ideas. I do not claim the same sort of completeness and finish for them as distinguishes Mr. Shcherbin's "essay."

I would do it this way:

To begin with, I would in the first place consider one idea as fundamental to my plan and follow it through unflinchingly, to wit:

1) that before trying to bring about an *immediate* rise in the education of the common people, one must see that literacy and a desire for reading is spread among them as quickly as possible;

2) since a good book greatly develops the desire for reading, it is necessary to provide the common people with most entertaining and pleasant reading matter;

3) that only after the common people get a taste for reading should an attempt be made to teach and educate them. And though in the first "readers," published for the common people, no one can prevent me from choosing articles that would be of the greatest usefulness for them, I would all the same put the entertainment value of these books above everything else, for it is necessary first of all to achieve one thing—the spread of a desire for reading among the peasants—and only afterward to set about educating them; for it is no use chasing after two hares at once, since one thing can do harm to the other.

Note: There can be no doubt whatever that an obstinate and intense desire to re-educate and teach *first of all* will harm the book so far as its interest and entertainment value is concerned; for it will be too *contrived,* too *selected,* dry to a point of pedantry, full of articles that the common people will find boring (for instance, *The Song of Igor's Campaign* Mr. Shcherbin has included in his proposed *Reader* "in order to educate the common people in accordance with their true national spirit," in other words in order to make the people "national"), with sections included with the idea of "inveigling the reader by the artistic *lure of an educational idea,*" and so planned that one section should follow the other. All this is likely to make the book extremely ponderous, reveal to the common people its secret purpose and thereby harm them greatly from the very beginning. As, indeed, we have already pointed out. It would therefore not at all be amiss to substitute entertainment for scholarship.

Clever people may tell me that there is little that is sensible and useful stuff in my book. It will include some fairytales, stories, all sorts of fantastic nonsense, without any system, without any direct aim—in a word, a lot of nonsense—and that the common people will never be able to distinguish my book from *The Beautiful Muslim Girl.*

Well, I reply, I don't care if they do not distinguish it at first. Let them even wonder which to give preference to. For it must mean that they *like* it if they are comparing it with one of their favorite books. It is quite impossible to ask them for precise criticism *immediately.* The important thing is that they will *like* my book, make a note of *who* published it (for I shall certainly put the name of its publisher on the cover), and when I publish a second book of the same kind, with the legend "Published by so and so, second part," they will without a moment's hesitation be glad to buy the second book too with pleasure, remembering how entertaining the first one was. And as I will continue to publish interesting, entertaining and at the same time good articles in that book, I shall little by little achieve the following results:

1) the common people will be so interested in my books that they will forget all about *The Beautiful Muslim Girl;*

2) they will not only forget it but will even give preference to my book, for it is the nature of good literature to purify taste and reason, and that is why I pin my hopes on it;

3) and, finally, as a result of the pleasure (most of all *pleasure*) my books will provide, the desire for reading will gradually spread among the common people. What do you say—will the results I achieve by this policy be important or not? *To arouse in the common people a desire for reading* is what I consider to be the first and the most important step, my real aim; for in my opinion it is in the ability and the knowledge of taking the first step that the true practical and sensible expression of the activity of every useful social worker lies. It is not luxurious living we want; all we want is to keep alive. Let us first do

195

that and then think of a better life. And how can it possibly be done without trying to remove the thought of guardianship by their masters from the minds of the common people? You are of course right in stating that a book is an important matter for the peasant; from a book he expects something serious and instructive. That is so. But he does not like to be instructed by his masters. He does not like to be looked down upon, to be under guardianship when he has the full right to do as he likes. "Look here, my dear peasant, you'd better learn something from my book. Stop reading *The Beautiful Muslim Girl*. It's rubbish. Now, in my book you will find an extract at the end from Lazhechnikov's *House of Ice*. It's a lot better than *The Beautiful Muslim Girl!* Have you ever heard of such a marvel as a house made of ice? What style! I've also heard that you like to read something religious. Well, here's something about Mount Athos, about the life of the monks in the monasteries there. How they live and pray. There's entertainment for you. You'll enjoy it after reading the serious articles in the preceding sections. You'd better think it over. You have such improper games, too. I'm told you are still playing knucklebones. Now, here is the magazine *Teacher* and you'll find all sorts of interesting games there. Instructive, too. Look, here are drawings of ducks—see how they swim? And here's a sportsman— he has shot them. And here is a riddle: five ducks were swimming in a lake, came a sportsman and killed three, how many were left? Well, guess, my dear child—I mean, my dear peasant, of course. A much better game than knucklebones." I would not try to persuade myself when compiling my book that the peasant would not realize what I am after. I am quite certain that he has enough sense to realize immediately the methods we employ to get him to do what we like and if he does not, he will feel it. Neither would I approach the authorities to assist me in the distribution of my book. For, you see, this could lead one to seek the help of the authorities to impose a ban on a book that the peasants read but that you consider to be unfit.

And, indeed, why hesitate? Collect them all and burn them! But, joking aside, how can a sensible man like Mr. Shcherbin count on the following methods for the sale of his book:

"In order to assure the widest possible distribution of the book, an appeal should be published in the press to all those who are anxious for the spiritual and moral enlightenment of the common people, landowners, factory owners, etc., to buy the *Reader* in order to give it as a present to the literate peasants."

Or, in another place:

"It is necessary to pass a decree that every pupil of a Sunday or village school should receive a copy of the *Reader*, which should become his own property and which should be at his disposal as he thinks fit. This would be a kind of legal act confirming the fact that the recipient of the book has been admitted as a pupil of the school. The same should apply to the parish schools of the Ministry of Education. Since the honorary trustees of the schools enjoy all the rights of civil servants without any regular duties and since they are as a rule people of means, it should be made their duty to purchase these books for the pupils of their schools, which will, anyway, amount to a very small annual expenditure. The *Reader* could be exchanged, sold or given as a present to the pupils and in this way change hands freely and at the same time still remain among the common people."

Good heavens! This is the surest way of giving the book an official stamp and ensuring that no one will have anything to do with it; it is the surest way to make it worthless in the eyes of the common people. And, finally, your words: "the book will still remain among the common people" prove that you recognize only one method as the best for the widest possible distribution of your book: the compulsory, almost forcible method, at any rate, something *imposed* from above, that is to say, the worst possible of all methods of distribution. You will achieve nothing in this way. It has been tried before. About twenty years ago books were distributed by official means, but the common people are not reading them, are they? Have they become popular? I don't suppose you will agree with me about this, but the following passage from your article really shows your utter ignorance of reality. Judge for yourself:

"There is still another method of the widest possible distribution of the *Reader* by means of the administration, namely to propose to the administrative chiefs of the rural districts and the village headmen to purchase the *Reader* at a reduced price and present it to the literate peasants in the big and small villages as though it were a reward for their literacy. The presentation to take place at the ordinary meetings of the village communes in the most patriarchal manner without any control by the authorities or any bureaucratic procedure. *Est modus in rebus.*

"It may be assumed that if the distribution of the book had been entrusted to the rural police, some peasants would not have declared themselves to be literate. The village headmen must explain at the meeting that 'this book is given to you as a present because you have learned to read and write. It is henceforth your own property: lose it, sell it, exchange it—the police will never ask you to account for it.' In any event, the book will not be destroyed, but will remain among the common people and will thus help to increase its popularity by constantly changing hands. This will create a *demand* for the book also in the towns, from market booksellers and village peddlers."

Just as if we lived on the moon or in Karamzin's *Marfa the Mayoress*. Why, this means making a philanthropist of everyone! "To propose to the administrative chiefs of the rural districts and the village headmen to purchase the *Reader at a reduced price* [!] and present it to the literate peasants [. . .] as though it were a reward for their literacy." That is to say, to assume even before the spread of education among the peasants such a love

198

for education, such a clear understanding of its necessity, that they will agree *voluntarily* to part with their money. Furthermore, to assume, even before the wide distribution of the *Reader* and before people know what it is all about, such a tremendous respect for it that it is given as a reward (you do not want to force people to give it as a reward, do you, but to make them do it of their own free will). Finally and above all, such an extraordinary and unheard-of event is completely contrary to the customs and habits of the common people: it is something monstrously German. Would it not be better to sew little pink ribbons on the shoulders of peasants as a reward for their literacy? Why, the peasants will never stop wondering what is behind it all when you offer them the chance to buy your *Reader* and at a reduced price, too. They will of course buy it if *ordered* to, but *of their own free will?* I am afraid they will never understand that. And see what a subtle, what a wonderful knowledge of the common people is revealed in Mr. Shcherbin's remark that if the distribution of the book were entrusted to the rural police authorities, some peasants would pretend to be illiterate. And how can you be so sure that the presentation of the books at the village meetings without the direct participation of the police would take place in a most patriarchal manner?

According to you, the village headmen would have to explain that the book was given as a reward for having learned to read and write and that the peasant receiving it could do whatever he liked with it. Now, we happened to read in manuscript a project for the promotion of literacy among the common people in which it was frankly stated that the best way of achieving a satisfactory result was to forbid the peasants to marry until they had learned to read and write. (The degree of despotism some liberals can achieve!) Needless to say, such a method, which is anyway quite impracticable, would only have brought about a general feeling of bitterness and disgust with literacy; but nevertheless this impracticable and draconic method seems to us much more realistic than Mr. Shcherbin's innocent method. Imagine a peasant who has just received as a reward a copy of the *Reader* at a village meeting. Confused and disturbed by such an unheard-of event, he takes it to his house very carefully and even fearfully, puts it on the table, sternly bids everyone in the house not to come near the table, then sits down on a bench, props his head on his hands and stares bewildered at the *Reader*. Soon the room is filled with curious neighbors and relations who are also bewildered by what had happened at the meeting.

"They tell me you've got a reward," says one. "From the authorities?"

"Yes, from the authorities."

"I hear it came straight from Petersburg."

"What kind of a reward, you silly man!" the host himself interjects. "A reward because I know how to read and write. It's all the better for myself, isn't it? Then what do they want to reward me for?"

"Why," a relative says, "so that looking at you, others should also try to get a reward. That's what Grishka said the other day."

"*The Reader,* price thirty kopecks," another neighbor reads. "I daresay when you try to sell it, you won't get five kopecks for it. They should have given you the thirty kopecks instead, Gavrila Matveich."

"I don't agree with you," sayd the relative. "Why, if they had given him thirty kopecks, he'd have spent it on drink in a bar, but here they gave him a book, *The Reader,* in which all the wisdom in the world is described."

"Half a moment, friend," the host interrupts again. "Why, then, did Grigory Savich say to me at the meeting 'Lose it, sell it, exchange it, give it to anyone you like, no one will ask you to account for it—it's your property'! If this book had been of any use to me, why should I be selling or losing it? No, it isn't that at all. It's the authorities. . . ."

"Yes, the authorities," others in the room echo with even greater embarrassment.

"Trouble!"

"Let's go to the police inspector! Saddle the horses, Mitya!" cries a peasant, jumping up with a determined expression from his seat.

Others will be jeering.

"See what a lovely present Gavrila has got!"

"Same as getting a medal, I suppose."

"Same old supervision!"

"Very often," Mr. Shcherbin adds, "the circulation of a book among the common people depends on *chance*. Sometimes a peasant may never come across a book that would be to his taste and that would answer his requirements. Such chances may be the result of the measures we pointed out and occur comparatively frequently."

No, Mr. Shcherbin, we reply. Nothing will result from the measures you propose. The only possible result would be a loss of credit by the book. You can't take a step forward without the administration. Even to make the common people *like* your book you resort to administrative measures. Why do you think the common people like a book? *The Beautiful Muslim Girl* must have something to make the people like it and buy it. You ascribe it to the fact that it is written in a high-flown and sentimental style which appeals to the common people and is to their taste. There is a tiny grain of truth in that. Indeed, a high-flown and sentimental style may have an appeal because it contains and enshrines a reality that, though impossible and senseless, is the complete opposite of the boring and burdensome reality of the peasant's everyday life. But that is not all. That is not the whole reason. The chief and foremost reason is, in our opinion, that this book has nothing to do with the peasant's masters or has ceased to have anything to do with them. Quite possibly its author in the simplicity of his heart wrote it for the highest society. But our literature met it with jeers. It was published by a small publisher who offered it for sale in the market places for a very low price. Rejected by the "masters," the book at once became popular among the common people, and I daresay the fact that it was not a book their masters liked helped it to find favor in the eyes of the common people. No doubt it was first bought by peasants, then it found its way among the parlor maids, the copy clerks, the footmen, the shop assistants, the artisans and similar people. Having become popular, it took root and began circulating in the barracks, and, finally, even in the villages. In the villages, though, its circulation was still very small. We emphasize this fact because the compilers of popular books have chiefly in mind the peasant who is a tiller of the soil. This is a big mistake. The peasant does not feel the need for reading as much as the townsman, such as the artisan or the shop assistant, or even as much as the former house serf. Books reach the peasant through this *higher class* of the common people, and it is a mistake to mix up these two classes, a mistake that is often made and gives rise to the mistaken idea of attempting to promote the circulation of books through the village societies. A book that appeals to the villager will find its way to him itself through the townspeople and the house serfs, the only existing methods for the circulation of books among the peasants. It is this method that should be taken into account. This higher class of the common people, which includes servants, artisans, copy clerks, etc., includes some low-grade civil servants and even landowners. Many of them have not received a proper education and it is they who read and hold in high esteem such books as *The Beautiful Muslim Girl;* other adventure stories are very popular with the higher and well-educated classes. A man who is incapable of any independent action and who accepts (as a matter of course and owing to his inability not to accept it) the reality that he knows so well as something extremely normal, as something absolutely immutable and permanent, quite naturally gets a certain hankering after, a certain temptation for, doubts, philosophizing and negation. Hence he is drawn to books that present him with facts or the possibility of facts that are diametrically opposed to the reality as he knows it and that decline to accept its immutability and its oppressive quiescence, particularly as these books are written in a popular style and provide one with an excellent opportunity of indulging in all sorts of exciting speculations and of enjoying a short spell of skepticism. That is why an ordinary man of the people and even a peasant loves most of all the fact that such books contain something that is contrary to their reality, which is always so monotonous and stern, and reveal to them the possibility of a different world that is quite unlike their own surroundings. Even fairytales, that is to say, stories that have no relation whatever to the real world, are liked by the common people perhaps for the same reason. As for anything of a mystical nature, one can easily imagine what its influence on the common people would be. And since all these books do not in any way attack the views held by the common people or overstep the boundaries of their philosophy, they are accepted as *their own,* and with the growth in the number of these books, the literature of the masters becomes more and more detached from the literature of the common people. That is why it is so terribly funny when Mr. Shcherbin offers to give *The Song of Igor's Campaign,* or, better still, the Proverbs to the common people. In other words, he offers what has naturally emanated from the common people, what composes their everyday reality—the Proverbs—to the common people. But what do the common people want proverbs for? To be more national than they are already? Do not worry, the common people will not forget their own proverbs. You'd better not forget them yourself.

In Mr. Shcherbin's book not everything is uninteresting for the common people. But the tone of the book, its upper-class origin, and the whole of its approach—all this will prove to be quite unacceptable to the common people. They will reject it *instinctively.* Besides, the above-mentioned methods of promoting its circulation will kill its success finally.

We repeat once more: in our opinion the best method (of the artificial ones) is the speculative one. There, too, if you like, is a high degree of artificiality, a high degree of chance, and that may make the success of a book very doubtful. But its highest degree of artificiality, its whole approach would not be visible from the outside, that is to say, the book would at first glance seem to be published solely for the sake of profit. And a man who embarks on so speculative an enterprise can hardly be a gentleman, can he? He cannot therefore be suspected of being a *deliberate* promoter of education among the common people. A man who is out to make a profit is intent on untying the purse strings of the purchaser of his goods and he does not *thrust himself* on people with his learned benefactions. But the problem is how to turn a *deliberate* educator into a businessman. If the book is published by some charitable institution or by some nobleman—an enlightener of humanity or, finally, simply by a scholar—is he a friend of humanity? None of them wants to make any money out of it. They would be only too glad to spend their own. In this case one must use a great deal of cunning in order to make sure the common people do not guess the book's true purport. So that it would certainly be much better if this friend of mankind really were a businessman. There is nothing very bad about it, in our opinion. The laborer is worthy of his hire, this has been said long ago. Let us imagine a charitable man, burning with the desire to do good, but who is poor. He, too, has to live and feed himself on the proceeds of his labor. But because he possesses a special talent for compiling books for the common people, that is to say, he knows the common people and what they need most and, in addition, is full of zeal for the spreading of literacy and education among them, he has found an occupation for himself: he publishes popular books, sells them and lives on the profit from their sales. And there is, in fact, no need at all to raise the price of such books. If they appeal to the readers for whom they are intended, they will sell in large numbers and, consequently, however small the profit from each book, it will add up to a large sum. It is entirely a question of the talent of the compiler: the more talented he is, the more copies of the book will be sold and the greater the profit. And to compile such a book in a talented way means to do so entertainingly, for the best book, whatever its subject, is always entertaining. To make sure of this, one must avoid every kind of "approach," all sorts of "sections," based on psychological studies of a peasant's soul; all sorts of sections turning out other sections; all sorts of articles written with the intention of enticing or encouraging, so that, in short, it should be very difficult (and not easy, as Mr. Shcherbin claims) to perceive "the essential qualities of the logic and the practical and psychological motives" which the publisher puts at the basis of his book. Logic and all the practical and psychological considerations must of course exist, if the compiler of such a book is an intelligent and sensible man; but it is desirable that they should be concealed as much as possible, so that it would be best of all if these basic things were to be concealed even from the compiler himself and were present in him in a naïve and unconscious way. But that is already an ideal; that would only be possible if the compiler of such a book regarded his work as his vocation from his early childhood and felt a most naïve and irresistible need to live with the common people and converse with them all the days and hours of his life. Such, it is said, are some *born* pedagogues who are passionately fond of living and associating with children and who must on no account be confused with learned and spurious pedagogues. The first, that is, the born teachers, too, can be very learned pedagogues, but without an inner stimulus and vocation the fact of their being learned would not be of much use. But it is difficult at the moment to have such compilers of popular books, though they will certainly appear in the future. Every new social activity finds its ideal worker in the end. In our country this kind of activity is only in its infancy, but it does promise to become a deeply felt need. Such social workers will subsequently be able to publish all the necessary hygienic, juridical and other scientific popular books for the common people, and they will publish them in a most excellent form, they will publish everything that is needed without any clever stratagems, and they will be able to do so well because they themselves will be national in the real sense of the word, so that the common people themselves will recognize them to be one of themselves, and their books will sell in thousands of copies, for, besides being useful and needed, they will be published in a talented fashion, for it is *talent* that is wanted *first of all* in order to approach the common people and associate with them, a naïve and born talent, which the present compilers of all sorts of "readers" do not seem to have had in mind. But for the present we publish such books in an *artificial* and *cunning* manner and in order to conceal this cunning manner it is necessary that this artificiality and cunning should be interpreted by the common people as due merely to the wish to make money. Therefore, the pedantic simplicity of such a title as "reader" could be eliminated. The common people are not at all such puritans as you think. They will not be offended by an alluring title and will realize that its function is to make them buy the book and not, as in the "reader," to make them read it because it is shameful to be an illiterate and an uneducated peasant, shameful before the charitable gentlemen who were at last forced administratively and officially to promote education among the ignorant peasant population. That is why every administrative promotion of the sales of the book must be avoided, for it is necessary that the common people themselves should obtain it in the market just because Uncle Matvey had heard that the book was very entertaining and recommended it to his nephew. A book, whatever its nature, never sells well except by its own merits, by itself, and it is the surest, most sensible, most dependable and most useful way of promoting its sales. In this kind of book everything must at least for the first time be sacrificed to entertainment and amusement. When compiling such a book, one must never, therefore, keep away from anything that seems to be contrary to everyday reality, which is often so abhorrent to ordinary, uneducated people. It would not at all be criminal, for instance, to try to stimulate the imagination of such people. The wonders of nature, stories of distant lands, of kings and peoples, of Russian Czars and their actions, of the punishment imposed on Novgorod, of pretenders, of the siege of Lavra, of wars and campaigns, of Ivan Tsarevich's death, of entertaining adventures of ordinary people, of travels, such as Cook's voyages, for instance, or the travels of Captain Bontecourt, wonderfully made up of the material left by Alexandre Dumas, which is highly entertaining for all classes and ages.

Good heavens, what's that? What homeric laughter, what terrible shouts of indignation all around! What do you mean? Translate Alexandre Dumas for a book intended for the common people? But what else is one to do if Alexandre Dumas has happened to have written these travels (for children, I believe) in a most brilliant manner, just as it should be written for the common people. The common people are not at all such puritans as it seems and they would not disdain to read Dumas at the right time, and—who knows?—Dumas may be just right from the point of view of practicability and the business-like methods of compiling such a book. The common people are not at all averse to reading, but they have so far had little chance of being tempted to read. Why keep feeding them with all sorts of essences of usefulness, good behavior and your good intentions? You will say that the common people are not as spoiled by their tastes as some high-class lady who simply must have her Dumas so that the book should not drop out of her hands from boredom. I agree with you; but a book is still something new to the common people and though they do not expect from it what an idle and stupid high-society woman demands, it will hardly be harmed by being entertaining. I myself happened to hear soldiers reading aloud in their barracks (one read and the others listened) the adventures of some chevalier de Chevarnie and the Duchesse de la Vergondière. The book (actually a thick magazine) belonged to one of the cadets. The soldiers read it with pleasure. When they reached the point in the story at which the Duchesse de la Vergondière gives up all her possessions and, after giving away several millions of her annual income to the poor grisette Rosa, marries the girl to the chevalier de Chevarnie and, becoming a grisette herself, marries Oliver Durand, an ordinary soldier, though of a good family, who refuses to become an officer for the only reason that he would have to curry favor with some influential official to get his commission, the soldiers were quite visibly impressed. And how many times did I myself have to read aloud to the soldiers and other low-born people the adventures of all sorts of Captain Polls, Panfilles, etc. My reading always produced an effect and I liked it very much; in fact, I enjoyed it greatly. I would be stopped, asked for explanations of all sorts of historic names, kings, lands, generals. I think Dickens would hardly have produced a similar effect. Thackeray would have been even less effective, while Skobelev's army stories made no effect whatever: the soldiers merely yawned with boredom. Oh, they certainly are highly sensitive! They would discover falsehood and deception in no time. And how quick they were to respond to humor! I shall no doubt be asked what useful purpose my reading served. Did it educate the listeners? What did they carry away from my reading? Well, to begin with, I had no intention of educating my listeners, but merely of giving them pleasure, and the reason why I wished to do this is that it gave me great pleasure myself. Even when I explained to them about the kings and their countries or, generally, made some useful remarks, that too gave me great pleasure. Second, it was reading and not something else and, whether it was useful or not, these people learned to look for pleasure in a *book*. The book, therefore, benefited by it. Third, though at the time it did not occur to me, afterward I could not help thinking that a book is still much better than a game of cards. Fourth, if you insist on usefulness at all costs, surely the impressions obtained from reading, as well as certain ideas and dreams, are worth something. No doubt it would have been much more useful if they had listened to *The Song of Igor's Campaign*, or to information about infusoria or had heard a few proverbs, or an account about Mount Athos or even about the chronicler Nestor (whose biography is included in the *Reader* not because it might be interesting to learn of the life of Nestor but because Nestor was a *chronicler*, which would make him an entertaining subject in the eyes of the common people—or would it?). Please, do not accuse me of trying to minimize the importance of all these articles. For all I know, they might be both extremely useful and entertaining to the common people. But it seems to me that it is not enough to choose them and publish them in the *Reader* for the common people to read them with avidity. It seems to me that they have first to be written with inspiration by a person who has a special vocation for this sort of thing as well as talent, which is indispensable for this kind of literature for the people.

I shall be asked, but where do you think you could now obtain articles for your book, even if you were to compile it in order to make money, without first obtaining official sanction for it, without getting the right kind of approach, etc., etc., etc? We reply, *now* we should also make use of our modern literature, though it is almost entirely an upper-class literature. But of course there is a good deal that can be chosen from it for the common people. One must only know how to choose. How to choose—we think that after all we have said about it no new explanations are necessary. We have been analyzing Mr. Shcherbin's article, but we do not claim that we are competent to make a more intelligent and more successful choice than he. We would like to make one observation, though: however profitable such a "reader for the masses" might be, we do not believe that at the present moment there is anyone who could compile a good one. We are, on the other hand, convinced that within a short time, a very short time, perhaps, we shall get a special section of literature devoted to popular reading. It may be only a guess, but we believe it will come true. Those who will provide that kind of literature will do so, as we have already mentioned, because they feel a special vocation for it. They may discover naïvely and without any effort the kind of common language in which they will be able to talk to the common people and will really merge with their views, needs and philosophy. They will be able to put into the right words all that we know and will find pleasure in this activity. It seems to us that they will not even have to conceal from the common people their own intellectual superiority. Then they will perhaps perceive in themselves new ideas and quite new opinions, living and positive ones, whose force and independence will stem from their new activity, from the need of this activity, which will be the result of our insistent and urgent need for union with the common people. All this, of course, is still merely guesswork, and though we should like to have said a great deal more in this sense about the future activity of our literature, we shall for certain reasons say nothing about it now. Besides, it is something that has to be dealt with as a separate subject. But in any event we do not wish to say anything against the present activities in the field of popular reading of our intelligent and well-intentioned men. May they be successful in their work. For it is from their activities that a more beneficial activity will emerge. And therefore if we were forced to disagree with Mr. Shcherbin, we repeat that we have rarely come across anything more intelligent and well-intentioned than his "essay." We cannot help being grateful to the author of this "essay" for his excellent and most useful work and we can only envy the periodical that published it.

V. The Latest Literary Controversies

WHEN PEOPLE HAVE NOTHING TO DO, when there is nothing serious to occupy their minds, they live a cat-and-dog existence and begin all sorts of controversies about principles and convictions. One reproves another for his beliefs, a second reproves a third for not seeing what is going on under his very nose, a third screams about books and book covers, a fourth does not care a hang about anything but himself, a fifth rests content with the immutable laws of nature, reduces everything and everyone to the same world water level and whistles as he contemplates everyone around him. And so on and so forth. You cannot enumerate everyone. The newspaper *Day* [*Den*] has issued only five numbers and already abuse is flying around freely. A "new question" has made its appearance concerning the universities and a whole stream of articles about universities have been published. Now we too would like to say what we think about these latest literary controversies and we too shall argue about principles and reprove others for not holding the same beliefs as we do. What's to be done? There is one rut for all of us. And we simply must say what we think: everyone does it . . . one must take part in the general movement, etc., etc.

Day is the same quiet, far from calm but far from becalmed *Russian Talk,* divided into newspaper pages. The same names, the same ideas, the same principles. Ivan

Aksakov is the editor, and the first number has articles by Khomyakov and Konstantin Aksakov (both deceased). The most remarkable parts of the paper are its "Slav" and "district" sections. No other Russian publication today has got this, not at least in the same unbroken continuity, and this makes the paper rather interesting. In fact, the whole of it is extremely interesting.

In certain quarters it has already given cause for annoyance. Askochensky, it is said, praised it enthusiastically and some have even hastened to bury the new *Day* (in print, of course). In one Petersburg journal some gravediggers even speculated as to what section the paper belonged in.

But the gravediggers are wrong.

There can be no question of any divisions into sections.

We are not interceding on behalf of *Day* or the views it stands for. But the name of the Aksakovs (all three of them) is too well known not to know whom you are dealing with. And, finally, what is this terror of thought? The moment a man thinks differently from you—destroy him, if you cannot do it literally, then at least by slander. What two-bit despots! What domestic terror nurtured on sour milk!

But enough. Let us say what we think about the new journal.

It is the same Slavophiles, the same pure, ideal Slavophilism, not a whit changed, whose ideals and reality are so strangely mixed up: for whom there are neither events nor lessons. The same Slavophiles with the same bitter hatred of everything that is not theirs and with the same inability for reconciliation; with the same intolerance and pettiness, and completely un-Russian formal approach to things. Here as an example is an extract from the first issue of *Day:*

"And how widely has this lie been spread and is being spread! The whole inner development, the whole life of our society is infected and contaminated as with leprosy. A lie! A lie in education, purely external, bereft of any independence and creativeness. A lie in the inspirations of art, which is trying to give expression to alien and fortuitous ideals. A lie in literature, dealing with problems of supercilious importance, problems created by historic conditions and alien to our national, historic life; in literature sick with alien illnesses and *indifferent to our national afflictions*. A lie in the denial of our nationality, *not by virtue of indignant and passionate love, but by virtue of inner dishonor, instinctively hostile to everything that should be sacred, such as honor and duty*. A lie in self-adulation accompanied by spiritual breakdown and disbelief in one's own powers. A lie in the worship of freedom existing side by side with impulses of the most refined despotism. A lie in piety, loyalty to one's religion, masking coarse irreligiosity. A lie in the triumph of savage dogmas, created by shameless ignorance, fearlessly insulting to social conscience and unyielding before the quite evidently indestructible strength of the fundamental bases of our national life. A lie in the thoughtless chasing after novelty under the foreign firm of progress and civilization. A lie in humanism and enlightenment of which our society, in its systematic inconsistency, boasts, irrespective of the fact that it admits without criticism the most incompatible principles, shuts its eyes from drawing the right conclusions, by-passing deliberately all fundamental questions, fawning upon all modern fads and pretending that its cheap ability to cover up without solving the most irreconcilable contradictions is a sign of great nobility and tolerance. A terrible, hitherto unseen combination of childish immaturity with all the infirmities of decrepit old age, and yet in spite of it all a cure is possible and, indeed, indubitable. We all feel it, we cannot even doubt it sincerely, and the day of our salvation is already dawning."

We do not think that that day is dawning for the Slavophiles. The Slavophiles possess the rare ability of being unable to recognize their own and to understand anything of contemporary reality. To see only the bad is worse than seeing nothing. And when something good does sometimes stop them, then if it bears no resemblance to the form of their ideals cast forever in one mold in Moscow, it is at once repudiated irrevocably and violently persecuted just because it dared to be good in a way that is different from the one that had been ordered once and for all in Moscow. However, their own ideal is not absolutely clear. They do occasionally betray a strong flair, subtle and precise, for some of the fundamental moments of the Russian national idiosyncrasies, though not by any means for all. Not a single Westerner understood or said anything better about the Russian village community than Konstantin Aksakov in one of his last essays, unfortunately unfinished. It is difficult to imagine anything more precise, clear, wide and fruitful. But the same Aksakov wrote an essay on Russian literature, published in the first issue of *Day*, which . . . but of that later. Let us reply to the above-quoted extract first.

Let us say frankly: the leaders of the Slavophiles are known to be honest men. If this is so, how can they say about the whole of our literature that it is "indifferent to our national afflictions"? How can they speak of "a denial of our nationality, not by viture of indignant and passionate love, but by virtue of inner dishonor, instinctively hostile to everything that is sacred, such as honor and duty?" What a fanaticism of hostility! What crude assurance about the innermost thoughts of their opponents, about their hearts and conscience! Is it only the Slavophiles who have been granted the privilege of loving their country and being honest? Who could have said a thing like that, who could have written it except a man in the last phase of fanatic frenzy? Why, one almost gets a whiff of the stake and the torture chamber here! We are not exaggerating. At the end of our article we shall quote another extract from *Day:* it hints at many things. . . .

But, of course, there were a great many lies; this is true enough. We accepted other people's interests for our own, but if we did, we did so because they *seemed* to be *ours,* of vital concern to us, and not at all because the Westerners were moved by "inner dishonor, instinctively hostile to everything that is sacred, such as honor and duty"! (How could you write a thing like that! One must first make sure of all sorts of things before making such a terrible accusation!) But why refuse to see the truth, why leave out of account the vital forces that are springing up on all sides, the longing for reality, for a return to the soil? If a lie did exist, our literature dealt with it for the past ten years almost invariably in a *negative* and not a *positive* way. The Slavophiles, for instance, seem to overlook the fact that during the period of the most violent sympathy with Western ideas the whole of our literature, including Gogol (before his illness) and all his followers, took up a negative attitude to the results of the same Western ideas. They have also overlooked the fact that this very passionately negative literature, with an unprecedented force of laughter and self-condemnation— honorable and marching with enthusiasm toward what it considered valiant and honest—this very literature was enthusiastically backed up by the most extreme Westerners. But the Slavophiles still stubbornly regard the Westerners as their enemies and speak of them with contempt and execration, forgetting, or rather refusing, to understand that the Western party and even its most extremist manifestations have been brought into being by an urgent desire for self-examination and self-analysis, the last spark of life in the dying Petrine reform and the first spark of consciousness which condemned it—that is to say, it was called into being by life itself. Did the Westerners lack the same feeling for the Russian national spirit as the Slavophiles? They did not, but the Westerners did not want to shut their eyes and stop up their ears like fakirs when faced with some facts they did not understand; they did not want to leave them without a solution and take up a hostile attitude toward them *at all costs* as the Slavophiles did; they did not shut their eyes to the light and were determined to discover the truth by their intellect, by analysis and by ideas. The Westerners would eventually have gone too far and admitted their mistakes. They did go too far and at last turned to *realism,* while the Slavophiles still cling to their confused and vague ideal, based, as a matter of fact, on some successful studies of our ancient way of life, on a passionate but somewhat bookish and abstract love for our country, on a sacred belief in our common people and their sense of truth and justice, but at the same time (why conceal it? why not say it?) on the panorama of Moscow seen from the Sparrow Hills, on an idealized conception of the Moscow great gentlemen of the second half of the seventeenth century, on the siege of Kazan and Lavra and other panoramas presented in the French style by Karamzin and his idea of Marfa the Mayoress, which they had read as children and, lastly, on the daydream of a final, partly physical, triumph over the Germans, who are not forgiven and are abused even after our triumph over them. We are not at all inclined to laugh when saying this and, besides, there is really nothing to laugh at; but we should like to point out the somewhat idealized element of the Slavophile party, which sometimes leads it to a total incomprehension of its own people and a total discord with reality. The Westerners were much more realistic than the Slavophiles and in spite of all their mistakes went further and kept moving, while the Slavophiles never budged from their place and indeed regarded this as something to be proud of. The Westerners bravely put the final question to themselves, solved it with a feeling of pain and, having achieved self-consciousness, returned to the national soil and recognized the importance of a union with their national sources and that salvation lay in a return to the soil. We, for our part, declare it to be a fact and believe this fact to be irrevocable, namely that in the present almost general (with the exception of some extreme and ridiculous exceptions) return to the soil, conscious or unconscious, the Slavophiles took hardly any part, if, indeed, they took part in it at all. The party that kept moving forward, however, went its own way, urged on by its own analysis of the situation. But having recognized the necessity of a return to the soil, it realized from its own former life and experience that it was no longer a matter of execrations but of reconciliation and union, that the Petrine reform, having had its day, had introduced into our country the great element of universal humanity, forced us to comprehend it and put it before us as our chief purpose in the future, as the law of our nature, as the most important aim of all the aspiration of Russian power and the Russian spirit. And note this: the majority of our society always sympathized with the Westerners. Do not despise it, this ever growing majority! Do not speak of it, as I can already hear occasionally, as too insignificant, too ignorant, too crippled by European ideas and as rotten even before it had time to pool its strength. Do not comfort yourself with that, do not think lightly of the instincts of our society, whatever they might be. Let us remember that our society sympathized passionately with the Westerners and shared all their mistakes and enthusiasms while always regarding the Slavophile movement as a masquerade. And what is the secret of this feeling of sympathy of the majority of our society? The secret is that life, that any kind of reality, that regeneration, that the pledges of the future, that even the return to the native soil itself and the first step toward it still rest with the realists, because Europeanism, Westernism, realism are still renascent life, the beginning of consciousness, the beginning of will-power, the beginning of new forms of life. The Westerners went along the road of merciless analysis and they were followed by everything that could go forward in our society. Realists do not fear the results of their analysis. Let there be a lie in this majority, let there be an accumulation of all the lies that you enumerate with such ardent enjoyment. We are not afraid of this gloating enumeration of our ailments. All these lies, if they exist at all, are the stations of the questing intellect and analysis carefully defined by fate. Let them be lies, but what moves us is truth. We believe that. Movement cannot be stopped and our society will reach the final result of at least its present efforts. You can be sure of that.

But you come out with a daily paper. You wish to stand aside from the general movement. You want to respond to the modern facts of life with a living, never-ceasing word, to make your way into the very midst of those interests that, as you say, are alien to you, with redoubled force. We welcome friends, but then you will not be our friends, will you? You will still continue to teach us with unbearable disdain, go on teaching, go on teaching forever, laughing at our mistakes, refusing to acknowledge our torments and suffering, condemning them with all the cruelty of frenzied idealism, and—and . . . But you have already begun. Look how the same Konstantin Aksakov, in his article in the first issue of *Day*, deals with the entire Russian literature. He regards it with hostility and skepticism, he refuses to find anything of his *own* in it, he does so with a lightheartedness that is quite intolerable from a man who is seriously concerned about its progress, with a sophistry that is both disdainful and insulting. Even if he were absolutely right in his judgment, this lightheartedness, this skepticism of his article, this self-admiration, this majestic separation of himself from everyone living next to him, this disdainful look which does not deign to stop seriously at anything, which does not deign to appraise anything—that alone would be heartless and thoughtless to a degree. To him, all our literature is nothing but an imitation of a foreign ideal and a longing to achieve it. He denies the existence of any manifestation of a social consciousness in our literature, he does not believe in the analysis that appears in it, in the self-condemnation, the pain and the laughter that are reflected in it. No, gentlemen, you have not lived with us, you have taken no part in our joys and our griefs, you have come from beyond the seas!

But of course the European ideal, the European views

and, generally, the European influence have been of great importance to our literature and are still reflected in it. But have we imitated them slavishly? Have we not experienced them as part of our own lives? Have we not worked out our own Russian view from those foreign facts? Have we not become convinced, have we not been made to realize by life itself that our conception of universal human values is perhaps the most important and the most sacred attribute of our national character? Have we not at last realized the importance of the soil and a return to it? Konstantin Aksakov maintains that all our attempts to return to our national values have proved unsuccessful in literature. "Ostrovsky's portrait of a merchant," he declares, "bears a vague resemblance to him and his speech can just be recognized as genuine." Is that all Aksakov has noticed? No, we do not believe it: Aksakov is merely pretending that it is so. Why, it sometimes happens even to a most serious person that he feels like doing something whimsical, of turning a somersault, of screwing a monocle into his eye and gazing at the universe—well, just as one does sometimes gaze at the universe in our country at four o'clock in the afternoon on Nevsky Avenue. And what do you think Mr. Aksakov demands? "Where," he asks, "is the real merchant? Where is his soul? Where is the thing that must live in him?" That is to say, he asks for the representation of the positive qualities of a Russian merchant—no more, no less, a representation that would fill the spectator with uncritical admiration. What do you say to that? What he wants is the last word in consciousness, the final degree of the beauty of an idealized person which appears to us only for a moment but which exercises such a powerful attraction on us. A bagatelle! We are not reproaching Mr. Aksakov for failing to discover in Ostrovsky the traces of positive Russian beauty which have already been observed elsewhere in his "Realm of Darkness," for not expressing his surprise at its appearance at so early a time, at so early an utterance of the new word, instead of reproaching and jeering at our literature.

219

A man may fail to notice lots of things when under the influence of a certain idealistic mood. But we find Mr. Aksakov's pronouncement hard to bear, as it is hard to bear the views of a gentleman wearing yellow gloves and carrying a riding crop in his hand addressing a laborer: "Why didn't you finish your work? Can you carry a hundredweight on your back? Mollycoddle!" What have you been doing, Mr. Aksakov? And if not you, then the rest of you Slavophiles? One reads some of your opinions and one cannot help coming to the conclusion that you place yourself entirely apart, that you look on us as if we were some alien tribe, as though you dropped from the moon on us, as though you did not live in the same kingdom as we or at the same time as we, as though it were not the same kind of life you were living! It is as though you were making some kind of an experiment, as though you were studying someone under a microscope. It is our own Russian literature, you know. Why, then, do you regard it so superciliously? Why do you examine it as though it were some tiny insect? Why, you are writers yourselves, my dear Slavophiles! You are so proud of your knowledge of the common people, so why don't you provide us with a representation of your ideals, your images? But as far as we know, you have never risen above Prince Lupovitsky. You will say it is rude and absurd to talk like that. Well, we are ready to agree with you, but only when you cease looking down upon your own Russians, when you cease regarding them like insects, like a heap of ants, and making fun of our efforts, our torments and our mistakes. Give up your supercilious tone and remember that you are Russians yourselves, that you are members of the same society as we, that we are all bound by one and the same fatalism, and you cannot look down upon us as inferiors or regard us in a detached manner, deeming yourselves always to be in the right. For some reason, you seem to be proud of the fact that you have got something of your *own*, something *special*, something that is different from what we've got. You always seem to be jeering at us:

"That's what those miserable people do not know! What basic things they simply do not know! How perverted and dull they have become!" But why don't you show us what you have got? Do not hide your treasures. Prove to us, not in all sorts of instructions and graveyard addresses, what you have achieved—shall we say, in the realm of art, since it is more innocent and more handy. Otherwise it does seem a little odd to an outsider: what is the matter with them, people will say, they maintain that they have grasped the meaning of the mystery of the Russian destiny and the Russian spirit, they have marked off for themselves the knowledge of the future of the Russian people and what the Russian people ought to be like, and yet when it comes to doing something tangible, there's nothing they can show us. They can't even show us what the Russian people ought to be like! And it is not as if there were no writers among them!

They have writers; what they lack is life.

Yes, what they lack is life. They have no feeling for reality. Idealism stupefies, fascinates, and—kills, and you yourselves have no clear understanding of the things you are so proud of knowing better than we. That is why we said that you possessed a gift for discovering certain basic elements of Russian life but not all. After all, there is no reason why you should not possess that gift, for you are Russians, you are honest people and you love your country; but your idealism is your undoing and sometimes you commit frightful howlers even in the understanding of the very basic elements of Russian life. Here, for instance, is another tirade from the second issue of *Day*. Have a good look at it:

"What do we see . . . even in our literature? What —*theories*? On one hand, empty and total negation, excitement without content or aim, a kind of phantom of life and movement, but in reality there is neither life nor movement. Everything is half dead and rotten and draws its strength from the attack of their enemies; on the other hand, coarse, dull, senseless *power* which imagines that

221

salvation lies only in coercion and lifeless mechanism. On one hand, the lie of destruction, on the other, the lie of construction; on one hand, unbelief, worshiping, like gods, transient human idols, on the other, imaginary belief, worshiping God, like an idol, and serving with the power of God's name their own selfish aims and advantages. Here we have servility before every last word of science, there coarse contempt of science, thought and the achievements of reason and spirit; here abuse and dishonest treatment of the word, there persecution of the word, love for darkness and dumbness and a secret sympathy for the speechless. Here and there you get the same murder of the spirit: there through external coercion and here through the impoverishment and the coarsening of the spirit; both here and there the same cringing and slavish attitude to everything foreign, a senseless submissiveness to imitation, betrayal of the national spirit coupled with an outwardly crude attempt to simulate the Russian national character. Both conflicting parties are sunk in inspissated darkness and they mutilate and destroy each other in this darkness. And when at last the common people raise their eyes, tired from the long slumber, and cast a look upon our writers and all kinds of artists (with a few exceptions, of course), upon these uninvited guests who arranged their wild revels at its bedside, listen to the deafening shouts, to the crash and thunder of their orders and their prophecies—what will they say? 'What have you done with the gifts of our rich native land which had been entrusted to your care? Where have you squandered her spiritual treasures? What has become of our customs, our religion, our legends, our past life, our long and bitter experience? What have you achieved in your leisure hours? What has happened to the wholeness and unity of life and spirit? Where is the learning cultivated by you? Where is my living, imaginative, free word? What rubbish have you deposited on my soil? No, you do not belong to me, you are hideous photographs of foreign peoples! Go to them if they will receive you. We do not know you, we do not need you, you are alien to us . . ." The common people will say when they awaken to consciousness, and the fresh wind of their resurrected spirit will sweep them away like dirt!

"But the time is not ripe yet. And though we are almost convinced that our voice is raised to no purpose, in conformity with the subject of our present speech, we too shall say, 'I am the voice of one crying in the wilderness. Make straight the way of the Lord. . . . Confess your sins!' "

Very well, but will the common people say this? Will they (and this is the main thing) pass this kind of judgment? Are you not ascribing your own opinions and your own judgment to the common people? You were talking about our artists and writers. We shall say nothing about the artists now and we are not going to guess the fate that will overtake our academy of arts. But of the others you mention, in our view the common people will say, "Don't worry, you are also Russians and we acknowledge you to be Russians for having at last realized that without us you would find life hard and wouldn't be able to do anything. All honor to you for having at once remembered us as soon as you grew up and matured and were capable of thinking. All honor to you for having grieved with our griefs and taught others to grieve, for having taken our part and decided at one accord to return to us, to your own native soil. Teach us now what you have learned in the foreign parts beyond the sea and describe to us in detail all your wanderings and sufferings. As for us, we shall teach you what you have so freely forgotten. You have made many mistakes, but people cannot be blamed for making mistakes. You never put up with deliberate mistakes among yourselves and this we prize above all. We all come from the same honorable soil and, as Russians, we are all equal. . . ." And if we are to quote texts, the common people will not quote the menacing text of the prophet but the merciful word of infinite love. So it seems to us. It seems to us that we shall deserve well of

223

them and that they will not sweep us away like dirt. Why, with you, too, they speak consciously; how then have you consciously put such words into their mouth? No, gentlemen, do not slander the Russian people, do not ascribe to them your own judgment.

There are more of your tirades, but we do not think it expedient to discuss them (so as not to make our article too long, of course). What strikes us as particularly strange is that you must of course have known that no one would discuss those tirades of yours or reply to them; but in spite of that you were carried away and—passed your final judgment. But what kind of judgment was it? You admitted yourselves from the very start that you would discuss only one aspect of the whole matter under discussion and would hear only one accused. But then what kind of court is it that hears only one party? But you did so and passed judgment too, that is to say, passed sentence on one party only. Was it well done? We leave it to your conscience. It concerned Russian literature, but this is not so important. What if it had been something more important? Believe me, it is not a good method. You are not promising good *Days* for us in the future. We wanted to welcome your paper sympathetically, but you seem capable of killing any kind of sympathy. And here is something else. In your forth issue a correspondent wrote about the peasants. It is difficult to imagine anything more self-satisfied and narrow-minded than this gentleman's opinions. The editor of *Day* dealt with his letter in his article in a most obliging manner and replied to his arguments again and again; he assured him that whereas he, the correspondent, saw only the peasant's stupidity and ignorance, there is nothing of the sort, but, on the contrary, a great deal of good sense. To some of his correspondent's revolting opinions, the editor replied with quite extraordinary good humor and forbearance and in one instance even hastened to declare that his correspondent was not at all an obscurantist. "We know only too well the ideas and actions of our correspondent," the editor wrote, "to allow the possibility of such a view." Well, of course, let us suppose not that the correspondent is not an obscurantist, but that every man must be allowed to have his own fantastic views and that an editor likes to publish them in order to be able to criticize them in the same issue of his paper. To one of these views the editor himself makes the following remark in connection with our now abolished serfdom:

"We even believe that, taking things as a whole, the personal relations of the landowners and their peasants were quite humane. Basing himself on the supposedly immutable laws of serfdom and naïvely convinced of his absolute human and divine legality, the landowner was not forced to justify serfdom by spreading slanders about the peasants and therefore treated them in a highly amicable and good-natured fashion. This is proved by the fact, among others, that the landowners were not against the education of their peasants or against the development of their communes, which were formed with their consent and not at all as a defense against the arbitrary powers of the landowners. We never had anything resembling the relationship between the feudal landowners and their vassals. The peasant was never a *villein* to the landowner but *God's slave, with the same Christian soul* as his own, though occasionally *with a peasant's feeble intelligence!* Sometimes terrible abuses took place, but they were never to become legal as in the West. Such taxes as were imposed there, such 'rights' of landowners as the famous *jus p.n.*, were quite unthinkable in our country. And when the critique of social consciousness exposed the whole inner untruth of serfdom and put an end to the blissful peace of unconscious, despotic, and, at the same time, good-natured relations between the peasants and their owners, all sorts of slanderous stories were really spread by certain landowners about their peasants and all sorts of false appraisals of serfdom, which did not, however, prevent the liberation of the serfs from taking place.

"Much stronger than the slanders against the peas-

DOSTOEVSKY'S OCCASIONAL WRITINGS

ants were the slanders against the Russian people spread by the frantic admirers of Western culture which refused to acknowledge the right of the common people to a free and original development."

Good? "Basing himself on the supposedly immutable laws of serfdom and naïvely convinced of his absolute human and divine legality, the landowner . . . treated [the peasants] in a highly amicable and good-natured fashion". . . .

To begin with, think of the state of complete idiocy a man has to reach to be convinced of the *divine* legality of serfdom. And if this is so, then who can guarantee that such a man will treat his peasant *amicably*? You say that we had nothing that resembled the feudal relations in the West. Well, no. There was not much difference between them. Ask the peasants.

"The peasant," you say, "was never a *villein* to the landowner but God's slave, with the same Christian soul as his own." But what about serf, boor, clodhopper, yokel —do you think these names were better than *villein*? And, besides, what exactly do you mean by a good-natured landowner? Well, a landowner, possessing the powers he did over the peasants, even if he was the most kindhearted man on earth, could not possibly in certain circumstances have treated them "amicably and good-naturedly." But why talk about it? So much has already been said about it and the whole thing is so clear to everybody that it is difficult not to understand it today.

Finally, you observe that the slanders of the Westerners against the Russian people were worse than the slanders of the landowners against the peasants, when the blissful peace of "good-natured" relations has been brought to an end by the increased supervision of the government. Well, no. It merely seems to you to be so. . . .

But enough. I expect we shall perhaps have several more encounters with the paper *Day* in the future.

226

FOUR "MANIFESTOES"

FROM

Time A N D *Epoch*

Four "Manifestoes"

I

Time: SEPTEMBER 1860

BEFORE PROCEEDING TO EXPLAIN why we consider it necessary to publish a new literary periodical, we must say a few words about what we understand the nature of our time to be and, particularly, the nature of the present moment of our social life. This will also serve to elucidate the spirit and the tendency of our journal.

We live in a highly remarkable and critical epoch. As proof of our view we need not emphasize those new ideas and needs of Russian society which have been proclaimed with such unanimity during recent years by the thinking section of Russian society. Nor shall we deal with the great peasant problem, the solution of which has begun in our own time. All these are only the signs and the facts of that prodigious change which is about to take place peacefully and with the consent of our entire nation, though when we consider its tremendous importance, we cannot help feeling that it is equivalent to the most outstanding events in our history and even to the great reforms of Peter the Great. This change consists chiefly of the total union between the educated section of our population with its national element and the participation of the whole of our great Russian people in all the events of our current life—the people who recoiled from the Petrine reform one hundred and seventy years ago and who have since been separated from the educated section, which carried on its own special and independent life.

We have mentioned signs and facts. No doubt the most important of these is the question of the amelioration of the conditions of life of our peasantry. Now millions and not only thousands of Russians will enter into Russian life, introduce their fresh, pristine forces into it and utter its new word. It is not the hostility of the classes, of the conquerors and the vanquished, as everywhere else in Europe, that must lie at the foundation of the development of the future elements of our life. We are not Europe and we must have neither conquerors nor vanquished.

The reform of Peter the Great has cost us too much as it is: it separated us from the common people. The common people repudiated it from the very start. The forms of life that were left to them by the reform were not in accordance with their spirit or their aspirations; they did not fit the common people, they were not opportune. The common people regarded them as alien, as due to the great Czar's wish to follow the example of foreigners. The very fact of the moral dissociation of the common people with the upper classes, with their leaders and guides, shows how much we had to pay for that new life of ours. But having repudiated the reform, the common people did not lose heart. They proclaimed their independence again and again, proclaimed it by extraordinary, convulsive efforts because they were alone and they found things difficult. They walked in darkness, but they went on their separate way regardless. They thought deeply about themselves and their position and tried to create their own views on life, their own philosophy, broke up into all sorts of mysterious, ugly sects, looked for new solutions of their problems, for new forms. It was impossible to recoil more from the old shores, it was impossible to burn one's boats in a braver fashion than it was done by our common people on entering upon the new ways they had been looking for with such torment. And yet they were calling the common people the custodians of old pre-Petrine forms, of the stupid dogmas of the old believers.

Of course the ideas of the common people, left without leaders and thrown back upon their own resources, were sometimes quite monstrous and their attempts at new forms of life hideous. But they had all arisen from one common cause, one spirit, unshakable faith in oneself, untried strength. After the reform there was only one case of unity between ourselves, the educated classes, and the common people—the campaign of 1812—and we saw how splendidly the common people behaved in that crisis. The trouble is that they do not know us, that they do not understand us.

But now the separation has come to an end. The Petrine reform, which continued up to our own times, at last reached the outermost limit of its influence. We cannot go any further; besides, it is impossible to go further, for there is no road; it has been completely traversed. All those who followed Peter got to know Europe, adopted the European mode of life, but did not become Europeans. Time was when we reproached ourselves for being unable to become Europeans. Now we think differently. Now we know that we cannot become Europeans, that we are incapable of squeezing ourselves into one of the European forms of life, forms Europe has produced out of its own national sources, which are alien and contrary to ours, just as we could not wear somebody else's clothes which did not fit us. We have at last come to the conclusion that we too are a separate, highly subjective nationality, and that our task is to create a new form, our own native form, taken out of our soil, out of our national spirit and our national resources. But we returned unvanquished to our native soil. We do not renounce our past: we realize its wisdom, too. We realize that the reform has widened our horizon, that through it we have come to understand our future importance in the great family of nations.

We know that now we cannot erect a Chinese wall as a protection against the rest of the world. We foresee, and we foresee with a sense of veneration, that the character of our future activity must be to the highest degree universal, that the Russian idea will perhaps be the synthesis of all those ideas that Europe is developing with such stubbornness and with such courage within its separate nationalities; that perhaps everything that is hostile in those ideas will find reconciliation and further development in the Russian nationality. Surely it is not for nothing that we spoke all languages, understood all civilizations, sympathized with the interests of every European nation, realized the reason and wisdom of phenomena that are quite alien to us. Surely it is not for nothing that we have manifested a power of self-criticism that has astonished all foreigners. They reproached us for it, they called us impersonal, people without a native land, without noticing that the ability to renounce one's native soil for a time is by itself already a sign of the greatest ability to examine oneself as soberly and impartially as possible; on the other hand, the ability to assume a reconciliatory attitude toward the things that divide the foreigner is the highest and the most noble gift of nature which is bestowed only on a few nationalities. The foreigners still do not have the slightest idea of our infinite powers. . . . But now, it seems, we too are entering a new life.

And it is before we enter this new life that a reconciliation has become necessary between the followers of the Petrine reform and our common people's fundamental ideas. We are not referring here to the Slavophiles and the Westerners. Our time is completely indifferent to their dissensions. We are referring to the reconciliation of civilization with the basic ideas of our common people. We feel that both sections must at last understand each other, must clear up all the innumerable misunderstandings that have arisen between them and then advance together in concord and harmony along the new glorious wide road. Union at all costs, regardless of any sacrifices and as soon as possible—this is our motto, our advanced idea.

But where is this point of contact with the common

people? How is one to take the first step toward unity? That is the question, that is the worry that must be shared by everyone who holds the Russian name dear, by everyone who loves the common people and holds dear their happiness. For their happiness is our happiness. It goes without saying that the first step toward obtaining an agreement is literacy and education. The common people will never understand us if they are not prepared for it first. There is no other way and we know that by saying this we are not saying anything new. But while the educated class has still to take the first step, it has to make use of its position and do its utmost to do so. The spread of education in an intensified form and as soon as possible is the chief task of our time, the first step to any activity.

We have only expressed the main and foremost idea of our journal and given a hint as to its character and the spirit of its future activity. But there was another reason that impelled us to found a new, independent literary periodical. We have noticed for some time that during recent years a kind of peculiar, acquiescent dependence on literary authorities has developed in our literature. We do not, of course, accuse our journals of selfishness and venality. No one in our country sells his convictions for money, as is the case almost everywhere in European journals, where writers change their odious service and their masters because others pay them more. But one can sell one's convictions not only for money. One can sell oneself, for example, out of an innate servility or fear to be thought a fool because one does not agree with the literary authorities. Mediocrity sometimes quite unselfishly trembles before opinions of literary luminaries, especially if those opinions are expressed boldly, insolently and impertinently. Quite often it is just this insolence and impertinence that provide the literary luminary with his great, though only temporary, influence on the masses. Mediocrity, for its part, in spite of its apparent arrogance, is almost always pusillanimous and submits readily. Pusillanimity begets literary servitude and there must not be any servitude in literature. The craving for literary power, literary superiority, literary prestige will induce even a distinguished old writer sometimes to undertake an activity so unexpected and strange that it willy-nilly arouses astonishment, lead his contemporaries into temptation and be sure to be passed on to posterity as some scandalous story about Russian literature of the mid-nineteenth century. And such things are occurring more and more often and such people enjoy an influence that lasts a long time, while the journals say nothing about them and indeed do not dare touch them. There are still in our literature a few fixed ideas and opinions that exist in the form of immutable truths solely because the leading literary men had declared them to be so a long time ago. Criticism gets more and more vulgar and petty. In some journals certain writers are completely ignored for fear of saying something they would not like. They engage in literary polemics for the sake of getting the better of their opponents and not for the sake of truth. Cheap skepticism, harmful by its influence on the majority of readers, successfully conceals mediocrity and is used in order to attract subscribers. The stern word of true and profound conviction is heard more and more seldom. Finally, the desire for making money, which is now so rife in literature, turns certain periodicals into essentially commercial enterprises, while literature, and the benefits it confers, is being pushed back into the background and sometimes no one bothers about it at all.

We have therefore decided to found a journal that is completely independent of literary authorities—notwithstanding our respect for them—with the aim of a bold and full exposure of all the literary quirks of our time. We undertake this exposure out of a most profound feeling of respect for Russian literature. Our journal will have no literary antipathies or predilections. We shall be quite ready to acknowledge our own mistakes and blunders, to acknowledge them in print, and we do not think we are ridiculous in being proud of that (though in anticipation). We shall not eschew polemics, either. We shall not be afraid to "tease" the literary geese occasionally; the gaggle of geese is sometimes very useful: it forecasts the weather, though it doesn't always save the Capitol. We shall pay particular attention to the section dealing with criticism. Not merely every remarkable book, but also every remarkable literary work published in other journals, will be analyzed without fail in our periodical. Criticism must not be allowed to go by default merely because books are now beginning to be serialized in journals and not published separately as before. Leaving personalities aside, ignoring everything mediocre, provided it is not harmful, *Time* will follow every movement in literature, however insignificant, drawing attention to both positive and negative facts and exposing without evasiveness mediocrity, every kind of evil intent, sham enthusiasms, misplaced pride and literary aristocratism—wherever they may appear. Everyday facts, current opinions, established principles, which have grown into clichés from too frequent use, strange and disappointing aphorisms, are as subject to criticism as a newly published book or magazine article. Our journal regards as its unalterable rule to declare frankly what it thinks of every honest literary work. A famous name makes it necessary for our judgment to be stricter and our journal will never descend to the now generally accepted trick of showering a famous writer with compliments so as to earn the right to make one unflattering remark about him. Praise is always chaste; flattery alone smells of the servants' hall.

I I

Time: OCTOBER 1861

The first year of the publication of our journal is drawing to a close and we are about to open the subscription lists for the second. The public supported us; it responded to our last year's announcement and thereby strengthened our confidence that the idea for the sake of which we had undertaken to publish our journal has been just. We do not say this because we want to boast of the fact that the support shown to us by the public has been such as has never been heard of for a long time among our periodicals. To the questions how have we served our idea, have we deceived the public in the expectations we aroused in them, or have we to any extent succeeded in our attempt to put before the public what we really believe in, we reply that we could not as yet do many things we should have liked and hoped to do. We are the first to admit it. If the public supported us to the end, to the last issue of our journal, it was because they believed in the honesty and sincerity of our idea; and this is the main thing we want and we shall not betray their trust. Almost a year has passed since we began publishing our journal and the circumstances that accompanied its publication have not shaken our conviction but strengthened it even more. We do not give up the hope of expressing our idea fully. And there is still a great deal to talk about. It is absolutely necessary to come to some decision. Events and facts must not be allowed to catch literature by surprise.

They all say that they are in favor of progress; you can't do without it, it is a *sine qua non*. But what sort of progress when we are *de facto* sitting on European textbooks? A forward movement is a normal and lawful phenomenon and God forbid that we should say anything against it. But having renounced what was futile and base in the facts of our past life, we soared into the air and almost renounced the soil itself. Without the soil nothing will grow and there will be no fruit, whereas for every fruit its own soil, its own climate, its own training is necessary. Without a firm soil under one's feet no movement forward is possible: you may slip backward or fall down

236

from the clouds. How can we possibly fail to agree that we measured many facts of our past life with too narrow a yardstick? We measured everything with our new yardstick hurriedly, our minds already made up beforehand. We were too eager to assure ourselves that we were right about everything, which means that at heart we were not sure whether we were not lying. Even as regards many facts of our lives which we thought belonged to "the realm of darkness" we failed to discern the power of the native soil, the laws of development, love. For all that we must cultivate a new, impartial and long-range view. We destroyed everything regardless simply because it happened to be old. The Lord preserve us from old forms of life. But it is not they that matter and it is not about them that we speak.

Migrants who wish to settle somewhere a thousand miles away from their own homesteads often weep, kiss the ground on which their fathers and forefathers were born; they think it ungrateful to abandon their old soil—their old mother because her breasts have withered and run dry. They take with them on their way a handful of earth, which they look upon as sacred, and they intend to bequeath this sacred handful of earth to their great-grandchildren as an eternally revered memory. But time passes and their great-grandchildren are astonished that their forebears should have so greatly revered that ordinary handful of earth. And they are right: for countless years they have had their own soil, a new soil that did service for them and that fed them. But what new soil have we got? Why, we are not even migrants. We simply soared into the air. And, indeed, our feeling now is like the feeling of an aeronaut who has risen seven thousand feet into the air. No doubt he can make many most interesting observations from such a height, observations that are perhaps a little too abstract, not very close and, above all, somehow unbearably supercilious; and yet, however much he professed to love science, he still longs to be back on earth. He is even a little frightened up there all by himself, it is hard to breathe and he could fall. For a balloon might burst like a soap bubble . . .

Let us at last agree to speak the whole truth: we love even our *Russian* land in a conventional bookish sort of way. We have become accustomed to the idea that we do not care anything about anything. We have grown so lazy that we are quite accustomed to having others do things for us, while we get everything ready-made, perhaps not so well done, but ready-made. On the other hand, a tremendous amount of vanity and malice has accumulated in us. This is not to be wondered at: sedentary life! We are craving for something to do and are angry as we lie about that there does not seem to be anything to do. Perhaps if we knew how to love, we might have found something to do; for it is possible to love even during a bilious attack. . . .

But for the time being all we have are controversies and arguments about, it is true, high matters: about Russian thought, about Russian life, about Russian science and so on. We have gone so far that some of our thinkers are asking *frankly,* "What sort of Russian thought have you in mind? What do the words *Russian soil* mean?" The frankness of these questions is a very significant fact and justifies many things. We are speaking seriously. For what it means is that, if we are not afraid to ask such questions, we want very badly to come to some decision. However, the Westerners of blessed memory were even more consistent: in extreme cases these too did not dodge the answer and declared openly that we had to become, for instance, Frenchmen at least. If they had not put it in so many words, they had at any rate opened their mouths to declare it and stopped short simply because they choked: the words stuck in their throats. If Belinsky had lived another year he would have become a Slavophile, that is to say, from the frying pan into the fire. There was nothing else left for him to do. Besides, in developing his idea, he was not afraid of any fire. He loved too much, Belinsky did! Many of our present thinkers have not gone farther than Belinsky, though they assure themselves that they have. Others refuse to acknowledge that they, too, are part of the people because they wear frock coats. Others still would like to order Russian national ideas from England, for it is generally agreed that English merchandise is best. And there are those who are just on the point of discovering new laws, a general formula for the whole of mankind, attempting to make a mold for some universal national form in which they wish to cast a universal kind of life without distinction of tribes and nationalities or, in other words, transform man into an effaced copper coin.

We shall follow the same ideas we expressed in our last year's announcement of our journal.

And though we have not said a great deal so far, we have served our cause conscientiously. What we consider to be the truth we like and hold dear. We stood up for literature. We regarded literature as an independent force and not as a means, though we recognize as lawful and normal many of the literary deviations of our time. We never bent our knee before authority. We never spared phrasemongering, egoism, self-satisfaction and pride amounting to a sacrifice of truth in others, and perhaps we were carried away to a point of hatred. We were carried away in many things—we admit it, but we are not sorry for it. We admit another mistake, too: sometimes it was with reluctance that we attacked certain opinions, which may not have been radically in agreement with our own and which may even have struck the public by their violence and unnecessary presumptuousness, but which were nonetheless honest and expressed without fear or favor, and whose intentions were honorable. We apologize for it because we promised impartial polemics. We do not think, however, that we have been too partial and we guarantee to remain impartial in the future, too. As for the polemics of ideas, we consider it necessary at the present time. Skepticism and a skeptical view kill everything, even the view itself, and in the end lapse into complete apathy and the sleep of death. For literature is today one of the main manifestations of Russian conscious life. We received everything from outside and gratis, beginning with science and ending with the most ordinary things in life; but literature we obtained by our own efforts, it is a product of our own life. That is why we love it so much and hold it so dear. That is why we pin our hopes on it.

III

Time: OCTOBER 1862

With the beginning of next year we shall enter into the third year of the publication of our journal. Our political program remains the same. We know that some of our ill-wishers are trying to distort our idea in the eyes of the public, are anxious to misunderstand it. We have many ill-wishers and it could hardly have been otherwise. We have acquired them suddenly, all at once. We have been too successful not to have aroused all sorts of hostile comments. We do not, of course, complain about it: some journal or book not only fails to arouse any comment for several years, but also fails to draw attention to itself in the literary world and among the public in general. Our experience was different and we are quite satisfied. At least we have aroused discussion and comment. This, surely, is much more flattering than to be completely ignored.

We quite naturally pay no attention to the petty and empty comments of hide-bound shouters who do not understand what we are about and who are incapable of understanding it. They fling themselves upon their prey instigated by those in whose service they are and who think for them. They are just men who never had an idea of their own. It is a sheer waste of time to talk to them. But our literature has both theoreticians and doctrinaires

240

and they have been constantly attacking us. They act consciously. They understand us and we understand them. With them we have had arguments and shall continue to have arguments. But let us explain why they have been attacking us.

With the publication of the first issue of our journal the theoreticians felt that we differed from them in many things. Though we agreed with them about the things everyone at the present time must be finally convinced of (about progress, that is), we could not agree with them about development, ideals and points of departure of the general idea. They, the administrators and the armchair students of Western ideas, at once realized that we had been talking of the soil and attacked us furiously, accusing us of phrasemongering, declaring that "soil" was just a meaningless word that we do not understand ourselves and that we have invented for the sake of creating an effect. And yet they understood us thoroughly and this is proved by the very fury of their attacks. One does not attack empty and meaningless words and mere chasing after effect with such bitterness. We repeat: there have been many publications that pretended to say something new and that were chasing after effect and yet failed to attract the slightest attention of the theoreticians. But they attacked us with quite unprecedented fury.

They knew perfectly well that an appeal to a return to the soil and union with our national sources were not empty sounds, empty words invented for the sake of creating an effect. Those words were a reminder and a reproach which made them realize that they are not standing on firm ground but floating in the air. We have joined issue against the theoreticians who not only refuse to acknowledge that *everything* is contained in nationality but reject the very concept of nationality. All they are concerned about are the principles of universal humanity and they believe that, in the course of their further development, nationalities will become effaced like old coins and that everything will merge into one form, one general type, which they are not, however, able to define themselves. This is the Western movement in its extreme form of development and without the slightest concessions. In their fury, they persecute not only the sordid and deformed aspects of different nationalities, aspects that in time are bound anyhow to give way to a correct development, but present in a misshapen form even those peculiarities of our nation which are the guarantees of its future independent development and which are the only hope of its independent and everlasting powers. In their aversion to filth and deformity, they fail to notice many things besides filth and deformity. No doubt, being sincerely anxious for the general good, they are a little too strict. Driven by their love of self-denunciation and exposure, they are only looking for "the realm of darkness" and do not see the fresh and bright sides. Inadvertently they sometimes are almost of the same opinion as the slanderers of our common people, the fine ladies and gentlemen who look down on them; without realizing it themselves, they condemn our people for their weakness and do not believe in their self-dependency. We, of course, do not confuse them with the ladies and gentlemen we have just mentioned. We understand and we know how to appreciate both the love and the generous feelings of these true friends of the common people; we have respected and we shall respect their sincere and honest activities in spite of the fact that we do not agree with them about everything. But these feelings do not prevent us from concealing our convictions. Silence would be a weakness; besides, we did not keep silent before. The theoreticians, plunging deeper and deeper into their bookish wisdom, not only do not understand the common people, they also despise them, without, needless to say, any evil intention and, as it were, by accident. We are absolutely convinced that the most intelligent of them think that they have only to speak to the people for ten minutes to be fully understood, whereas the people would not even listen to them whatever they might be saying. The common people still do not believe in the sincerity of our sympathy and are indeed surprised that we should not have our own but their interests at heart and are puzzled as to why we should be doing it all. For hitherto we have been speaking to the people in a kind of bird language. But the theoreticians stubbornly refuse to see that, and for all we know, not only arguments but also facts would not convince them that they are floating in the air in utter solitude and without any support from the soil and that all the things they are so keen on are of no importance whatsoever.

As for our doctrinaires, they do not, of course, repudiate our national character, but they look down upon it. The whole point is that one has to understand the common people and their national character. They understand them in the old way; they believe in all sorts of social strata. The doctrinaires want to teach the common people, they are willing to write popular books for them (though so far they do not know how to write even one); they have not grasped the most important axiom, that the common people will read their books only when the doctrinaires themselves with all their hearts and minds become one with the common people and not merely pretend to be their friends, that is to say, when the interests of the common people become our interests and our interests their interests. But such a return to the soil is quite unthinkable to them. It is not for nothing that they go on talking so much about their learning, their professorial distinctions and almost their ranks. The most gracious of them will go so far as to raise the common people to *their* level, teaching them every science and in this way educating them to *their* own standard. They do not understand our expression, "Union with our national source," and attack us for it, as though it were some mysterious formula concealing some mysterious meaning. "What's so new about the national character?" they say to us. "We've heard it discussed a thousand times before, and in the not so distant past, either. Why do you consider it to be a new idea? What is so special about it?"

243

We repeat: everything depends on the right under-standing of the words "national character." There is no mysterious meaning in our words about a union. One has to understand it literally. Yes, literally. We are still con-vinced that we have expressed ourselves clearly. We have declared frankly and we declare again that it is necessary to unite with the common people morally and as closely as possible; that it is necessary to merge with them com-pletely and become one with them morally. That is what we have said and are still saying. The theoreticians and the doctrinaires cannot of course understand such a com-plete union. Those who for a hundred and fifty years have been accustomed to regarding themselves as a special kind of society cannot understand this either. We agree that it is a little difficult to understand it entirely. It is sometimes difficult to understand from books what is very easily understood from the facts of real life. However, we need not go into too detailed explanations. We are not afraid for our idea. It has never happened that a just idea should not be understood at last. Life and reality are for us. And, good Lord, the objections some people raise against us: they are afraid for science, for civilization! "What will happen to science?" they clamor. "And have we all to turn the clock back, to put on peasant smocks and get registered?" To this we reply now, too, that there is no need to be afraid for science. Science is an eternal and superior force, inherent in everybody and necessary for everybody. It will never disappear and will find a place for itself everywhere. As for the peasant smocks, there will perhaps not be any left when we achieve a true un-derstanding of the meaning of the common people and the national character. Perhaps it will be just because we shall return to the common people in all sincerity and not as a joke that the peasant smocks will begin to disappear. This observation, of course, we make for the timid ones and those who have never done a stroke of honest work in their lives as a special consolation for them. We have the utmost respect for the peasant smocks. It is an honest apparel and there is no need to have an aversion to it.

We freely confess that we find it more difficult to publish a journal than anyone else. We are introducing a new idea about the fullest possible national and moral independence, we are vindicating Russia, our national roots, our national principles. We have to speak passionately, we have to prove and convince. Those who expose the evils of our time have it much easier than we. All they have to do is to expose, attack and whistle to be understood by everybody, frequently without having to give an account of what exactly they are exposing, attacking or whistling at. God preserve us from talking disdainfully about the exposers. We have always respected an honest, generous and bold exposure, and if an exposure is based on a profound and vital idea, it cannot be achieved easily. We are exposers ourselves; we refer you to our journal during the whole of its existence. All we wish to say is that it is easier for an exposer to find sympathy. Even those who think differently from him or those who are not entirely in agreement with him are ready to join him for the sake of exposure. Needless to say, we and the exposers, both the sensible and the cheap ones, repudiate the rottenness of some of our borrowed jetsam and our native filth. We are all for regeneration and we are so no less than they. But we do not want to throw out the gold together with the dirt, while life and experience convince us that there is in our earth something of our own, something native that is deposited in the natural, ancestral foundations of the Russian character and customs and that our salvation lies in the soil and the common people. It is not for nothing that these people defended their independence. Some of our cheap critics jeer at our common people; they say they did nothing and achieved nothing. It is easy not to want to see. It is just this that we want to show. The future will show it too when science develops; we believe in it. The very fact that our people have preserved their independence for so many centuries is significant, for any other people in their place after so many trials and tribulations, which Providence visited upon them a thousand times, would have long ago turned into a tribe of savages. There may be a lot of filth on it. But in their views on life, in some of their already formed communes and societies, there is so much meaning, so much hope for the future, that the Western ideals cannot be entirely accepted by us. They will never suit us, because they have not been the result either of our history or of our common heritage, because there were other circumstances that brought them about and because the right of nationality is stronger than any right that may exist among other peoples and societies. This is too well-known an axiom. Must we repeat it? Must we also repeat that those who consider that our common people are bankrupt of any ideas, those who are ready to condemn them for their filth and deformity and regard them as incapable of independence are despising them? As a matter of fact, it is only our journal that fully recognizes our national independence even in the form in which it expresses itself now. We proceed straight from this, from our nationality as an independent point of departure, just as it is now—ill-favored, savage, after living for two hundred years in gloomy solitude. But we believe that all the methods of its development reside in it. We do not go to ancient Moscow for our ideals; we do not claim that before everything has been transformed in the German fashion our nation cannot be regarded as proper material for a future everlasting edifice. We proceed straight from what already exists and all we want is the fullest possible freedom of development for what already exists. Given such freedom of development, we believe in the Russian future; we believe in its independent possibility.

And who knows, perhaps we shall be called obscurantists by people who do not realize that we are perhaps going incomparably farther and deeper than they, our exposers. For we believe that in the *natural* sources of the character and customs of Russia there are incomparably more wholesome and sensible guarantees of progress and regeneration than in the idle dreams of the warmest regenerators of the West who have already condemned their civilization and are looking for a way out of it. Let us take one of many examples. There, in the West, they consider the extreme and most unattainable ideal of prosperity something that we have already possessed for a long time in a natural though not in a developed and properly organized state. For instance, with the exception of a limited number of artisans and poor civil servants, no one in our country should be born poor. Every human being, on emerging from his mother's womb, is already registered as belonging to a piece of land, so that he really should not die of hunger. If in spite of this we still have so many poor, it is solely because these national principles still remain in their natural, undeveloped state, without even being brought to the attention of our most progressive people. But with February 19 a new life has already begun.

We have remained inactive for a long time as though bewitched by a terrible force. Meanwhile, a powerful desire for living began to manifest itself in our society. It is through this desire to live that society will attain an awareness that it could achieve nothing without a union with the common people. But this coming-out onto the right road must take place without any leaps, without any dangerous *salto mortale*. We are the first to desire this. That is why we are so anxious that the union with the common people should be made at the right time. At any rate, progress and life are better than stagnation and dull, heavy sleep, which reduce everything to numbness and paralysis. Our society already has sufficient enthusiasm and a precious and sacred power anxious to find an application and a solution. Therefore, God grant that this power be given some legal and normal solution. No doubt, any freedom granted for finding such a solution, even the freedom of the press, would not exceed the lawful limits and would take a normal, regular course. We wish it sincerely.

247

We respect every noble beginning; in our age, when everything is in a state of confusion and when everywhere the questions of foundations and principles are debated, we try to take a broader and more impartial view, without losing our distinctive personality, for of course we have our own convictions which we are ready to defend against anybody. But for all that, we sympathize warmly with everything that is honest and sincere.

But we hate the empty-headed shouters, who disgrace everything they touch, who befoul some pure and honest idea by the very fact of being in favor of it: the whistlers, who whistle for bread and merely for the sake of whistling; the people who ride on a stolen phrase as a child rides on a stick, and who whip themselves up with the little whip of routine liberalism. Their convictions do not cost these gentlemen anything. They do not acquire them by suffering. They are quite ready to sell them without a moment's hesitation for what they had bought them. They are always on the side of those who are stronger. With them it is only words, words, words, and we have had enough of words; it is time we had a bird in hand.

We are not afraid of authorities and we despise servility in literature. And there is a lot of this servility in existence, especially in recent times, when everything in literature has grown turbid. Let us say one more thing: we hope that during the past two years the public has become convinced of the impartiality of our journal. We are particularly proud of that. We commend what we consider to be good even in the journals hostile to us and we have never praised anything out of friendship. Alas, has one really to boast about so simple a matter today?

We are for literature, we are for art. We believe in their independence and irresistible power. Only the most extreme theoretician on the one hand and the most vulgar mediocrity on the other can deny this power. But mediocrity and routine depend on someone else's authority. Ignorance is their staunchest ally. We are not for art for art's sake. We have made that sufficiently clear. And the fiction we have published proves that, too, quite sufficiently.

I V

Epoch: SEPTEMBER 1864

. . . The political orientation of our journal will remain the same. The study and analysis of our social and rural problems from a Russian national point of view will, as before, remain the chief aim of our publication. We are convinced as before that there can be no progress in our society before we become real Russians. And the mark of a real Russian at the present moment is to know what things in Russia today one ought not to abuse. One must not denigrate, one must not condemn, one must know how to love—this is what a real Russian is most in need of today. For he who is capable of loving and is not mistaken in what in particular he ought to love in Russia knows also what he ought to condemn. He knows unmistakably also what to wish, what to censure, what to complain about and what to solicit; and he is able to say a useful word, too, better and more understandably than anyone else, much better than any professional exposer. We have learned to abuse many things in our country, and, to do people justice, the abuse was sometimes very clever and even to the point. But more often these people talk absolute nonsense, for which our coming generations will blush for us. But, on the other hand, we have still not learned and we still do not know what one ought *not* to abuse in Russia. No one will praise us for that, either. Indeed, what is it all of us are mostly mistaken and so furiously in disagreement about? Is it about the precise nature of the good things we possess? If only we could reach an agreement about this point, we should at once also agree about the bad things we possess. The inability to do so is a dangerous and damning sign for our society. That is why the common people still do not understand us. The common people and we love our country in different ways: this is the chief thing that divides us. Our expression "soil" strikes others as funny, though they know perfectly well what it means. The soil is something to which everyone clings and holds on. And one holds on only to something one loves. What is it that we love and know how to love in Russia sincerely, spontaneously, with all our being? What is it that we consider so dear to us in our country? Is not the idea that we are a distinct, separate, historic entity still considered as something shameful and reactionary by many people in our country? Do not the same people consider nationality, in the highest sense of the word, as something like a disease of which all-leveling civilization will rid us?

In our view, any idea that finds its way to us from outside, however beneficial in itself, can be justified, strike root and be of real benefit to us only if, without any outside suggestions and recommendations, our national life evolved this idea naturally and practically as a result of the generally realized pressing need for it. No nationality in the world, no state that is in any way stable, has hitherto ever been formed in accordance with a program recommended and adopted from outside. Everything living came into being and lived by itself. All the best ideas and decrees in the West were evolved independently throughout the centuries as a result of an organic, spontaneous and gradual need. Those who formed the Parliament in England had, of course, no idea of the form it would take afterward. Why, then, do our exposers refuse us our own kind of life and laugh at our expression: "organic, independent life based on the soil"? But laughing disdainfully, they are themselves mistaken and confused about the contemporary facts of our national life and do not even know how to define them: organic or introduced from outside, good or bad, healthy or diseased. Unable to formulate their definitions with precision, they are beginning to be afraid of definitions and seek refuge more and more in abstractions. Our conception of good and evil, or what is harmful and harmless, is becoming more and more distorted in our sick society. Who among us, honestly speaking, knows now what is *good* and what is *evil*? Everything has become a matter of controversy and everyone talks and teaches as he pleases. In saying this, we do not, of course, claim to know everything ourselves or to have never made any mistakes. On the contrary, like everyone else, we too can be talking nonsense sincerely and conscientiously. We have said this without wishing to reproach anyone; we have merely been expressing our distress at such a state of affairs. All the same, it does seem to us that our point of view makes it possible to find out more correctly and unmistakably and define more precisely what is happening all around us (we are not praising our journal now, but our point of view). Holding this view, we cannot remain bewildered by the recent facts of our national life, not knowing what attitude to take up toward them, that is to say, afraid for our general convictions and afraid of failing to see the irresistible fact, constantly at a loss and confused and trying to resort to prudent shifting and shuffling.

No country will renounce its own life. It would rather be in difficulties than not to live at all or live the way others do. Wise men and reformers appear among different nations also organically and are successful only if they are in organic contact with their peoples. It is said that when we were discussing the amelioration of the conditions of our peasants, a French prefect published his own project in France. In his opinion, there was nothing easier than the problem of the liberation of the serfs: all one had to do was to publish a law to the effect that anyone born in Russia between such and such a date was born free. *Et c'est tout.* Easy and humane. We laughed a lot at that Frenchman, quite wrongly, in our opinion. To begin with, he has, of course, offered a solution in accordance with the ideals and the spirit of his own nation and could not but be a Frenchman in doing so. According to the view of a Frenchman, a man without land, a proletarian, is still to be regarded as a free man. But according to the fundamental, inherently Russian idea, one cannot be a Russian without a general right to land. Western science and life have only reached the stage of personal right to property, so how could the Frenchman be wrong? How could he be wrong if we ourselves reduce our fraternal, wide conception of our right to own land to the much lower level of economic development according to Western science? Second, in what way are our own thinkers and theoreticians better than this Frenchman?

Every healthy land power believes in itself and its own truth and this is the first sign of a people's health. This belief of a people in itself and in its own powers is not a sign of stagnation but, on the contrary, a guarantee of life and energy and does not by any means exclude progress and prosperity. Without this faith, for instance, the White Russian people would never have been able to resist and save themselves. People, however coarse they may be, will never cling to something that is rubbish, provided they realize that it is rubbish, and will always be able to change it according to their own will and judgment. Neither have any people ever given up science of their own free will. On the contrary, if anyone respects science sincerely, it is the common people. But here again the same condition applies: it is absolutely necessary that the people should arrive at their respect for science themselves, by their own independent living process. It is then that they will come to you themselves and ask you to teach them. Otherwise they will never accept science from you and will never give up their own rubbish. But people come to their conclusions in a practical way, through their own experience. And to possess one's own incontestable experience, one must live independently, one must undergo this experience in practical life. So what is the conclusion we derive from this? The conclusion is that one must never interfere with independent national life, but, on the contrary, do all one can to widen this life and as much as possible be in favor of its individuality and originality. Our own Russian progress can come into being and manifest itself in any way only in as far as our national life develops and the sphere of its independent activity widens, in both the economic and the spiritual field, as it gradually frees itself from its centuries-long seclusion. We repeat: this is what we must first of all try to achieve and assist in bringing about. Till then we shall only get a confusion of tongues in our educated society and its extreme spiritual impotence. We see how our present generation is vanishing by itself, feebly and without a trace, manifesting itself by the strange and, for posterity, inconceivable admissions of "superfluous men." We speak, of course, only of the elect among "the superfluous" men (for there are elect even among the "superfluous"); mediocrity, on the other hand, still believes in itself, and what's so annoying is that it does not notice that it is making way to new, unknown, healthy Russian forces, brought at last to life during the present reign. And thank God for that!

Of course, in our literature, we all, all except a tiny minority, love Russia, wish her to be prosperous and seek everything that is good for her. One thing, though, is not so good: we all wish and search each in his own way and crawl in all directions like crabs out of a sack. Almost all of us have quarreled with one another several times and are no longer on speaking terms. It is true that there was nothing else left for us to do, for we are solitary people who are for the time being unwanted and unwelcomed by anyone. All the same, if some signs of independent life did sometimes appear in our society (that is to say, among its educated section), it was only in literature. That is why, in spite of the confusion of tongues and conceptions and all sorts of quarrels, we still regard our literature with respect as a vital factor and, in its own way, an absolutely organic one.

253

In condemning others for their quarrels and dissensions, we do not wish to exclude ourselves; we did not escape our fate, either; we do not apologize or justify ourselves; we can say one thing, though: what always mattered to us was not getting the better in an argument but truth. No doubt there are people among our literary men who have become clever at adopting opinions that are likely to help them in their careers, but even here it is not a question of any serious phenomenon but rather of a ridiculous one; a case of comic mischances, wounded pride and pretensions that are more like caricatures than sad and shameful facts. We promise to follow attentively the progress and development of our literature and draw attention to everything that we think significant and remarkable. We shall not try to avoid arguments and serious polemics and are even ready to attack everything that we consider harmful to our social conscience; but we shall avoid any *personal* polemics, though we do not claim that we have not hitherto been guilty of it, even if accidentally. We loathe such polemics and we cannot understand how one can bring oneself to defame people by abuse and deliberate libel, as some do simply because they do not happen to share their own point of view. We cannot and will not praise what is bad and justify it *out of principle*. To publish a journal so that every one of its sections should stress the facts that seem to confirm our views, to see in any given thing what we wish to see in it and ignore everything else and deliberately overlook it, to call it a "movement" and to imagine that this is correct, impartial and honest—this we cannot do, either. This is not our view of a "movement." We are not afraid of investigation, of light or of accepted authorities. We are always ready to praise what is good even in our most fierce opponents. We are also ready to admit our mistakes as soon as they are pointed out to us.

SMALL SKETCHES

SMALL SKETCHES

(*During a Journey*)

I MEAN A JOURNEY on a steamer or a railway. The former roads, the journeys "with a horse," as a peasant expressed it recently, we, the inhabitants of our capital cities, are beginning to forget completely. I suppose journeys by road, too, are quite different now from what they used to be. I, at any rate, have heard a great deal of interest from all sorts of people, and as I do not entirely believe the stories of the roads being infested with brigands everywhere, I am planning to go on a journey almost every summer somewhere in the wilds of the country along the old roads for my own edification and information. Meanwhile, be so kind as to follow me to the railway station.

Well, here we are. We enter one of the carriages. Russians of the educated classes are always an object of interest to an observer eager for instruction, especially when they appear in a mass in public. More especially during a journey. In our country, railway passengers are not particularly keen on talking to each other, and it is the first moments of a journey that are especially characteristic in this respect. Everyone seems to regard his fellow passengers with suspicion, everyone is feeling uncomfortable, everyone eyes his neighbor with the most mistrustful curiosity invariably mixed with hostility, trying at the same time to pretend, not only that they do not notice, but also that they do not want to notice one another.

257

In the compartments patronized by the intelligentsia the first moments of looking for a place and getting to know your fellow travelers are for many people absolutely moments of suffering, impossible anywhere else—abroad, for instance, just because there everyone knows his place and at once finds it. In our country, however, it is difficult to find one's place without the guard or, generally, some guide—not only anywhere on the train, but even with a reservation in your hand. I am not talking only about arguments about seats. If you just happen to ask some fellow passenger sitting next to you something of urgent importance, you do it in a most cowardly and sickly sweet tone of voice, as though you had made up your mind to do something extremely dangerous. The man you put your question to, of course, immediately gets frightened and stares at you with quite extraordinary nervousness; and though he replies much more patiently and sweetly than the person who asked him for the information, both of them all the same, in spite of their mutual sweetness, continue to feel certain entirely unjustifiable misgivings: "I only hope it doesn't degenerate into a fight!" Though this supposition rarely comes to anything, at the first moment, wherever Russian educated people gather among strangers, it invariably flashes through all the educated Russian heads, though only in the form of an unconscious sensation.

"And this," one pessimist with a "bleeding heart" observed to me furiously, "is not only because they do not trust the European nature of their education, but because deep inside his European soul every one of them is all but convinced that he deserves a good beating. No, I'm sorry," the same pessimist corrected himself with a shout, "I am wrong. Our European will never admit that he deserves a good beating. To attribute such an admission to him would be doing him too great an honor. The consciousness, however remote, that you deserve to be flogged is already the beginning of virtue, and what do we know of virtue? Telling lies to oneself is implanted in us much more deeply than in others. With us everyone can feel that he deserves to be flogged, but he never admits even to himself that he really and truly ought to get a good thrashing."

I am quoting this pessimist's opinion because of its rather eccentric nature and because it is somewhat interesting; I am not entirely in agreement with him, being inclined to a more conciliatory opinion.

The second period of the traveling Russian educated society, that is, the period of starting a conversation, always begins soon after the first, that is, the period of apprehensive spying-out the land and nervous twitchings. It is only at first that they do not seem to know how to start a conversation; afterward they get so carried away that sometimes it is impossible to stop them. Nothing can be done about it: extremism is our national characteristic. Besides, it is also the fault of our mediocrity; say what you like, but there are terribly few talented people among us, in whatever field you may look for them; on the other hand, there are terribly many people belonging to what is called "the golden mean." The golden mean is something cowardly, impersonal and at the same time also bragging and provocative. People are afraid to start a conversation so as not to compromise themselves. They feel ashamed and shy: the intelligent ones because they consider every independent step to be beneath their intellect, and the foolish ones out of pride. But as Russians are by nature the most gregarious and communicative people in the whole world, what happens is that during the first quarter of an hour they get so worn out with suffering and finally become so oppressed with one another's presence that they are only too glad for anyone to break the ice and start any kind of conversation. In the train this breaking of the ice sometimes takes place in a most amusing fashion, but nearly always somewhat differently than on steamers (I shall explain that later). Sometimes a man of genius suddenly and quite unexpectedly makes an appearance amid this general mediocrity and "golden mean" and by his example carries everyone along with him. All of a sudden, amid the general tense silence and convulsive but vain attempts to seem natural, such a man, without any invitation, without the affected lisping that, according to our ideas, is so much a part of a real gentleman who suddenly finds himself among strangers, and without the slightest horrible affectation in the pronunciation of the most ordinary words, which has become such a habit with certain of our gentlemen after the liberation of the serfs as a sign of their extreme dissatisfaction with the reform—such a man, on the contrary, begins telling everyone and nc one in particular in the tones of a gentleman of a previous era no more and no less than the story of his life—to the utter and incredulous amazement of all his listeners. At first they all look flustered and exchange questioning glances, though cheered by the thought that "At all events it is he who is talking and not we." Such a story, full of the most intimate and sometimes even quite wonderful details, can go on for half an hour, an hour or, indeed, as long as you please.

Gradually everyone in the compartment begins to feel the magic influence of genius; they become aware of this because, to their own surprise, they do not feel at all offended in spite of their wish to be so. Above all, everyone is amazed at the fact that the gentleman does not seem to flatter anyone; he is not trying to ingratiate himself with anyone, nor does he seem to be in need of any listener as some ordinary, mediocre chatterer is in need of one; he speaks simply because he is no longer able to keep his hidden treasure to himself. "If you like, listen to me, if not, don't, it makes no difference to me. I'm telling you all this merely to make you happy"—this is, I think, what he might have said; yet he does not even say this, because everyone now feels absolutely free, whereas at the very beginning (well, it could hardly have been otherwise), when he had just begun speaking so unexpectedly, everyone, of course, during the first few moments, felt as though personally offended. Gradually they begin to pluck up courage, start interrupting him, putting questions to him, going into details, but, of course with all the necessary precautions. The gentleman at once listens to what they have to say with quite extraordinary courtesy, though without any sign of wishing to curry favor with them, corrects them if they are wrong about anything and immediately agrees with them if they are even just a little bit right. But whether he corrects them or agrees with them, he undoubtedly gives them pleasure; they feel it with all their being every minute and they are quite at a loss to decide how he manages to do it so well. For example, a moment before they have been contradicting him, and though he had been saying just the opposite, it now seems that he had really been saying the thing they have found it necessary to point out to him and is in complete agreement with them, so that they feel flattered while he keeps his own independence untarnished. Sometimes, indeed, one of them feels so overwhelmingly flattered after one of his successful objections in the presence of the other passengers that he begins to regard the public with the air of a real conqueror for all his intelligence. Such is the fascination of true talent. Oh, he had seen everything, known everything, been everywhere, gone everywhere, sat everywhere, and it was only the day before that everyone had said good-by to him. Why, thirty years ago he had been to see a celebrated cabinet minister of the last reign, and then the Governor-General B., to complain about a relative of his who had quite recently won general fame by the publication of his memoirs, and B. at once asked him to sit down and offered him a cigar. He had smoked several of B.'s cigars and he had never smoked such superb cigars again in his life. Well, he looks about fifty, so he might well have remembered B.; but only the day before he was seeing off the famous Jewish financier F. before he had escaped abroad, and just a minute before their parting, F. disclosed all his latest secrets to him, so that he is now the only man in Russia who knows all the facts about that affair. While he was talking about B., his listeners were still calm, particularly as the whole story seemed to turn on smoking cigars; but at the mention of F., even the more serious of his listeners assumed an air of the greatest interest; they even bent forward to listen to him and swallowed every word of his avidly without the slightest sign of envy at the fact that he was on friendly terms with so eminent a financier while they were not. The balloon *Jules-Favre*—one blow and it bursts; in the Franco-Prussian war he flew in quite a different one; this one was new. Here *un mot de Jules-Favre*, about Prince Bismarck—he had whispered it a year before in the prince's ear in Paris as a secret—still, you needn't believe him if you don't want to; it can be seen that the teller of the story does not seem to care very much whether you believe him or not, but he certainly knows everything about the new excise laws as well as what has been said the other day at the meeting of the State Council; indeed, he knows it better than the members of the State Council themselves. For instance, the joke about publicans cracked during the discussion. Everyone smiles and looks very interested because it certainly sounds genuine. A colonel of engineers informs his neighbor in an undertone that he heard almost the same thing the day before and that he thinks it is almost certainly true. The prestige of the narrator at once rises. He had traveled by rail with G. a thousand times, a thou-sand times, and this is quite a different kind of story; here is a story that nobody knows and nothing at all is going to happen to the Stranger, for a certain person is involved in it and that person is determined to put an end to the affair. The person had forgiven and said that he would not intervene, but only to a certain point, and as both had gone beyond that point, he would, of course, intervene. He was there himself and he had seen it all; as a matter of fact, he had signed his name in the post office register as a witness. But, of course, there was going to be a reconciliation. But about hounds and about a certain breed of hounds our gentleman speaks as though his whole aim in life revolved around hounds. In the end, of course, it is as clear as can be to all his listeners that he had never traveled with G., did not sign his name in the register, did not smoke cigars with B., had never owned a hound and had never been within a mile of the State Council; nevertheless, everyone, even an expert, realizes that he knows everything and quite well too, so that there is absolutely no reason in the world why one should not listen to him, for there is no danger of compromising oneself. But what matters is not the news but the pleasure of listening to it. One can notice, however, an omission in the know-all's stories: he hardly mentions the school question, the universities, classicism or realism, or even literature, as though he does not even suspect the existence of those subjects. You ask yourself who he can be and you can't find an answer. All you know is that he is a man of undoubted talent, but you cannot guess his profession. You feel, however, that he is a type and, like every other sharply defined type, must needs belong to some profession, and that if you cannot guess which, it is because you are ignorant of that particular type and have not met it before. His appearance in particular puzzles you: he is immaculately dressed and apparently he has a first-class tailor: in the summer he wears summer clothes, a calamanco jacket and trousers, spats and a summer hat, but it looks rather threadbare on him, so if he did have a good tailor, he *did* have him and perhaps has him no longer. He is tall, spare, yes, very spare indeed; carries himself very straight, more so than his age warrants; looks straight before him; has a bold presence and quite an irresistibly dignified air; not a trace of impudence—on the contrary, personified benevolence, but without sugariness. A small wedge-shaped beard, going gray, not altogether an imperial, but of an unmistakably nobleman's trim. His manners are irreproachable and we are generally very impressed by good manners. Does not seem to smoke a lot, perhaps not at all. No luggage—just a small bag in the shape of a reticule, undoubtedly of foreign make but now quite unpardona-

263

bly worn, that is all. It all ends by the gentleman's sudden and unaccountable disappearance, usually at some unimportant country station, at a junction of someplace nobody ever travels to. After his departure, someone who had been listening to him more attentively than anybody else and nodding in agreement declares in a loud voice that he was telling "terrible lies." There are always two or three men who believed everything he said and who are eager to start an argument; opposing them are two others who had been resentful from the very start, and if they did not at once object to the stories of "the liar," it was simply because they were too shocked to speak. Now they heatedly protest. The public laughs. A man who had hitherto been very modestly and gravely silent offers a suggestion, based on personal knowledge, that the gentleman belongs "to a special type of the old nobility, a type of nobleman who has been a hanger-on for most of his life, a small landowner, perhaps, a ne'er-do-well from his mother's womb, who really does have connections in the highest social circles and has spent all his life in the company of great noblemen and statesmen—a highly useful type in society, especially in the wilds of the country, where he is often to be seen and where he is particularly fond of visiting." For some reason, everyone agrees with this unexpected opinion at once, and, the arguments cease; but the ice is broken and conversation starts. Even without joining in the conversation, everyone feels at home and they all feel that they can breathe freely at last. And yet it is all thanks to the man of genius.

However, if one does not take into account the so-called accidental brawls and a few inevitable "surprises," sometimes rather unpleasant ones and, unfortunately, still too frequent, it is quite possible to have a pleasant trip on our railways. With precautions, of course.

I have already expressed my opinion in writing that the problem of having a pleasant and cheerful trip on our railways consists mainly of "knowing how to let other people tell lies and trying to believe them as much as possible, for then you, too, will be allowed to tell a little lie with effect, that is, if you should be tempted to do so; the benefit is therefore mutual." Here I should like to confirm that I am still of the same opinion and that I mean it not at all in a humorous but in a most positive sense. As for lies and especially railway lies, I have already stated at the time that I do not really consider lying to be a vice but, on the contrary, a natural function of our national good humor. We have practically no vicious liars; on the contrary, all Russian liars are kindly people. I am not saying, though, that they are good.

Nevertheless, one is sometimes surprised to hear quite a new kind of conversation in a railway compartment: people discussing serious subjects, such as the eagerness of people to teach all sorts of social subjects of public importance. Such teachers do come forward. I have written about this too, but what is particularly striking is that the majority of those who wish to learn and study are women, married and unmarried, and not at all with close-cropped heads, I assure you. Tell me, where today can you meet a married or unmarried woman in a railway carriage or even in the street without a book? Perhaps I am exaggerating a little, but it cannot be denied that a great many of them walk about with books, not with novels, but with books dealing with pedagogic or scientific subjects. They even read Tacitus in translation. In short, there is a great deal of zeal and eagerness, most noble and enlightened, but—this somehow does not prove anything. There is nothing easier, for example, than to persuade such a girl student to believe anything you like, especially if you know how to talk well. A deeply religious woman will suddenly, before your very eyes, express her agreement with almost atheistic theories and with a recommendation to apply them. As for pedagogy, all sorts of queer ideas are dinned into them and the things they are capable of believing is hardly credible! One cannot help shuddering at the thought that on her return home, such a woman will at once begin to apply the things she had been taught to her children and to her husband. The only comforting thing is that she probably did not understand her teacher and that at home she will be saved by her motherly instinct and common sense, which has been very strong in Russian women ever since the beginning of Russian history. But common sense is one thing and the need of real and true scientific education quite another, and this is not the sort of thing you glean from books while reading them in railway carriages. Here the most praiseworthy steps can be turned into lamentable ones.

Another good thing about our railways is that—again, not counting all sorts of "accidents"—one can travel almost incognito all the way, in silence and without speaking to anyone, if one really doesn't wish to talk. Today it is only the priests who start a conversation with you by asking who you are, where you are going, on what business and what your expectations are. But it seems that even this benign type is about to disappear. On the contrary, even in this case there have recently been unexpected encounters such as one can hardly believe are possible.

On the steamers, as I have already said, the conversations are started in a somewhat different way from those on the railways. There are natural reasons for this, but, to begin with, the public is a more *select* one. I am of course referring only to the first-class passengers, the public *aft*. The public on the bow, that is to say, the second-class passengers, are hardly worth talking about, for they are just ordinary passengers. There you find the small fry, bundles of luggage, a mob of people, widows and orphans, mothers breast-feeding their babies, whole co-operative associations of workmen, peasants and their wives with loaves of black bread in sacks, stewards, the galley. The first-class public, everywhere and at all times, completely ignores the second-class public and has no conception whatever about it. Perhaps the opinion that the first-class passengers on a steamer are always even more *select* than the same kind of public in the first-class carriages on the railways may appear to be strange. As a matter of fact, it is not true, for as soon as the passengers disembark and arrive at their respective homes, they lower their tone, which becomes natural. But while the family is on board, it quite involuntarily raises its tone insufferably to that of high-society people, and this is done solely in order to appear no worse than anyone else. The reason for this is that on board a steamer there is more elbow room and more leisure for showing off than on a railway; therefore, as I have said, the reason is quite a natural one. On board a steamer, people are not so huddled together, the public does not run the risk of forming a dense *crowd,* one is not in such a terrific hurry, one is not so much on the spur of necessity, one does not depend on the bell, on the last minute, on sleeping or crying children. Here you are not forced to reveal some of your instincts in such natural and exaggerated forms. On the contrary, everything here is like a formal drawing room. On going out on deck, you are like a man entering a house in response to an invitation. At the same time you are compelled to share the company of the other passengers for the five or six hours of your journey or perhaps even for a whole day, and there is no doubt in your mind that it can't be helped and that you would have to make the acquaintance of your fellow passengers. The ladies are almost always better dressed on a steamer than in a railway carriage, your children are wearing their most charming summer clothes, if, that is, you have any respect for yourself. No doubt here, too, one occasionally comes across ladies with bundles and fathers of families who behave exactly as if they were at home, some even carrying their children in their arms as well as their decorations on their chests—just in case. But these are only the lower strata of the "genuine travelers," who take the matter of a voyage seriously and in a rather plebeian fashion. They are not influenced by a higher idea but merely by a heightened instinct of self-preservation. The real public at once ignores these miserable creatures, even if they happen to sit beside them, and, anyway, they themselves realize their position immediately, and though they stick firmly to the seats for which they had paid, they meekly and completely efface themselves.

In short, space and time change conditions radically. Here even the "man of genius" could not embark on his autobiography and would be forced to find another approach. Indeed, he might not have been successful at all. Here a conversation can hardly be started because of being cooped up together on a journey. Above all, the tone of the conversation must be strictly "drawing room," that is the whole point. It goes without saying that if the passengers are not acquainted with one another it is more difficult to break the ice than in a railway carriage. General conversation on a steamer is almost unthinkable. But personal suffering as a result of the lies one is telling and the airs one is putting on, especially during the first moments of the journey, is considerably greater than in a railway carriage. However small your powers of observation, you will most likely be surprised at the amount of lying one is capable of in a quarter of an hour, how many lies those splendidly attired ladies as well as their self-respecting spouses will tell. All this, of course, you come across in its purest form more often on so-called pleasure trips during the holidays, on trips lasting at most from two to six hours. They tell lies with everything: their manners, their beautiful poses; everyone seems to be looking at himself in a glass every moment. The squeaky scansion of sentences, both unnatural and disgusting, the most incredible pronunciation of words in a way that no one would bring himself to pronounce if he had the slightest respect for himself are, I believe, more often heard on steamers than in railway carriages. Fathers and mothers of families (that is, before conversation on deck has become general) try to speak to one another in unnaturally loud voices, doing their utmost to pretend that they are not in the least impressed by their new surroundings, but failing ignominiously to keep it up: they talk to each other of all sorts of trifling matters that are terribly out of place and do not conform to the situation in which they find themselves, and sometimes a husband will be talking to his wife as if he were a stranger addressing a woman he had met for the first time at a strange house. They cut short their conversation suddenly and without any obvious cause and, generally, exchange words in a rather abrupt fashion; they look round at their neighbors nervously and uneasily, listen to the replies they get from one another with distrust and even with panic and sometimes even blush for one another. If, however, they should happen, that is to say, be forced by some circumstance, to talk about something that has a direct bearing on their present situation and about which every husband might have to talk to his wife at the beginning of a journey—about some household or family matter, for example, about their children, about little Michael's cough or about the fresh breeze lifting little Sonia's dress a little too high, they look abashed and begin to whisper quickly to make sure that no one can hear them, though there is nothing indecent or reprehensible in what they are saying; on the contrary, everything they say is worthy of the highest respect, particularly as all those children and their worries about them are shared by everyone on this steamer. But it is this very simple idea that does not enter their heads and, indeed, even to harbor it seems to them beneath their dignity. In fact, every family group is more inclined, though rather enviously, to accept almost every other family group on deck as, first, a notch higher in the social scale than itself and, second, as inhabiting a sort of special world, something like the ballet, but by no manner of means like themselves, with household worries, children, nursemaids, an empty purse, money owing to the shopkeeper and so on. Such an idea would have been much too offensive to them, even cheerless; it would have destroyed their ideals, as it were.

On steamers, the people who are first to begin talking to one another, almost before everyone else, are the governesses—speaking in French, of course, to their charges. In middle-class families the governesses are mostly of one sort, that is, very young girls, all having recently completed their studies at school, all of them not really good-looking, though never absolutely ugly, either. They all wear dark dresses, all with pinched-in waists, all trying to show a leg, all with an expression of proud modesty on their faces, but at the same time looking entirely at ease, a sign of their irreproachable innocence, all fanatically devoted to their duties, everyone clasping a French or English volume of highly moral contents, mostly some travel book. There, you see, she picks up a two-year-old girl in her arms and, without taking her eyes off her, calls in a severe but affectionate voice to her six-year-old sister, who has been playing too long with other children (the little girl wears a straw hat with forget-me-nots, a short white dress with lace trimmings and a pair of most charming children's booties), saying in her governess French: Vera, *venez ici,* and invariably stressing the connective sound *zi.* The mother of the little girls, a plump woman of the highest society (her husband is there too, a gentleman of European aspect, quite obviously a landowner, very tall, stout rather than lean, his hair beginning to go gray, a fair beard, a little too long but of unmistakably Parisian cut, in a white fluffy hat, summer clothes, of rather doubtful rank)—the mother immediately realizes that by picking up two-year-old Nina, the governess is undertaking a task not agreed to in their contract. Wishing to make it clear to the young girl that she is not going to be beholden to her for that, she remarks in a quite extraordinarily affectionate voice, which, however, excludes any idea in the governess's mind of her right to any further familiarity, that she supposes little Nina to be a little heavy for her and that she ought to call for the nursemaid; at the same time she looks around anxiously and imperiously for the nursemaid, who has slipped away unnoticed. Her European husband makes an identical movement, as though wishing to run off to look for the nursemaid, but he changes his mind and stays there, unable to conceal his satisfaction at having changed his mind and not having gone to look for the nursemaid. He seems to be running errands for his wife, a lady of a higher social standing than he, and cannot help resenting it. The governess hastens to put her ladyship's mind at rest by assuring her in a loud and singsong voice that she "really loves darling Nina," accompanying her words with a passionate kiss. There follows another peremptory shout to Vera with the same *zici*, but love simply flashes from the eyes of the loyal girl even for the guilty Vera. At last Vera comes running up, skipping and hypocritically fawning upon her governess (a six-year-old child, still regarded as a little angel, and already lying and cheating!). The mam'selle at once, without any need whatever, begins to set right the little girl's straw hat: that was the only reason she had called her. . . .

The journey on the steamer lasts only six hours and it is almost a pleasure trip. I repeat: a journey lasting two or three days somewhere on the Volga and from Kronstadt to Ostende would no doubt have had quite a different effect: necessity would have dispelled the drawing-room atmosphere, the ballet would have faded and been torn in shreds and the shamefully concealed instincts would have leapt out without the least attempt at disguise and, indeed, rejoicing in their right to leap out. But there is a great difference between three days and six hours, and everything remains in its "purest state" on our steamer from beginning to end. On a lovely June day at ten o'clock in the morning we are sailing along the calm surface of a wide lake. The bow part of the ship is dropping away from the "passengers," but then there are the riff-raff there we do not want to know anything about; we, on the other hand, form, as I have already said, the *"salon."* Still, even among us there are people who are a problem everywhere and with whom you do not know what to do. For example, among our passengers is a German doctor and his family, consisting of a Mutter and three German skew-mouthed young ladies whom it is difficult to imagine any Russian marriageable male proposing to. None of our rules applies to them. The old doctor is completely at ease: he is wearing his German oilskin traveling cap of a rather stupid shape and he puts it on on purpose to show his spirit of independence, at least so it seems to us. But, as it were, in recompense for this discordant note, we have on deck a stunningly beautiful young married woman and a colonel of engineers, an elderly woman with three rather mature but highly chic daughters of Petersburg high, though not the highest, society, girls full of all sorts of mischief who quite evidently know their way about in the world. There are besides two coxcombs, a cadet officer and a cavalry officer of a famous guards regiment, who, however, keeps himself at a disdainful distance from the rest of the passengers, considering them all to be his social inferiors, a fact that apparently pleases us all no end. But it is the *authorities,* occupying the best places, who attract the greatest attention. His Excellency, however, gives the impression of a very good-natured man. He wears a cap and informal dress. Everyone finds out at once that he is a civil servant of the highest rank and, so to speak, the "boss" of the province, and it is even said that he is on his way to "inspect" something or other. It is much more likely that he is simply taking his wife and family to their summer home not far away. His wife is a remarkably handsome woman of thirty-six or -seven, a member of the highly aristocratic family of S. (a fact that is very well known on the steamer), and she is traveling with her four children (all girls, the eldest of whom is ten) and a Swiss governess, but, to the disgust of our ladies, her manners are those of a lower-middle-class woman, though she does give herself insufferable "airs." She wears her everyday clothes, "and this is now the fashion among them, among those ma-trons," one of the general's daughters drawls in an undertone, enviously examining the smart cut of the modest dress of the wife of the boss of our province. A tall, spare gentleman of about fifty-six or fifty-seven, whose hair has gone almost completely gray, also attracts considerable attention. He is sitting down by himself almost in the middle of the gangway on a folding chair with his back turned resolutely to the public and keeps looking lazily and abstractedly at the water. Everyone knows that he is a court chamberlain of the previous reign, and though he is no longer of any particular importance today, he still is, of course, a man belonging to the most exalted circles of society, a rich landowner who has spent a great deal of money in his lifetime and who for some reason has recently been wandering abroad for a rather long time. He is dressed rather carelessly in civilian clothes, but his bearing is that of an unmistakable Russian milord without even an admixture of a French hairdresser, which is quite a rarity among the genuine Russian Englishmen. He has two valets with him on the steamer and an English setter of quite remarkable beauty. The dog walks about the deck and, anxious to strike up an acquaintance, pokes his nose between the knees of the sitting passengers, evidently bestowing his favors indiscriminately on everyone in turn. And though it is a nuisance, no one objects; indeed, some of us try to stroke the dog with the air of experts who know how to appreciate the nice points of an expensive dog and who perhaps intend to acquire exactly the same breed of setter the very next morning. But, like a real aristocrat, the setter accepts our blandishments with absolute indifference and does not stay between our knees a long time, either, and though he does wag his tail a little, he does it merely out of genteel politeness, indolently and indifferently. The milord apparently has no acquaintances on board, but from his flabby and doughy face it is quite clear that he does not need anyone, not out of principle, but simply because he really does not need anyone. To the administrative importance of "the boss of the province," he, on his folding chair, is utterly indifferent, and this indifference of his is absolutely lacking in principle. But it is not difficult to guess that a conversation between him and the "boss" of the province is quite unavoidable. The administrator keeps walking past the folding chair, wishing with all his might to start a conversation. Though married to a high-society lady, he recognizes, with the straightforwardness natural to him, that he is far beneath the milord in the social scale—without, of course, any loss of personal dignity; and now he has to find a solution to this last ticklish problem. There is a gentleman of "second-class" nobility on deck and it was as a result of his efforts that the "boss" and the milord managed by chance and without any formal introduction to exchange a few words. This exchange took place after the "second-class" nobleman had informed them about the mishap that had happened to the governor of a neighboring province, also a well-known aristocrat. While abroad, this governor, in a hurry to join his family at a watering place, broke his leg in a railway carriage. Our governor was greatly struck by the news and was very anxious to learn the details of the accident. The milord knew all the details and very considerately mumbled a few words through his false teeth, without, however, looking at the governor, so that it was impossible to say whether he was talking to him or to the bearer of the sad news. The governor hovered over the folding chair with his hands behind his back, waiting for the milord to vouchsafe a few more details and unable to disguise his impatience. But the milord was most unreliable and might, in fact, suddenly fall silent and forget what he was talking about. At least, he looked like one who would behave in this manner. The "second-class" nobleman, too, was hovering over him, trembling with impatience and wondering what he could do to prevent the milord from falling silent. He conceived it to be his most sacred duty to bring the two high-placed gentlemen together and introduce them to each other.

It is a remarkable fact that many such "second-class" gentlemen can be met on a journey especially in the proximity of "elderly" personages, and they are there for the simple reason that on a train or a steamer there is nowhere you can tell them to go to. But actually they are not told to go anywhere, because they know how to make themselves useful, provided, of course, that the conditions are favorable and the time is right. Our gentleman even has some sort of order round his neck, and though he is wearing civilian clothes, they look like some kind of uniform and his cap, too, has a curious kind of band, so that he is quite presentable. Such a gentleman begins by placing himself before the superior person and, without uttering a word, by his figure alone, introduces himself as a man who will never presume to be in any way offensive: "You see, sir," he seems to say, "I am second class and it would never occur to me to pretend to be on the same level with you. I assure you, sir, I shall never try to climb to the top of the ladder. You cannot possibly take offense, sir, and I should be most happy to divert you, so that you can always look down upon me, for I know my place, sir. I shan't forget it to my dying day, sir." There can be no doubt that the reason these gentlemen are so anxious to please their superiors is because they hope to derive some benefit, but the "pure type" of such a gentleman behaves as he does without the slightest hope of gain but simply out of the sort of inspiration peculiar to civil servants; he feels that in a case like that he can be useful and this makes him genuinely happy. In circumstances like these he is so simple-hearted that even the lackey in him seems to disappear completely. In the end, he does benefit after all, for this is not only a fact but a logically inevitable result.

Everyone on deck suddenly becomes extremely interested in the conversation that is beginning between the two "superior" personages. Not that they show any wish to join in—this would have been going a little too far, but they are just as happy to look on and listen. Some of them are already taking a walk near them, but it is the "European" husband of the "society lady" who is suffering most of all. He feels that he could not only go up to them, but even join in their conversation and that, indeed, he

has a certain right to do so: high-placed officials and noblemen are one thing, but, after all, Europe is Europe,
say what you like. And he is quite sure that he can talk
about the governor who broke his leg abroad no worse
than anyone else. He is even about to stroke the setter so
as to have some subject to start with, but he draws back
his already outstretched hand and suddenly feels an irresistible urge to kick the dog. Gradually he assumes a
kind of withdrawn and offended expression, walks away
for a moment and becomes absorbed in the sparkling waters of the lake, his gaze wandering far away to the
horizon. His wife, he notices, is looking at him with most
malicious irony. He cannot bear this and he returns again
to where the two exalted gentlemen are conducting their
"conversation," walking up and down near them, like a
soul in purgatory. And if at that moment this sinless soul
is capable of hatred, it hates the "second-class" nobleman,
hates him with all the force at its command, and but for
that man nothing of what has happened would have happened.

"Te-le-graphed here," the lean milord drawls, his eyes
fixed on the setter and hardly replying to the governor,
"and im-a-gine, sir, at the first moment I was com-plete-ly
taken aback . . ."

"He isn't a relation of yours by any chance, is he?" the
governor of our province is about to ask, but resists the
temptation and waits.

"Just im-a-gine," the milord goes on mumbling inco-
herently, "his fa-mi-ly is in Carlsbad and he te-le-
graphed . . ." he repeats, the word "telegraphed" exer-
cising some strange fascination over him.

His Excellency is still waiting, though there is an expression of extreme impatience on his face. But the milord falls silent suddenly and seems to forget all about the
conversation.

"I . . . er . . . I believe, sir," the governor makes
up his mind at last to ask with an expression of shy in-

certitude, "that . . . er . . . his chief estate . . . er . . . is the province of Tver."

"Both of them are ve-ry . . . er . . . thin, Jacob and Aristarchus. Brothers, both of them. One brother is now in Bes-sa-rabia. It's Jacob who broke his leg, sir. Aristar-chus is in Bes-sa-rabia. . . ."

The governor jerks up his head and looks completely at a loss.

"Ve-ry thin, both of them. His estate belongs to his wife, sir. Née Ga-ru-nin. His wife, sir. Née Ga-ru-nin . . ."

"Oh!" exclaims the governor, looking very pleased. He seems to be glad she is "née Garunin." Now he under-stands.

"An extremely good-natured person, I believe, sir," he exclaims warmly. "I knew him . . . I . . . er . . . mean I hoped to make his acquaintance here. A most honorable man, sir!"

"Extremely good-natured, Your Excellency!" the pert little gentleman of the "second class" interjects warmly, his eyes shining with unfeigned enthusiasm. "A most good-natured man, sir! Just as you, sir, were so good as to express it just now: a most good-natured man, sir!"

Having said this, he looks around importantly at the other passengers, feeling himself morally superior to everyone else on deck.

This is more than the European gentleman, who has been wandering round the "conversation," can bear. Alas, he is fated to put up with things like that!

What was so "fateful" about that was that his wife, the "high-society lady," had as a girl been almost a friend of the wife of "the boss of the province," née S., also un-married at the time. As a matter of fact, the "high-society lady" is also "née" something or other and also regards herself as a being of a somewhat superior type than her husband. Before stepping on board, she knew perfectly well that the wife of the governor of the province would be on the same steamer and she counted on "meeting" her again. But, alas, they did not "meet" and from the very first step, from the first glance, it became abundantly clear that they could not possibly "meet"! "And it's all because of that insufferable man!"

For his part, the "insufferable man" knows perfectly well what his wife is thinking. Indeed, he has learned to know his wife's wordless thoughts all too well during the seven years he has been married to her, and yet he, too, was born in "Arcady." Why, he himself had once owned eight hundred serfs in the same province! They had spent seven years abroad on the redemption money he had received on the liberation of the serfs and the money he had got from the sale of his oakwood (over eight hundred acres!) three years ago. And now they have come back to their native country, they have spent four months there, and are now on the way—they did not know why themselves—to the ruins of their estate. What is so awful is that the "high-society lady" does not seem to want to know that they have neither redemption money nor woods left. But what annoys her most of all is that four months after their return from abroad she still has not succeeded in "meeting" anyone. The "case" of the governor's wife is not the first one. "And it's all because of him, it's all because of this nonentity!

"What if he wears a European beard! He has no rank, no connections, no social standing of any kind! He could not do anything himself. He could not think of anything. He couldn't even get married. Didn't know how to. And what made me marry him? Fell for his beard! What do I care whether he talked to John Stuart Mill or helped to unseat Thiers. He won't get anything for it here, will he? Besides, he lies. If he really had been unseating Thiers, I would have seen it. . . ."

The happy husband knows perfectly well that this is what his "society lady" is thinking at this moment. She did not tell him she wanted to "meet" the wife of the governor of the province, but he knows that if he does not arrange such a meeting, she won't let him forget it for the rest of his life. Besides, he is anxious for her to be the first to admit that he can talk not only to Mill but also to native generals at home, that he too is a somebody and not just anybody. Alas, it was this voluntary admission by his wife of his perfections that constituted the chief ambition of his remiss life, and even its aim from the very first hours of his marriage. How it all happened is too long a story, but it was so and that was all there was to it. Suddenly he makes up his mind, walks up to the milord nervously and stops in front of him looking terribly embarrassed.

"I . . . er . . . sir, was also in Carlsbad," he mumbles desperately to the governor, "and, just imagine, sir, the same thing happened to me . . . er . . . I mean with my leg. Have you been talking about Aristarchus Yakovlevich?" He turns terribly quickly to the milord, unable to endure the governor's stare.

The governor jerks up his head and gazes with some surprise at the gentleman who has run up and is trembling all over while speaking to him. But the milord does not even raise his head and—oh, horrors!—stretches out his hand, and the European gentleman feels very clearly the milord pressing against his leg with his hand and pushing him back forcibly. He gives a start, looks down and suddenly becomes conscious of the reason: having thoughtlessly placed himself between a bench and the milord's folding chair, he did not notice that he had brushed against his lordship's cane, which was beginning to slip and was about to fall from the bench. He jumps back quickly, the cane falls and the milord bends down growling to pick it up. At that very moment a terrible yelping is heard: jumping back, the gentleman sees that he had stepped on the setter's paw. The setter is yelping horribly, absurdly; the milord turns around on his folding chair and addresses the gentleman furiously in his drawling voice:

"I'd be in-fi-nitely ob-liged to you, sir, to leave my dog alone!"

"It's not me, sir," Mill's collocutor mumbles, wishing he

could sink through the deck. "It's the dog, sir. It's the dog's fault. . . ."

"You can't believe how much I have had to suffer because of that me-di-ocrity!" he hears his wife whispering furiously behind him in the ear of their governess, and he does not even hear it but feels it with all his being, while perhaps his wife has not even been whispering anything to the governess.

But it no longer makes any difference: he is not only ready to sink through the deck, but to get lost somewhere on the bow of the steamer, or hide himself under the wheel. At least, he couldn't be seen anywhere on deck for the rest of the journey.

It all ends with the administrator, unable to keep it up any longer, introducing his wife to the milord and going off to the cabin, where, thanks to the efforts of the captain, a card table has been put up. We all know our administrator's little weakness. The "second-class" gentleman has got everything ready, including the right kind of partners he could find on board. These include a civil servant supervising the construction of the nearest railway with a salary of quite astronomic dimensions, whom His Excellency had occasion to meet before, and the colonel of engineers, who, though unacquainted with the governor, agreed to make up the party. The colonel looks rather morose and a little dull (from an excess of self-importance), but he is an excellent partner. The railway official is a little trivial, but he knows how to control himself; the "second-class" nobleman, who made up the fourth of the party, behaves exactly as he is supposed to behave. The governor is very pleased.

Meanwhile, the milord becomes acquainted with the governor's wife. That she was the daughter of Count S. he has completely forgotten, but now he suddenly remembers that he knew her as a sixteen-year-old girl. The governor's wife treats him in a rather haughty and offhand manner, but this is just put on. She is knitting something and hardly looks at him; but the milord is getting more and more charming; he becomes animated, and though he mumbles and sputters, he is such an excellent raconteur (he speaks French, of course) and remembers such delightful anecdotes, such truly witty stories . . . And the society gossip he knows! The governor's wife smiles more and more often. The fascination of a charming woman has a most strange effect on his lordship. He keeps pushing his chair nearer and nearer till at last he goes completely limp and starts giggling very peculiarly. . . . The unhappy "society lady" finds it too much to bear, she get a nervous tic (*tic douleureux*), retires to the ladies' cabin together with Nina and the governess. Vinegar fomentations are applied, moans can be heard. The governess feels that "the morning is lost" and sulks unashamedly. She refuses to talk, puts Vera in a chair, and becomes absorbed in a book, which, however, she does not read.

"This is not the first time she's been acting like that during the three months she's been with me," the suffering lady thinks as she looks her up and down. "She ought to talk, she ought to! She ought to amuse me, to pity me. She's a governess, she must cringe, she must look after me. It's that contemptible man's fault, it's all his fault!" And she goes on throwing hateful glances at the girl. She is too proud to start talking to her herself. The girl meanwhile is dreaming of the Petersburg she has only just left, the side whiskers of her cousin, his friend the army officer, two students. She dreams of a place where lots of men and women students gather and where she has been invited to come.

"To hell with them," she finally decides. "I'll stay another month with these savages and if I'm still feeling bored I'll run away to Petersburg. If I don't have enough to eat, I'll become a midwife. I don't care a damn!"

The steamer at last arrives at its destination and everyone rushes to the gangway, as though eager to leave the close air of some dungeon. What a hot day! What a beautiful sky! But we do not look up at the sky. We are in a hurry. The sky won't run away.

The sky is quite an ordinary thing; the sky is a simple business; but life is anything but a simple business.

THE SURRENDER
OF METZ

Maréchal Bazaine*

A MONTH AGO THE TRIAL OF Maréchal Bazaine began at Trianon. In spite of the "critical" time and the possibility of great political changes in France, the trial of Maréchal Bazaine is followed with the utmost interest by the French as well as by the rest of Europe; indeed, the longer it goes on, the greater the interest grows. The picture of the quite recent past, so fatal for the French, is again being unfolded in vivid colors: the almost fantastic start of the terrible war, the quick, almost unheard-of fall of the dynasty, politically the most important in Europe; then all those hitherto unsolved mysteries, the vacillations of people, the conflicts, the intrigues—at the moment when France was calling upon everyone to aid her. If the French could now, at so *critical* a time for all of them, make use of this great historic lesson, they might discover in this "trial of Bazaine" even now, at its very beginning, the fatal malady that had been sapping the strength of France for such a long time.

Maréchal Bazaine has been put on trial because, having shut himself up in the first-class fortress of Metz with an enormous army and all the necessary military impedimenta and having enough provisions to withstand a long siege, he surrendered the whole of his army to the Germans. He did this not only without repulsing an attack

* *The Citizen,* October 1873.

(the Germans did not even besiege the fortress but were merely surrounding it), as has been prescribed by all the military laws for all the armies in the world, but taking no advantage of the most favorable opportunity for distracting and even weakening the enemy forces invading France. He surrendered his army with all its arms, impedimenta and banners, which he did not even attempt to destroy, no doubt at the request of the Germans and after apparently engaging in special secret negotiations with them which had nothing to do with military matters. This is the gist of the indictment. No doubt a great deal more will come out in the course of the trial, but no doubt a great deal too will remain a mystery—until history clears it up. The maréchal is accused of treason—to whom? Let us consider this question. It is interesting in view of the present condition of France.

At the end of the reign of Napoleon III Maréchal Bazaine was held to be one of the ablest generals of the Emperor's army. When, sixteen months ago, the question of his being put on trial was being discussed and written about a little too persistently, one of his fellow marshals (a pity we have forgotten which one it was, but it might have been "the most honest soldier of them all") exclaimed, "What a pity! *Il était pourtant le moins incapable de nous tous!*"—that is, "he showed himself to be *the least incapable* of us all in this war!" And it was this "least incapable" marshal who was put in command of some of the most important units of the French troops in this so rapidly and so fantastically begun war against the Prussians. There was no commander-in-chief at the time; the Emperor himself, without being a military man and without assuming the title of commander-in-chief, was in charge of many things and, of course, interfered a great deal in the conduct of the war, but that was not the chief trouble. All those old generals, Canrobert, Niel, Bourbaki, Ladmirault, Frossard and so on, now appearing as witnesses in court, speak of Bazaine with the greatest respect. Their evidence has aroused the greatest interest among the spectators.

The Surrender of Metz

Above all, they all testify to Bazaine's quite extraordinary bravery, in the battle of Saint-Privat, for instance, in which he fought in the first ranks in spite of being in command of the troops, "though," some of the marshals add, "he did not realize the importance of that battle." Whether he realized it or not, in that battle things went so far that for lack of ammunition the soldiers were forced to fire only one bullet every two minutes from their quick-firing *chassepots,* and large units of troops joined battle without having had anything to eat for the last twenty-four hours. But even that was not the chief trouble, though, as is well known, the lack of organization in the supply of the French army with provisions and weapons astonished the whole of Europe. We remember a telegram Napoleon III sent to the Empress Eugenie in Paris (long before Sedan) with the request to order in Paris as quickly as possible two thousand cast-iron caldrons. What was comforting about that telegram, at any rate, was the fact that though there was nothing to cook the meal in, they had at least the food, for otherwise why this telegraphed order to purchase caldrons? But, according to the testimony of Marshal Canrobert, the French soldiers had been fighting at Saint-Privat without having had anything to eat or drink for twenty-four hours; they had nothing to eat the next day, either, and the day after. . . . By that time, of course, the caldrons might have arrived from Paris, but —they were a little too late, as everything else all through this unusual campaign has been a little too late. The Emperor, too, was a little too late in retreating to Paris with all the troops left over after the heavy defeats, which would have been, if not the saving of him, then at least the best way out of the terrible mess he had found himself in. But what happened to him is something we have mentioned recently in one of our reviews when speaking of one of the most characteristic and fatal features of his reign, namely that, bent on strengthening and safeguarding his dynasty in France, he was forced to do a great many things that, far from bringing happiness, were most

287

definitely likely to bring unhappiness to the French nation. Thus, this powerful ruler was and continued to be, even while on his throne, not a Frenchman but merely a party man, a leader of his party. A retreat to Paris even with a routed army, but with an army all the same (an army that might very well have been of assistance to France in the struggle that followed), frightened him; he was afraid of the discontent of his country, the loss of influence, insurrection, revolution, Paris, and preferred an unconditional surrender at Sedan, throwing himself and his dynasty on the mercy of the enemy. No doubt, not everything that was said at his meeting with the King of Prussia is known to history. All the secrets will perhaps not be revealed for a long time, but it is impossible not to draw the conclusion that Napoleon III thought that he was more likely to preserve his throne by his and his *army*'s unconditional surrender. For, by surrendering his soldiers, he, of course, counted on weakening his enemies the revolutionists. The *party man* did not spare a thought for France.

Maréchal Bazaine did not think of her, either. Having shut himself up in Metz with his fairly sizable army, he almost ignored the government of national defense formed in Paris after the Emperor had been taken prisoner. He, too, preferred to surrender, and thereby deprived France of practically her last army, which could have been very useful to her even if they had been besieged in Metz, by, among other things, neutralizing a considerable number of the invading enemy forces. It is impossible to imagine that by surrendering so prematurely and in so humiliating a fashion Maréchal Bazaine did not enter into some secret arrangements with the enemy or, at any rate, that he did not accept certain promises, which, needless to say, were not kept. But even if there had not been any conditions or promises at all, it is quite clear that the marshal, like his Emperor, preferred to give up his army to the Prussians rather than to remain its custodian—for the benefit of the revolution.

The Surrender of Metz

Though the marshal is lying "gallantly" at the trial now and quite obviously intends to go on lying, he does not altogether conceal his feelings and impressions at the time of his surrender. He declares openly that there was no legal government in France at the time and that he could not consider the chaos reigning there as a serious government. Such, at any rate, is the meaning of his words in court. But "if there was no government for you, then *la France éxistait!*" exclaimed the President of the Court, the Duke of Aumale.

This was the trial's starting point. These words of the Duke created a tremendous impression among the listeners and throughout the whole of France. To the accused marshal they were evidently said to make him realize clearly that he was not being judged by a party or revolution or some illegal government which, if he liked, he need not recognize, but by France, whom he had betrayed in the interests of his party.

It is impossible to acquit a traitor to his country, but are those who are trying the traitor right?—this is the point we wanted to make. On the contrary, aren't the judges themselves guilty of the chief malady that is sapping the strength of a great nation, of the disaster that hangs over it like a dark cloud? Do they now realize this disaster and are they at all capable of realizing it? And isn't the marshal like the ancient scapegoat upon whom the sins of the entire people were dumped?

And, indeed, what could he have possibly seen at the time from Metz? Suppose the party man had given place to the citizen at the sight of the disasters that had befallen his country and he felt a sincere wish to come to her aid— what could he have discerned in the Paris of those days? It is true that after its triumph the revolution of September 4 did not proclaim a republican government but a government of national defense. But those at the head of that government could not but inspire in Bazaine, a field general and, though a party man, still an active and energetic man, a feeling of natural disgust. That mediocre maniac General Trochu, all those Garnier-Pagès, Jules Favre and the rest, though honest men and worthy of respect, were flabby, wretched mummies, banal heroic phrasemongers of every first day of every Paris revolution whom, alas, the Parisians do not seem as yet to have got tired of—those were the people his searching and observant eye saw from Metz. But even if they were mediocrities, even if whatever affairs they had been involved in while they were in power, today and in 1848, were doomed to fail, they were still citizens, honest men at heart, sons of their fatherland! But were they? They were only republicans. *La république avant tout, la république avant la France*—that was their constant war cry. That was why the marshal, had he wished to be a citizen and given up his party even for a time so as to save his country, would have had to join, not saviors of his country, but also party men. But he hated that party and could not, of course, bring himself to help it. Shortly afterward a man separated himself from those comic mediocrities of self-styled rulers and flew in a balloon to the other end of France. He proclaimed himself Minister of War and the entire nation, eager for some kind of government, at once declared him its dictator. This man showed tremendous energy; he ruled France, he raised armies, he equipped them. He is now accused by some people of squandering a great deal of money for which, they say, he could have raised and equipped five times as large an army. Gambetta is entitled to reply boldly to his accusers that in his place they would perhaps have spent five times as much money without raising a single soldier. And yet this energetic and intelligent man, with whom Bazaine would not have found it shameful to work, still proclaims, *"La république avant la France!"* Now he would no longer say that; he is patiently and cunningly waiting his turn and, whenever necessary, supports the great citizen Thiers, who had taken his place three years ago. But at heart he still believes in *la république avant la France;* he still is a party man first and foremost! (It is this, it seems, that makes him so popular with the republicans.)

And so everywhere there are parties and party men. It is true that a few comforting facts seem to have come to light during this disastrous year for the French. The Bretons, born legitimists, came forward with their leaders and fought for their country and fought bravely. With a picture of the Virgin on their banners, they joined the government of republicans and "atheists," *for the time being.* The Orleans Dukes, too, fought the enemy in the ranks of the newly recruited French army. But did they fight for their country? Now it appears quite certain that they did not. In view of their present role in France, that is, their conspiracy against France in favor of the "legitimate" king, it is permissible to conclude that three years earlier they had roused themselves in the hope that there was at last a good chance for their party, which had been waiting for it so long. And, to be sure, they were not mistaken in the possibility of such a chance: they slipped into the National Assembly in great numbers during the first election of frightened France and now constitute their own oligarchic majority in it.

Parties everywhere! It is true that if one were to add up all these parties together, the total number of their adherents (except perhaps the Communist Party) would be very small compared with the total number of Frenchmen. The rest of the Frenchmen remain indifferent. They too, as before the appearance of Gambetta in that fateful year, are crying for a dictator to ensure their lives and their livelihoods. Their motto is the well-known French proverb: *"Chacun pour soi and Dieu pour tous"* ("Everybody for himself and God for everybody"). But even here, it would seem, every man has to belong to his own party and—what can the word "Fatherland" mean to such a man?

This is the misfortune of France: the loss of the general idea of unity, its total absence! It is claimed for the legitimists that they are now trying to resurrect and implant this idea by force. But even the best of them are not thinking of it, but only of the triumph of their party. The most enthusiastic of them are not thinking even of legitimism. The accession to the throne of the Comte de Chambord is for them merely the triumph of the Pope and the Catholic Church ("Union," "Universe"). This is already a party within a party.

And so party men are now trying Maréchal Bazaine for having remained an adherent of his party! Is he not like the ancient Jewish scapegoat we have compared him to? Things have gone so far that it is quite impossible to put anyone on trial in France for quite unquestionable treason to his country, for they are all party men. But will the French realize this by finding Bazaine guilty?

THE TRITON

THE TRITON

YESTERDAY, July 27, on Yelagin Island, at sunset, the weather being exceedingly calm and lovely at the time, the ladies and gentlemen who were taking a stroll around the pond were startled by a most amusing occurrence. A triton, a "water sprite" in Russian, suddenly appeared on the surface of the pond, his green hair and beard dripping wet, and, keeping afloat on the waves, began to play about and do all sorts of tricks. He dived, screamed, laughed, splashed, knocked his strong, long, green teeth together, gnashing them at the strollers. His appearance produced the sort of excitement that is usual on such occasions. The ladies dashed toward him from all sides to offer him sweets, holding out their boxes of chocolate to him. But the mythological creature, keeping up his character of a watery satyr, began making such gestures before the ladies that all of them started running away from him with shrill laughter, hiding their more grown-up daughters in front of them, so that the triton, perceiving this, shouted a few extremely unceremonious expressions after them, which merely increased their merriment. He soon disappeared, however, leaving only a few watery circles on the surface of the water and a doubt in the mind of the public. People began to wonder and refused to believe what they had seen with their own eyes—the men, of course, the ladies insisting that it was a genuine triton, exactly like one of those on the bronze table clocks. Some declared that it must have been a certain Pierre Bobo who emerged from the waves for a lark. This theory, needless to say, did not hold water, because Pierre Bobo would have come to the surface in his cutaway coat and—his lorgnette, though it were wet. The triton, on the other hand, was exactly like the ancient statues, that is to say, without a stitch of clothing. But soon skeptics appeared who maintained that the whole thing was nothing but a political allegory, closely connected with the Near Eastern question, which had just then been resolved at the Berlin Congress.

For a few moments it was even thought to be an English trick performed by the Great Jew in pursuance of British interests with the cunning aim of diverting our public, beginning with the ladies, by a series of esthetically playful pictures from their warlike fervor. However, objections were immediately raised, based on the fact that Lord Beaconsfield had been seen in London at the time and that it was too big an honor for the Russian bear to expect his lordship to get into a Russian pond with political aims for the esthetic delectation of our ladies, that he has his own lady in London, anyway, etc., etc. But the blindness and the passion of our diplomats are uncontrollable: they began shouting that if it was not Lord Beaconsfield himself, then why should it not have been Mr. Poletika, the editor of the *Stock Exchange News*, who is so eager for peace, and that it was him the English might have chosen to represent the triton. But this theory too was soon abandoned, for though Mr. Poletika might well be able to go through the same motions as the triton, he would have lacked the latter's antique grace, for which everything is forgiven and which alone could have attracted our holiday-making ladies. Just then a certain gentleman came on the scene with the news that Mr. Poletika had at that particular hour been seen at a certain spot on the other side of Petersburg. Thus the theory of the antique triton emerged on the surface again in spite of the fact that the triton himself had long ago been sitting under the water.

What is so remarkable about this incident is that it was the ladies who were particularly in favor of the antiquity and mythological nature of the triton. They were so anxious that this should be so, of course, in order to cover up the frankness of their taste by, as it were, its classical content. In the same way we place completely nude statues in our rooms and gardens just because they are mythological figures and, therefore, also classical antiques, and never think, for example, of putting naked servants in their place, which could well have been done in the days of serfdom; it could have been done even today, particularly as the servants would have performed it all no worse and, indeed, much better than any statues; they would have been more natural, anyway. Just think of the thesis of a natural apple and a painted apple. But as there would be no mythological angle about it, it cannot be done. The discussion, conducted strictly from the point of view of pure art, had, it is said, gone so far as to be the cause of several family quarrels between husbands and their better halves, who took up the cudgels of pure art against the political and contemporary movement, which their husbands believed explained the extraordinary event. In this latter sense the opinion of our famous satirist, Mr. Shchedrin, had a special and almost colossal success. Having been present at the pond when the triton had made his appearance, he expressed his disbelief in the whole thing and, I am told, intends to include the episode in the next issue of the *Contemporary* in the section "Moderation and Accuracy."

The view of our humorist is very subtle: he believes that the triton is simply a disguised or rather a naked police officer who, at the beginning of the season and immediately after the Petersburg spring disturbances, had been ordered to spend the whole of the summer in the pond on Yelagin Island, so popular with strolling holidaymakers, so as to listen under water to criminal conversations, should such occur. This conjecture produced a stunning impression, so that even the ladies stopped arguing and fell into thought. Fortunately, our famous historical novelist, Mr. Mordavtsev, who happened to be on the spot, related a historical fact from the history of our Northern Palmyra, a fact generally forgotten and unknown, but one that made it quite clear that the creature that had come to the surface of the pond was a genuine triton and a very ancient one, too. According to the information obtained by Mr. Mordavtsev from ancient manuscripts, the very same triton had been brought to Petersburg as far back as the times of Anna Mons, with whom Peter the Great was so greatly taken that, according to Mr. Mordavtsev, he carried out his great reform in order to please her. The antique monster arrived together with two dwarfs, who had been very fashionable at the time, and the jester Balakirev. All of them had been brought from the German town of Karlsruhe, the triton in a cask of Karlsruhe water, so that, on being transferred to the Yelagin pond, he might find himself in his natural element. But when they had emptied the Karlsruhe cask into the pond, the malicious and sardonic triton, paying no attention to the fact that a great deal of money had been spent on him, dived in and never appeared on the surface again, so that he had been completely forgotten till the memorable July day of this year, when he suddenly took it into his head to remind the public of his existence. Tritons can live in ponds for hundreds of years in the greatest comfort.

Never has a scholarly explanation been taken up by the public with such enthusiasm as this one. Last of all came the Russian natural scientists, some even from other islands, such as Sechenov, Mendeleyev, Beketov, Butlerov and *tutti quanti*. But all they found was the above-mentioned circles in the water and a steadily increasing skepticism. They did not, of course, know what to make of it and stood there looking lost and denying the phenomenon, just in case. The greatest sympathy was won by one very learned professor, a zoologist: he came last of all, but he was in utter despair. He inquired eagerly of everybody about the triton and almost burst into tears at the thought that he would not see the creature again and that zoology and the world had lost such a subject. The policemen in the vicinity of the pond told the zoologist they were sorry but knew nothing about it, the military gentlemen laughed at him, the stockbrokers regarded him haughtily, and the ladies, like chatterboxes, surrounded the professor and told him merely about the triton's indecent gestures, so that our modest savant was in the end forced to stop up his ears with his fingers. The distressed professor kept prodding his stick in the water near the place where the triton had disappeared, threw pebbles into the pond, shouting "Come along, come along, here's a lump of sugar for you!" but all in vain. The triton did not come to the surface. However, all the others were quite satisfied. Add to this a lovely summer evening, the setting sun, the tight-fitting dresses of the ladies, the sweet expectation of peace in all hearts, and you will be able to finish drawing the picture yourself. The remarkable thing is that the triton uttered the few highly obscene words in excellent Russian in spite of the fact that he was a German by origin and had, besides, been born in ancient Athens at the same time as Minerva. Who had taught him Russian?—that is the question. Yes, indeed, they are certainly beginning to learn Russian in Europe! At all events, he had enlivened society, which had fallen asleep under the uproar of war, which seems to have put everyone to sleep, and awakened it to all sorts of inward questionings. Thanks for that! In this sense, one ought to pray not for one but for many tritons and not only in the Neva but also in the Moskva river, and in Kiev, Odessa and everywhere else, even in every village. In this sense one might even breed them on purpose: let them wake up society, let them all come to the surface . . . but enough, enough! The future is ahead of us. We breathe the new air with our expanded chests, eager to put more questions, so that perhaps everything, including the Russian finances, will be settled satisfactorily.

NINE LETTERS

FROM THE FOURTH AND
LAST VOLUME OF

The Letters of Dostoevsky

I. Immorality, Christ and Dichotomy

Letter to Nikolai Peterson, Disciple of the Mystical Philosopher Nikolai Fyodorov.

Petersburg,
MARCH 24, 1878

Dear Nikolai Pavlovich,

I have long ago made the necessary arrangements for the dispatch of books for the Kerensk library and I expect you must have received them all by now.

Now about the manuscript in the December unsigned letter. In my *Writer's Diary* I did not reply because I had hoped to find your address in the list of subscribers (Kerensk, postmark) and write to you personally, but I kept delaying from day to day because I did not feel too well. At last your letter of March 3 arrived and explained everything. I did not reply because I had fallen ill again. I therefore beg you to excuse this delay.

First of all a question: who is this thinker whose ideas you have communicated to me? Please let me know, if you can, his real name. He interests me greatly. Let me know at least something in greater detail about him as a person, if at all possible, that is.

I can now tell you that I am virtually entirely in agreement with his ideas. I read them as if they were my own. Today I read them (anonymously) to Vladimir Sergeyevich Solovyov, our young philosopher, who is now delivering lectures on religion, lectures that are attended by almost a thousand people. I read to him your exposition of the thinker's ideas, for in his ideas I found a great deal that is similar to mine. This gave us a wonderful *two hours*. Solovyov is greatly in sympathy with your thinker and intends to put forward almost the same ideas in his next lecture (he has still four out of twelve lectures left). But here is a positive and firm question which I intended to put to you already last December:

The most essential thing in the exposition of your thinker's ideas is without a doubt the debt of resurrection owed to our ancestors who have lived before us, a debt which, if repaid, would put an end to the births of children and bring about what is described in the Gospels and the Apocalypse as the First Resurrection. But in your exposition, I am sorry to say, not everything is clearly defined. How do you understand this resurrection of our ancestors, in what form do you imagine it and believe it to be? I mean, do you understand it as something abstract, allegorical, for example as Renan does, who understands it as human consciousness becoming so clearsighted at the end of mankind's existence on earth as to make it possible for those men of the future to have a clear idea of what, for instance, has been the influence of a certain ancestor on humanity, how he exerted that influence and so on, and that to such a degree the role of every man who lived before would be clear to everyone and his actions would be elucidated (by science, by the force of analogy), and all this to such an extent that we shall, of course, also realize how much those who lived before us have each by their influence upon us become embodied in us and hence also in those last people on earth, allknowing and harmonious, who will bring the human race to an end.

Or:

Your thinker imagines directly and literally, as religion hints at, that the resurrection will be real and personal, that the gulf that separates us from the souls of our ancestors will be filled up, will be conquered and, having been conquered by death, they will be resurrected not only in our consciousness, not allegorically, but actually, personally, in their bodies. (N.B. Not, of course, in their present bodies, for the very fact of immortality, the abolition of marriage and of the birth of children shows that the bodies at the first resurrection, which has been fixed to take place on earth, will be different bodies, not the present ones, that is to say, as perhaps Christ's body was after His resurrection and before His ascension.)

An answer to this question is necessary—otherwise everything is unintelligible. I must tell you that we, that is, Solovyov and myself, at any rate, believe in a real, literal and personal resurrection and that it will come to pass on earth.

Therefore, please let me know, my dear Nikolai Pavlovich, if you can and wish, your thinker's views and, if possible, in detail.

As to the question what a people's school should be, I am of course entirely in agreement with you.

My address is the same as before, that is, near the Greek Church, Greek Avenue, Strubinsky's house, apartment No. 6.

N.B. This address till May 15 (though you can address your letters there after that date, too, in spite of the fact that I shall not be there, for the letters will be forwarded to me.)

Yours with deep respect,

F. Dostoevsky

Dostoevsky's views on immortality were pretty well consistent during most of his adult life. This becomes abundantly clear from a comparison of some of his reflections on the subject jotted down in his notebook on April 16, 1864, a day after the death of his first wife, Maria Dmitriyevna, with the above letter written fourteen years later and only two years before his own death.

The full text of this hitherto unpublished entry is as follows:

"April 16. Masha lies on the table. Will I ever see Masha again?

"To love your neighbor as yourself, according to Christ's commandment, is impossible. The law of personality on earth prevents it. The *I* prevents it [And yet] Christ alone was able to do it, but Christ is eternal, an eternal ideal toward which man aspires and is bound to aspire according to nature's law. And yet after Christ's appearance as *an ideal of man in the flesh* it became as clear as daylight that the highest and last development of personality must (at the very end of its development, at the very point of achieving its goal) reach the point at which man will find out, realize and become convinced, utterly convinced, that the greatest use a man can make of his personality, of the fullest development of his *I,* is in one way or another to destroy this *I,* to give himself up wholly to all and everyone, selflessly and wholeheartedly. And that is the greatest happiness.

"Thus the law of *I* becomes merged into the law of humanism, and in this union of the two both I and everyone (apparently extremes), while destroying themselves for each other, achieve at the same time the highest goal of one's own individual development, each one separately.

"This is Christ's heaven. The whole history of humanity and, to a certain extent, of each individual is merely the development, the struggle, the aspiration for and the achievement of this goal.

"Once achieved, humanity will no longer have to develop any further, that is to say, to struggle and aspire toward this ideal, to catch a glimpse of it every time it falls from grace, to strive for its achievement everlastingly, or, in other words, there will no longer be any necessity to live.

"But to attempt to achieve so great a goal is in my opinion absolutely senseless, if on the attainment of the goal everything becomes extinct and disappears, that is to say, if at the attainment of the goal there is no life left for man.

"Hence there is a future life in heaven.

"What it is like, where it is, on what planet, in what center, that is, in what final center, or, in other words, in some universal world, that is to say, in God—we do not know. We only know one aspect of the nature of the future human being, who can hardly be called man, hence we can have no idea what sort of being it will be."

To define one of the characteristics of this future being, Dostoevsky quotes St. Mark 12:25: "For when they shall rise from the dead, they neither marry nor are given in marriage; but are as the angels which are in heaven." He therefore makes the following deduction: "They neither marry nor are given in marriage, for there is no longer any need for it: there is no need to develop and attain one's goal by means of the replacement of generations. Man on earth," he concludes, "strives for an ideal which is contrary to his nature. When man does not carry out the law of striving for the ideal, that is to say, when he does not sacrifice his *I* to the love for other people or another human being (Masha and I), he becomes aware of suffering and he calls this condition sin. Hence man is bound to suffer continuously and this suffering is balanced by the heavenly joy of the fulfillment of the law, that is, by sacrifice. This is where the earthly balance manifests itself. Otherwise life on earth would be meaningless."

Letter to Yekaterina Yunge, daughter of the Vice-President of the Russian Academy of Art.

Petersburg,
APRIL 11, 1880

Dear Katerina Fyodorovna,

I am sorry I have been so long answering your wonderful and very friendly letter. Do not consider it negligence on my part. I wanted to say something sincere and heartfelt in my reply, but I am afraid my life goes on in such a disorderly fashion and even turmoil that I really very rarely belong to myself. Even now when I have at last found a free minute to write to you I shall hardly be able to put down even a small part of what my heart would have liked to tell you. I cannot but value your opinion of me: the lines your mother showed me from your letter to her touched me and indeed surprised me. I know that I have many faults as a writer and I am always the first to feel dissatisfied with myself. I must tell you that in some gloomy moments of inward analysis I am only too painfully aware that I have literally not expressed a twentieth part of what I wished to express and perhaps even could have expressed. What comforts me is my constant hope that if one day God will grant me enough inspiration and strength I shall express myself more fully, that I'd express everything, in short, that is locked in my heart and in my imagination. At the recent dissertation of the young philosopher Vladimir Solovyov (son of the historian), who was defending his treatise for a doctorate, he

307

made the following profound remark: "Mankind," he said, "I am deeply convinced, *knows much more* than it has hitherto succeeded in expressing in science and art." Well, the same is true to me: I feel that much more is hidden in me than I was able so far to express as a writer. But, all the same, speaking without any false modesty, I can't help feeling that in what I have already expressed I have said something that has come straight from the heart and that is true. And I assure you solemnly that though I have met with more sympathy than perhaps I deserve, the literary critics, even if they praised me (which was seldom), spoke of me in so superficial and facile a manner that they seemed not to have noticed at all what I gave birth to with so much pain in my heart and what poured out so truthfully from my soul. So now you can judge what a great pleasure it was to read so subtle and profound an appraisal of me as a writer in your letter to your mother.

But I keep talking of myself, though it is difficult not to talk of oneself when addressing so profound and sympathetic a critic as you. You write about yourself, about the state of your mind at the present moment. I know you are an artist, a painter. Let me give you a piece of advice straight from the heart. Do not give up your art but devote yourself even more than ever before to it. I know, I have heard—forgive me—that you are not very happy. Living in solitude and tormenting yourself with your memories, you are liable to make your life too dismal. There is only one refuge, one remedy: art and creation. Do not attempt, at least for the time being, to write your autobiography: you might find it a very painful task. Forgive me for trying to give you advice. I'd very much like to see you and have a talk with you. After the sort of letter you wrote to me you have become dear to me, a human being near to my heart.

What do you mean by complaining about your dichotomy? Why, it's a most ordinary characteristic of people, who, it is true, are not altogether ordinary. It is something peculiar to human nature as a whole, though it is very rarely met with in such force as in you. That is why you are so close to me, for I too suffer from absolutely the same kind of dichotomy and I have done so all my life. It is a great torment, but a great delight, too. It is a sign of a powerful awareness, of a need to give an account of yourself, of the presence in your nature of the recognition of some moral duty toward yourself and toward mankind. This is the meaning of your dichotomy. Had you not been so mentally developed, had you been more limited, you would have been less conscientious and you would not have suffered from that dichotomy. On the contrary, you would have suffered from great conceit. Nevertheless this dichotomy is a great torment. My dear Katerina Fyodorovna, do you believe in Christ and His promises? If you do (or wish to believe very much), give yourself up to Him fully and the torments of this dichotomy will be greatly alleviated and you will obtain spiritual consolation, and this is the main thing.

I am sorry to have written such a confused letter. But I'm afraid you don't know what a wretched letter writer I am and how I dread writing letters. But I shall always reply to you, if you will write to me again. Having found a friend like you, I shall hate losing her. Meanwhile good-by.

Your devoted friend and kindred in soul,

F. Dostoevsky

Excuse the untidiness of my letter, the corrections, etc.

Yekaterina Yunge was not only an artist but also a social worker. She died in 1898 at the age of fifty-five after writing her autobiography, which made her famous. Her correspondence with Dostoevsky began after her letters to her mother, in which she spoke enthusiastically of *The Brothers Karamazov*, had been shown to Dostoevsky by Countess Sofia Tolstoy, a close friend of her mother's. Having received Dostoevsky's expression of thanks for her analysis of his great novel through her mother, she wrote him a long letter in which she expressed her admiration of him "as a writer and thinker" and described her concern for the dichotomy of her character which forced her always to do things she was conscious she ought not to do. In reply, Dostoevsky wrote the above characteristic letter.

III. THE BROTHERS KARAMAZOV:
A REQUEST

---

*Letter to Vladimir Mikhailov,
writer and pedagogue.*

Petersburg,
MARCH 16, 1878

Dear Vladimir Vasilyevich,

I received your wonderful, intelligent and sympathetic letter on November 19 of last year and now it is March 16, 1878. And yet it is only now that I am answering you—can you forgive me? It is true that in the December issue of my *Writer's Diary*, which came out in January, there were a few words addressed to you, but that does not make it any easier. I am not trying to justify myself, but there are two reasons I should like to put forward: a too morbid and disturbed state of mind up to the very last number of my *Writer's Diary*. I simply decided not to reply to any of my correspondents until the publication of the last number. Well, after that and almost till the other day—deterioration in my health, repeated epileptic attacks and a feeling of deep depression. The second reason—my terrible, invincible and quite appalling aversion to writing letters. I love to receive letters, but I find it almost impossible and indeed quite absurd to write letters myself. Besides, I simply have no talent for expressing myself in letters. I write a letter and suddenly I receive in reply an opinion or a retort on certain ideas I was supposed to have expressed in that letter which I could not possibly have expressed. If I ever get into hell, I shall most certainly be sentenced to write a dozen letters a day for my sins. No less. This is the second reason, which I beg you to believe.

Your letter produced a wonderful impression on me and I felt at once that you were a man after my own heart. I receive many friendly letters, but I have not many such correspondents as you. I feel that you are a man *close* to my heart and now that life is passing and one wants so much to live and do things, now meeting a man so close to one's heart fills one with gladness and strengthens one's hopes. There are, then, men in Russia, quite a lot of them, in fact, who are her life and strength. It is they who will save her, if only they could unite. It is in order to unite with you that I press your hand warmly with all my heart and reply to you.

I read the whole of your letter three times and I hope you will forgive me for letting someone else read it too. I want to spread your ideas here, to make some people here understand your (true) Russian spirit. (I have read your letter, among others, to Apollon Nikolayevich Maykov, the poet. He was enraptured by it and even took it home with him.) I agree in many things with that man.

I shall write nothing about the details of your letter. One could write a great deal about what is happening here, but I can't write briefly and, anyway, I can't write letters. But if you ask me something, that is to say, if you want to get a reply from me about something, I shall reply, I promise. And now one request: you are not unwilling to write to me, as you say in your letter. I value this very greatly and *I count on you*. Among other things, what interested me very much in your letter was that you were very fond of children and that you liked to be in their company. So this is what I'd like to ask you, dear Vladimir Vasilyevich. I am contemplating writing a big novel and I hope to start on it soon. In this novel there will be a great number of children, most of them young children between the ages of seven and fifteen. There will be many of them. I am studying them and, in fact, I have studied them all my life. I am very fond of them and I have children of my own. But the observation of a man like you (I realize it) will be priceless to me. So please write to me about *children, anything you know about them yourself*. About the Petersburg children who used to call you uncle and about the Yelisavetgrad children, and about any others you know. (Incidents, habits, answers, words and sayings, features, family life, religion, wickedness and innocence; nature and teacher, Latin, etc., etc.—in a word, anything you yourself know about them.) You will be of immense help to me, I shall be very grateful and shall be waiting impatiently for the information. I hope to be in Petersburg till May 15, after which I shall probably be in Staraya Russa (with my children). Till May 15 my address will therefore be the same.

I am enclosing a photograph of myself and I ask you again to forgive me. I may have been uncivil to you, but I like you.

And now *au revoir*. Believe in my sincerity and my profoundest respect for you.

All yours,
Fyodor Dostoevsky

Mikhailov is the author of *Stories Told to a Twelve-Year-Old Boy*. His letter to Dostoevsky has not been preserved. During the Russo-Turkish war of 1877 he was active in the Red Cross and it was apparently to him that Dostoevsky addressed the following notice in the December issue of his *Writer's Diary* he mentions in his letter: "I press warmly the hand of the correspondent who sent me a letter dealing with the Red Cross. I am very grateful to him and I ask him to go on writing to me. I shall certainly send him what he requested."

IV. The Brothers Karamazov: An Elucidation

Letter to an Unknown Correspondent.

Petersburg,
NOVEMBER 8, 1879

Dear Madam,

It was the servant Smerdyakov who killed old Karamazov. All the details will become clear during the subsequent development of the novel. Ivan Fyodorovich only took an indirect and distant part in the murder solely because he refrained (intentionally) from dissuading Smerdyakov during their conversation before his departure for Moscow and failed to express to him clearly and categorically his disgust at the murder he (Smerdyakov) was planning (which Ivan Fyodorovich clearly perceived) and in this way *seemed* to have given his *permission* to Smerdyakov to commit the crime. Smerdyakov, on the other hand, needed this *permission*. The reason for this will again be explained later. Dmitry Fyodorovich is quite innocent of his father's murder.

When Dmitry Fyodorovich jumped off the fence and with his handkerchief began to wipe the blood off the head of the old servant he seemed by his words, "Bad luck, old man," etc., to have told the reader that he was *not* a parricide. If he had killed his father and, ten minutes later, Grigory, he would not have got down from the fence to the servant who had collapsed on the ground, except perhaps to make sure whether an important witness of his crime was alive or not. But he seemed not only sorry for the old man, he even went on to say, "Bad luck, old man," etc. If he had killed his father, he would not have been standing over the dead body of the servant uttering words of commiseration. It is not only the subject of the novel that is important to its reader, but also a certain knowledge of a man's soul (psychology), which every author has a right to expect from his readers.

However, I am flattered by your interest in my novel and I remain, Madam, with the utmost respect,

Your obedient servant,

F. Dostoevsky

The letter was written in reply in the inquiry of a woman correspondent who was obviously puzzled (as well she might be) by the ending of chapter IV of the seventh book of *The Brothers Karamazov,* which had just then been published in the October issue of the *Russian Herald.* Dostoevsky rather unfairly makes his readers believe that Mitya was about to kill his father by interrupting his narrative at the crucial moment with the sentence: "Mitya was beside himself and suddenly pulled the brass pestle out of his pocket. . . ."

V. Children's Reading

Letter to an Unknown Correspondent.

Petersburg,
December 19, 1880

Dear Nikolai Alexandrovich,

Important as the questions many people write to me about are, I have made up my mind that, having undertaken to renew the publication of my *Writer's Diary*, I ought to stop my correspondence with them: the publication of a monthly journal is such a heavy burden and I have so little strength left that if I were to reply to all the letters and inquiries (and there are hundreds of them), I should have no time left to do my writing and indeed anything at all. You will therefore excuse me if I reply to your letter very briefly.

You do not mention how old your son is, so I shall merely make a general statement: give your son to read only those books that produce *beautiful impressions or give rise to lofty thoughts.* If he is over sixteen, let him read Zhukovsky, Pushkin, Lermontov. If he is fond of poetry, let him also read Schiller, Goethe and Shakespeare in translations in Herbel's edition. He must read Turgenev, Ostrovsky and Leo Tolstoy, especially Leo Tolstoy. (Gogol without a doubt must be read in his entirely.) In short, all the Russian classics. It would be a good thing if he liked history. Let him read Solovyov, Schloesser's *World History* and historical works like William Prescott's

Conquest of Mexico. Finally, let him read Walter Scott and Dickens in translations, though these translations are difficult to obtain. Well, I have already given you quite a number of items. If he reads it all attentively and willingly, he will become a literarily cultured person. If you wish, you can let him have Belinsky too. But wait a little longer before you let him read other critics. If he is under sixteen, let him have the same books and merely ask yourself whether he would be able to understand them. If he is, give them to him. Dickens and Walter Scott can be given to children of thirteen.

But, of course, the scriptures above all, the New Testament in translation. If he can read it in the original (I mean Church Slavonic), all the better.

The New Testament and the Acts of the Apostles are *sine qua non.*

It is not I but my wife who runs a bookselling business, though, of course, it is my responsibility. It is rather difficult to compile a catalogue of all the above-mentioned books, for many of them are difficult to obtain, but the prices of some of them are included for your information.

Wishing you every success in your undertaking,

I remain,

Your obedient servant,

Fyodor Dostoevsky

It is clear from this letter that Dostoevsky wrote it at the instigation of his wife, Anna, who had just then started a bookselling business under the name of Fyodor Dostoevsky, Booksellers. The last page of the letter contains a list of books in Anna's handwriting.

VI. A Page from the Past

Letter to a Forgotten Friend.

Petersburg,
MARCH 27, 1878

Dear Leonid Vasilyevich,

I hope you have already received the *Diary* for the last
two years. It was posted after your letter.

Your friendly and warm reminder of our past life in
Petersburg, our meetings and the people we used to know
disturbed me. But do you know what worried me in particular? The fact that I have *completely forgotten* not only
you but also Yurasov, whom you mention in your letter.
You are not confusing me with my third brother, Nikolai
Mikhailovich, are you? I must tell you that I suffer from
epilepsy, which deprives me completely of my memory,
especially of certain events. I don't know if you will believe
me, but I do not recognize people in the street to whom I
was introduced only a month before. In addition, I completely forget my own works. This winter I reread one of
my novels—*Crime and Punishment*—which I wrote ten
years ago, and more than two thirds of the novel was completely unfamiliar to me, just as if I had not written it, to
such an extent had I managed to forget it. Still, I can't
help thinking that, surely, I could not be so forgetful as
not to remember a man whom I used to visit (though as

317

far back as in 1860), at whose house I met all sorts of people. Yurasov, for instance. I simply cannot remember Yurasov now. I repeat, are you sure you are not mistaken?

Nevertheless, I can see from your letter that you *have* met me and that you do know me.

As for the people of those days, the people who had come with a *new* word, they have most certainly done their work and have had their day. It is no less certain that new people are coming (or will come soon), so that there is nothing to grieve over or to be sad about. Let us be worthy of meeting them and recognizing them. With your mind and heart you will not of course reject them or let them pass by without recognition. It is a tremendous time for Russia now and we have reached a most interesting point. . . .

I would have liked to send you a photograph of myself so that you could decide for yourself whether you are mistaken or not. But I am afraid I have not got one. I have given them all away and I am very sorry I cannot send you one.

Let me press your hand warmly,

Your obedient servant,
Fyodor Dostoevsky

Nothing much is known of Leonid Grigoryev, to whom this letter is addressed, except that he lived at Anapa "among the common people." Nikolai Yurasov, on the other hand, is known from his name being mentioned by Chekhov, who met him in Nice and found him to be "a most excellent fellow, a model of goodness and a man of indefatigable energy." He was an artist by profession, but at the time Chekhov knew him he was writing a play dealing "with the life of Russians in Nice. He reads the proofs," Chekhov wrote to a friend on March 5, 1899, "and coughs over them."

VII. A Famous Writer's Troubles: Impostors and Literary Small Fry

Letter to an Unsuccessful Inventor.

Petersburg,
MAY 6, 1878

My dear Iosif Nikolayevich,

I have read your letter with the utmost surprise. You write first: "You *probably* know that my military-technical project, with which I specially arrived in Petersburg before Easter, has failed to attract the attention of the government. . . ." But, my dear sir, why should I be expected to know that? You were so good as to pay me a visit once and after that I never saw you again and (it goes without saying) never heard of you. And now you suddenly choose me to be your *rapporteur* and demand that I should submit your project to His Highness, and you add the following strange lines: "In short, I am *absolutely* sure that in the present case you are most certainly the best man for the role *which fate itself seems to have thrust upon you.*"

These are terrible words, my dear sir: *fate*(!) thrusts upon me such an awful burden and yet who am I and what am I? I am a sick man who the doctors insist should leave Petersburg to take the waters abroad and, besides, I happen to be burdened with a family and have to take my children for a cure at the watering place of Staraya Russa. And, last but not least, I have to work for a living and I have my own cherished dreams and plans. For instance, I have just made plans for writing a new novel and this summer, in spite of my cure abroad (for I have no rest), I intend and indeed I must sit down to it. But now it would seem I have to give everything up, for "fate itself" has chosen me, since, according to you, in this particular case "I am the best man for the role which fate itself seems to have thrust upon me." So that I have to abandon my children and my work, forget all about my health, don a frock coat and try to obtain an audience with His Highness in Kronstadt or Sveaborg, solicit, petition, write reports, etc.

Now seriously. As I was thinking over this strange business, that is to say, the strange nature of your letter and your proposition, it occurred to me that you must have been driven to make it by someone else. For, you see, it is impossible that you who did not consider it necessary to inform me about your affairs or to honor me with a visit before your departure from Petersburg should suddenly appoint me your representative, your *rapporteur,* adding that it is a decision of *fate itself!* Are you quite sure that it was not Varvara Ivanovna Pribytkova who made you believe that I would be ready to do you this service at once, leaving aside all my own affairs and flying off on your business wherever I was told to go. I confess I am almost sure that in some way or other she must be involved here. Many women like to make promises, to patronize, to put in a word for someone—and so she told you that so far as I was concerned she could twist me around her little finger. But let me assure you that I know the lady only very slightly and that she has never said anything to me about your affairs. Three days before I received your letter she suddenly came to see me with a strange request to open some box and your package—I do not know what for. I believed it was to be a witness of something for some reason. I realized, of course, that she wanted to dump something on me and make me responsible for something, *but I refused to have anything to do with it,* for I understood very well what it would have involved me in if I agreed to open the box and the package. That was all that happened between us. *I never promised her anything, I never heard anything from her,* so that the whole thing descended upon me like a bolt from the blue.

Be that as it may, I should like to make it quite clear to you that it is physically impossible for me to be of any service to you because I shall be leaving Petersburg in a day or two, first for Staraya Russa, and that I shall not be back till autumn.

And now, accept the assurances of my sincere respect and devotion,

Yours,

F. Dostoevsky

P.S. For God's sake, excuse the corrections and do not consider it negligence on my part. I cannot write without corrections.

Iosif Nikolayevich Livchak, a teacher of a Vilna secondary school, first met Dostoevsky in the spring of 1877, at the beginning of the Russo-Turkish war, when he arrived in Petersburg with a plan for the ferrying of troops across rivers. He was closely connected with the spiritualist movement, which was rather in vogue in Russia at the time, and was a friend of Varvara Pribytkova, a well-known spiritualist. His Highness mentioned in the letter is the Grand Duke Konstantin Nikolayevich, commander-in-chief of the Russian navy.

VIII. Letter to an Unsuccessful Writer

*Letter to Alexander Voyevodin,
journalist and scholar.*

Petersburg,
APRIL 24, 1878

Dear Alexander Dmitriyevich,

You will no doubt realize that I was unable to reply to your letter of March 16 at once because I had to see your manuscript first. But I am sorry I could not read it immediately, because I had not the time or the health even for my own most pressing affairs, let alone for those of other people.

I have, besides, to tell you that there was a great deal I could not understand in your letter. You write: "reply categorically, yes or no," and at the same time you add: "I have nothing to lose." What then am I to reply to? Shall I write about your subject of suicide? But I hardly think you were expecting a reply from me in a letter. It is quite impossible to write a letter on such a subject, all the more so since I know neither you personally nor your ideas. From your manuscript I find it very difficult to form an opinion of you. One could conclude that you were a highly sensitive man who loved art and was interested in contemporary literary trends. But this is not enough. Moreover, though I have read more than half your manuscript, I found it to be so confused and so personal (I mean it

322

seems to have been written for you alone) that I confess it gave me a great deal of labor but provided very few explanations.

Does your question "yes or no?" refer to *The Diary of a Schoolboy*? But I could hardly find the heading of that chapter and I am afraid I did not quite grasp what it was about. Are you writing a story or are they genuine letters? Finally, you state that you have a hundred pages. Where are those hundred pages? In short, I repeat I am entirely in the dark.

If you would like to call on me, you will always find me at home between two and three in the afternoons or eight to nine in the evenings. Perhaps you will be able to explain something to me.

I thank you for your kind words about me and I assure you I know how to value them.

Always at your service,
Fyodor Dostoevsky

Voyevodin's book *On the Banks of the Neva* was only published in 1901. He was obsessed by the problem of suicide, which forms the central theme of the book, whose hero, a would-be suicide, keeps proving to himself that he has a right to commit suicide but is at the same time afraid of death. The subject of suicide interested Dostoevsky greatly, as is shown in the case of Kirilov, one of the characters in *The Devils*.

IX. LETTER TO AN UNSUCCESSFUL WRITER

Letter to Pelageya Guseva, minor lady novelist.

> Petersburg,
> Kuznechny Pereulok,
> Near Vladimir Church,
> House No. 5, Flat No. 10.
> OCTOBER 15, 1880

Dear Pelageya Yegorovna,

Instead of reproaching me so bitterly, you ought to have borne in mind just a little the fact that there might be accidents and all sorts of other circumstances. I spent all summer with my family in Staraya Russa (a spa) and have only returned to Petersburg five days ago. Your first letter of July, addressed to the *European Herald*, reached me very late, at the end of August. And what could I possibly have done in Staraya Russa for you so far as *Ogonyok* is concerned, a magazine I do not know and am doing my best not to know? I did not reply to you—I'm sure you won't believe me why: because if there is a man condemned to hard labor, it is I. I spent four years in a convict prison in Siberia, but my life and my work there were much more tolerable than my present life. From June 15 to October 1 I have written about twenty printers' sheets of my novel and three printers' sheets of my *Writer's Diary*. And yet I cannot write just anyhow. I must write artistically. I owe it to the god of poetry, the success of what I have written and, literally, to the whole of the reading public of Russia who are waiting for the end of my novel. That is why I literally sat writing day and night. From August till today I have not answered a single letter and I am snowed under with letters and requests. I assure you I have not the time to read a single book or even newspapers. I have not even time to talk to my children. And I do not talk to them. My health too is bad. You can't imagine how bad. The chronic catarrh of my respiratory organs has turned into emphysema—an incurable disease (breathlessness, not enough air) and my days are numbered. My epilepsy, too, has grown more violent from overwork. You at least are well, one must have pity. Even if you do complain of ill-health, your illness is not fatal and may the Lord grant you many more years of good health, and—well—you must forgive me.

Your second letter with reproaches of September I received only the other day. All my letters came to this apartment and were not forwarded to Staraya Russa as a result of my own wrong instructions (owing to a misunderstanding, of course) and I got ten letters all at once.

I know no one on *Ogonyok* and please note I have no connections with the editors of any other magazine. They are almost all my enemies—I don't know why. My position, on the other hand, is such that I cannot run about editorial offices and ask for favors: yesterday they abused me and today I appear there to talk to the man who had abused me. That is literally impossible for me. However, I shall do my best to get your manuscript back from *Ogonyok*. But where am I to send it? Every literary hack I visit to beg to publish your novel will look upon me as someone who is trying to get goodness only knows what favors from him. On the other hand, I ought really to read your manuscript first and I have literally not a free moment even for my most sacred and most pressing duties: I am terribly behind-hand with everything, I have neglected everything, not to mention myself. It is dark now,

six o'clock in the morning, the city is awakening, and I
have not yet gone to bed. My doctors tell me that I must
not overwork, that I ought to sleep at night and not sit for
ten or twelve hours bent over my writing desk. Why am I
writing at night? Because as soon as I get up at one o'clock
the doorbell starts ringing: one man comes to ask for one
thing, another for another, a third comes with some demands, a fourth insists that I should solve some insoluble
"cursed" problem for him as otherwise he would be forced
to shoot himself. (And I have never seen him in my life
before.) Then a student delegation arrives, followed by
one of women students, schoolboys, charitable societies—
to read something for them at a public meeting. What
time is there left for me to think, to read, to work, to live?

I shall send someone to the editorial offices of *Ogonyok*
and ask for the return of your manuscript, but to read it,
to place it—I have no idea when or how I could do that.
For *I literally cannot do it*, having no time and *not knowing whom to approach*. You think I do not want to go there
out of pride, do you? But, good heavens, how can I be expected to go to Stassyulevich, or *Golos* or *Molva* or anywhere else where I am being abused in the most indecent
manner? If I took your manuscript to them and it turned
out a failure they would say: Dostoevsky cheated us, we
believed him to be an authority, but he swindled us and
got our money by false pretenses. They will publish this,
they will spread it abroad, they will traduce and malign
me—you don't know what the literary world is like!

Do not be surprised at me for indulging in such words.
I am terribly tired and my nerves are in a shocking state.
Would I otherwise have spoken to any man or woman
like that? Do you realize that I have a pile of manuscripts
sent to me by mail by people I do not know with requests
to read them and send them to the periodicals with my
recommendation: you see, I am supposed to know everyone at their editorial offices! If you have been told that
your novel is diffuse, then something must be wrong with
it. I simply don't know what to do. If I do do something, I

shall let you know. If you don't like such vague promises, get someone else to deal with it. But I should never have done it for another: it is only for you, in memory of Ems. I have *most certainly* not forgotten you. I enjoyed reading your letter (the first one) very much. But don't write to me about it in your letters. I press your hand warmly, like a friend.

All yours,

F. Dostoevsky

P.S. Literally, the whole of the literary world is hostile to me; only all the readers in Russia love me passionately.

Dostoevsky met Pelageya Guseva, a minor poet and short-story writer, in Ems in the summer of 1875. They quite probably met again during Dostoevsky's visits to Ems in the following years, and, unfortunately, Dostoevsky perhaps got a little too friendly with her.

INDEX

About Kuzma Ostolop 162, 164
About Wise Kerim 187
Aksakov, Ivan (1828-1886) poet and literary critic, one of the most active Slavophile leaders and a close friend of Dostoevsky. 212
Aksakov, Konstantin (1817-1860) critic, poet, dramatist. One of the first rabid Slavophiles who went so far as to dress up in what he believed to be ancient Russian costumes, being mistaken in the streets by the peasants for a 'Persian,' as his enemies, the Westerners, mockingly declared. xiv, 212, 214, 218, 219
Alexander II (1818-1881) hailed at first as the Great Liberator for having granted freedom to the serfs in February, 1861, but later on in his reign denounced by the Russian radicals as a reactionary. After many attempts on his life assassinated on the 13th of March, 1881. xii
Alexander of Macedon (356 B.C.- 323 B.C.) 189
Andrey Alexandrovich (*see* Kraevsky)
Askochensky, Victor (1820-1879) journalist and writer, author of a History of Russian Literature. 91, 212
Aumale (Duke of) (1822-1897) general and French historian. 289
Axle and the Linchpin, The 187

Barbier, Henri Auguste (1805-1882) French poet. 155
Barsky, Vasily (1701-1747) famous Russian pilgrim and traveller. 192
Battle Between the Russians and the Kabardinians, The 180, 183

Bazaine, Achille (1811-1888) marshal of France. xv, xvi, 285-6, 288-90, 292
Beaconsfield, (Lord) (1804-1881) Benjamin Disraeli, Prime Minister of England. 296
Beautiful Muslim Girl, The 195-6, 202
Beketov, Nikolai (1827-1911) Well-known chemist and philosopher, professor of Kharkov University. Dostoevsky struck up a close friendship with him while they were still students in 1846. 298
Belinsky, Visarion (1811-1848) famous Russian literary critic who first recognized Dostoevsky's genius and for a time became Dostoevsky's closest friend and protector. Eventually he became very critical of Dostoevsky's stories and the friendship came to an end. vii, xi, 66, 86-7, 238, 316
Benedictov, Vladimir (1807-1873) a romantic poet who for a short time was extremely popular. 189
Béranger, Pierre Jean (1780-1857) French lyrical poet. 150-1
Berg, Nikolai (1823-1884) poet, translator, journalist. 191
Berlioz, Hector (1803-1869) French composer and musicologist. 281
Bismarck, Otto von (Prince) (1815-1898) 262
Bontecourt, (Captain) 207
Book of the Wisdom of Jesus Son of Sirach, The 192
Borichevsky, N. A. 191
Boris Godunov 144
Bourbaki, Charles (1816-1897) French general. 286
Brothers Karamazov, The 309-10, 313-14

329

Index

the sentimental school, follower of Karamzin, author of songs, elegies, short odes, epigrams, fables, and narrative poems. 187

Dobrolyubov, Nikolai (1836-1861) brilliant critic of *The Contemporary*. Worked hand in glove with Chernyshevsky. Author of a brilliant analysis of Ostrovsky's plays published under the title of *The Realm of Darkness*. xiv, xv, 89, 91, 100-4, 106-9, 117-20, 131-132, 134, 136-7

Dostoevsky, Anna (1846-1918) Dostoevsky's second wife. xv, 316

Dostoevsky, Maria (1828-1864) Dostoevsky's first wife. 305

Dostoevsky, Mikhail (1820-1864) Dostoevsky's elder brother, official editor of *Time* and *Epoch*. xii

Dubensky, Dmitri (d. 1863) writer, historian of literature. 189

Dudyshkin, Stepan (1820-1866) literary critic, journalist, champion of the theory of art for art's sake. 66, 87, 144, 149

Dumas, Alexandre (1830-1870) French novelist. 47, 52, 66, 207

Enumeration of Christian Duties 192

Epoch xiii, xiv, xv

Ernst, Heinrich Wilhelm (1814-1865) German violinist. 6, 21, 27

Eugénie (Empress) (1826-1920) wife of Napoleon III. 287

European Herald 324

Favres, Jules (1809-1880) French lawyer and politician. Member of Government of National Defence. 262, 290

Fonvizin, Denis (1745-1792) Russian eighteenth-century dramatist and essayist, author of the two brilliant comedies, *The Brigadier* and *The Minor*. 87, 146

Fourier, Charles (1772-1837) French philosopher and sociologist. x

Frossard, Charles (1807-1875) French general. 286

Gambetta, Léon (1838-1882) French statesman. 290, 291

Garnier-Pagès, Louis Antoine (1803-1878) member of the French provisional government in 1848, author of the *History of the Revolution of 1848*. 290

Goethe, Johann Wolfgang von (1749-1832) German poet and dramatist. 154-5, 315

Gogol, Nikolai (1809-1852) Russian novelist, dramatist, short story writer, humourist. x, xi, 13, 21, 23, 33, 73, 148-9, 177, 192, 215, 315

Goncharov, Ivan (1812-1891) Russian novelist, author of *Oblomov*. ix, 8

Government Inspector, The 51

Grech, Nikolai (1787-1867) reactionary critic and novelist. 49

Griboyedov, Alexander (1794-1829) author of famous verse comedy *The Misfortune of Being Clever*, Russian ambassador to Persia, assassinated by Persian mob in Teheran. 68

Grigorovich Dmitri (1822-1892) Russian novelist and short story writer, close friend of Dostoevsky with whom he shared lodgings in Petersburg in 1846. vii, 50, 161

Grigoryev, Leonid 319

Gromeka, Mikhail (1852-1883) literary critic. 70

Guseva, Pelageya short story writer and novelist. 324, 327

Home Annals viii, 66, 86-8, 138, 142-4, 156-7, 161-2

Hugo, Victor (1802-1885) French novelist and poet. His novel *Les Miserables* was greatly thought of by Dostoevsky. 49

Idiot, The xiv

Iliad, The 97, 126-7, 132, 144

Index

satirist, editor of *Home Annals*. xvi, 66, 69, 70, 99, 297

Sand, George (1803-1876) pseudonym of Amandine née Dupin, Baronne du Devant, French novelist. 66, 70, 87

Schiller, Friedrich (1759-1805) German poet and dramatist. xi, 155, 315

Schloesser, Friedrich (1776-1860) German historian, author of *Universal History*. 315

Scott, Sir Walter (1771-1832) Scottish poet and novelist. 20, 316

Sechenov, Ivan (1829-1905) physiologist. 298

Selected Passages from a Correspondence with Friends x, xi

Sermon on Drunkenness, A 192

Shakespeare, William (1564-1616) English dramatist. 7, 136, 154-5, 315

Shamil (1797-1871) leader of Caucasian troops against Russian army. 47

Shchedrin (see Saltykov)

Shcherbin, Nikolai (1821-1869) Russian educationalist. 161-2, 164, 166, 168-71, 181-4, 188, 190, 192-3, 197, 199, 200-1, 203, 205, 209-10

Shevtsov, Nikolai (1831-1876) scientist. 191

Skobelev, Ivan (General) popular writer of army stories and playwright. 208

Sluchevsky, Konstantin (1837-1904) poet. 50

Snitkin, Anna (*see* Dostoevsky, Anna)

Sollogub, Vladimir (Count) (1814-1882) short story writer and dramatist. vii, viii

Solovyov, Vladimir (1853-1900) philosopher and poet. 303, 305, 307, 315

Song of Igor's Campaign, The 189, 194, 203, 209

Song of the Merchant Kalashnikov, The 191

Stock Exchange News, The 296

Stories Told to a Twelve-Year-Old Boy 312

Suvorov, Alexander (Count) (1729-1800) Russian field marshal. 191

Talleyrand, Charles Maurice (Prince) (1754-1838) French statesman. 181

Teacher 196

Thackeray, William Makepeace (1811-1863) English novelist. 208

Three Musketeers, The 47

Tikhon Zadonsky (Timofey Kirilov) (1724-1783) monk of the Zadonsk monastery, famous theologian and Greek Orthodox propagandist. 192

Time xii, xiii, xiv

Tolstoy, Alexey (Count) (1817-1875) Russian poet and dramatist. 191

Tolstoy, Leo (Count) (1828-1910) Russian novelist. 191, 315

Tolstoy, Sofia (Countess) Count Alexey Tolstoy's wife. 309

Trochu, Louis Jules (1815-1896) French general. Governor of Paris, President of the Government of National Defence. 290

Tsyganov, Nikolai (1797-1831) composer of folk songs. 191

Turgenev, Ivan (1818-1883) Russian novelist and short story writer. vii, ix, 100, 315

Two Peasants 184

Vladimir, Saint (Grand Prince) (d. 1015) converted the Russian Slavs to Christianity. 192

Voskoboynikov, Nikolai (1838-1882) writer. 90

Voyevodin, Alexander (pseudonym of Galitsky, Nikolai), writer, author of *Diary of a Schoolboy*. 322-3

World History 315

Writer's Diary, A 310-12, 316, 324